Women in Place

Women in Place

The Politics of Gender Segregation in Iran

———

Nazanin Shahrokni

UNIVERSITY OF CALIFORNIA PRESS

University of California Press
Oakland, California

Library of Congress Cataloging-in-Publication Data

Names: Shahrokni, Nazanin, author.
Title: Women in place : the politics of gender segregation in
    Iran / Nazanin Shahrokni.
Description: Oakland, California : University of California Press, [2020]
Identifiers: LCCN 2019023565 (print) | LCCN 2019023566 (ebook) |
    ISBN 9780520304277 (cloth) | ISBN 9780520304284 (paperback) |
    ISBN 9780520973008 (ebook)
Subjects: LCSH: Muslim women—Government policy—Iran. |
    Discrimination in public accommodations—Iran.
Classification: LCC HQ1735.2 S534 2020 (print) | LCC HQ1735.2 (ebook) |
    DDC 305.48/6970955—dc23
LC record available at https://lccn.loc.gov/2019023565
LC ebook record available at https://lccn.loc.gov/2019023566

Manufactured in the United States of America

28 28 27 26 25 24 23 22 21 20
10 9 8 7 6 5 4 3 2 1

CONTENTS

List of Illustrations　　　　　　　　　　　　　　　　　　　　*vii*

Preface and Acknowledgments　　　　　　　　　　　　　　　*ix*

1. The Politics of Gender Segregation in Iran　　　　　　　　　*1*

2. Boundaries in Motion: Sisters, Citizens, and Consumers Get on the Bus　　*30*

3. Happy and Healthy in Mothers' Paradise: Women-Only Parks and the Expansion of the State　　　　　　　　　　*57*

4. Soccer Goals and Political Points: The Gendered Politics of Stadium Access　　　　　　　　　　　　　　　　*81*

5. Re-placing Women, Remaking the State: Gender, Islam, and the Politics of Place Making　　　　　　　　　　　*109*

Notes　　　　　　　　　　　　　　　　　　　　　　　　*127*

References　　　　　　　　　　　　　　　　　　　　　　*135*

Index　　　　　　　　　　　　　　　　　　　　　　　　*151*

ILLUSTRATIONS

FIGURES

1. A sea divided: barrier at the Caspian Sea   *11*
2. A world apart: riding gender-segregated buses in Tehran   *32*
3. Tehran's shrinking living space   *64*
4. "Wuthering Heights," the Mothers' Paradise on Abbas Abad Hills, Tehran   *72*
5. The distribution of women-only parks across Tehran   *72*
6. Access denied!   *90*
7. White Scarf Girls facing the police   *97*

TABLES

1. Gender Segregation Regimes   *21*
2. Privatization of the City's Bus Lines and Buses   *51*

PREFACE AND ACKNOWLEDGMENTS

A story has no beginning or end: arbitrarily one chooses that moment of experience from which to look back or from which to look ahead.
—GRAHAM GREENE, 1951

I can trace that moment all the way back to a hot summer afternoon on July 30, 1995, in Isfahan. There were twenty-five hundred of us: women athletes from universities across Iran. Wrapped up in our school uniforms of black scarves and long, loose, dark dresses, we were indistinguishable, like a flock of dark-feathered birds. Excited to have flown all the way from Tehran, the capital, to Isfahan to attend the Second Students' Sports Olympiad, we marched toward Piroozi Sports Complex to attend the opening ceremony. The boys were already seated inside. We could hear the sound of their drums, whistles, and chants as we stood outside sweating, waiting in line to get inside from the back door, the "women's entrance," located in a small alley too narrow to contain the restlessness of our wings. One by one we had to pass through what I called "the tunnel of horror." A few members of the organizing committee, including Parvaneh Nazarali, the head of Women's Sports, had formed a tunnel-like passage. Wrapped up in their long black chadors, their frowning faces were all we could see, their eyes searching for immodest suspects. As we passed through the entrance, we were presented with a long list of "not-to-do's": "Do not laugh out loud!"; "Do not whistle and chant!"; "Do not talk to the boys!"

Inside the stadium, after what seemed like the longest hour of my life, we were guided toward *our* section, the "women's section." I slouched on my seat and scanned my surroundings. Most of my teammates, Shahid Beheshti University volleyball players, were ecstatic, grasping every opportunity to do what they had been told not to do: as the disciplining gaze of the officials moved away, the girls would whistle, clap, chant, and even do a few dance moves; as the gaze moved back they would stop, as if they were playing freeze dance. Ironically, the restrictions had added an extra layer of excitement. What to me was a source of humiliation, to many of my teammates was a source of hilarity. For me there was pain in playing *by* the rules; for them there was pleasure in playing *with* the rules.

These were my thoughts when Guity Shambayati, who had a habit of taking my inquiring mind and critical words seriously, encouraged me to write my first piece for *Zanan* magazine, then the most reputable feminist monthly in Iran. Soon after its submission, Shahla Sherkat, the editor, called me on the phone and asked if I wanted to become a journalist. In 1996 I officially joined *Zanan*. It was Shahla Sherkat, not my first-grade teacher, who taught me how to write. That small room in Ziba Street, from which *Zanan* operated, is where I thrived as a writer.

Throughout years, mockery of the rules, such as my teammates' playing "freeze dance," and "hide and seek" with the officials, made many of these rules and bans essentially ineffective. In 2008, when I attended a (mens) basketball game between two of Iran's leading teams and sat next to a female guard at the "women's section," she complimented me on my "appropriate" look and manners. Age might have made my manners appear more "lady-like"—after all, thirteen years had passed, and I was the product of the gaze that had for years regulated my appearance and bodily movements—but at the same time, I was wearing a white scarf, loosely tied with a knot under my chin, with a portion of my hair uncovered, and a blue tunic style dress with jeans. With this outfit, I would not have passed the "propriety test" back in 1995. When the young woman next to me started jumping up and down, chanting with excitement as her favorite team scored points, the female guard looked at me, shrugged her shoulders, and said: "The youth *these* days are out of control! What can I do? It's a basketball game after all!" A compromise, perhaps, which was the flip side of rules not taken seriously for decades.

In the years that followed the Second Students' Sports Olympiad, Parvaneh Nazarali and her colleagues at different state offices continued to hurdle over various obstacles in the masculinist (and "Islamist") domains of sports and the state in their efforts to promote women's access to public spaces, particularly to sporting events and opportunities. To them, I learned later, the door at the end of that small alley in Isfahan signified a delta that would open up to an ocean of opportunity. What I and many others labeled as a space of proscription was to them a space of possibility that they had fought very hard to carve out. The inclusion of women athletes in the opening ceremony had come at a cost, and they were determined to maintain this "success," come what may. The few strands of hair sticking out of our long black scarves, in their view, did not just undermine Islamic propriety but also made them susceptible to harsh criticism from their male peers and superiors, which could potentially jeopardize the future of women's sports and their further access to public facilities. The villains (heroes?) of the opening vignette, I realized, were themselves; caught up in a giant web of rules and regulations, they had to navigate a perilous route between ideological imperatives and political skirmishes and practicalities. This realization, along with the unique insights of Hosein Gha-zian, *Zanan*'s adviser and a sociologist, inspired in me the desire not to fall into facile assumptions but to dig deeper, beyond the obvious, and compelled me to pursue a postgraduate degree in sociology, not chemistry, which I had majored in. My life as a sociologist thus started at Allameh Tabataba'i University in Tehran, where I was immersed in a fascinating new adventure of discovery and became well versed in the alphabets of social science.

But that intellectual journey soon took me outside Iran. First I went to Montreal, Canada, where I was embraced by Homa Shams and Enayat Shahrokni, my aunt and uncle, who created a home away from home and facilitated my transition to North America. My conversations with Shirin Shahrokni and Karoline Truchon were, and continue to be, elevating. At Concordia University, Homa Hoodfar, whom I had met at an SSRC workshop on cities and citizenships in the Middle East in Beirut in 2001, provided me with research opportunities and opened doors for me as I applied for PhD programs. At that same workshop, I had met Norma Claire Moruzzi, Kaveh Ehsani, and Arang Keshavarzian, who have ever since watched over me and ceaselessly offered their wisdom, friendship, and support. This "mentoring team" represents to me the best that academia has to offer. They are a model of academic rigor, integrity, care, comradery, and tutelage. Such a rarity!

Then I landed at the University of California at Berkeley, where I eventually earned my PhD in sociology in 2013. I used to joke and say that I was made in the USA (since I was actually born in the United States) and that I was remade in the USA. The intellectually stimulating environment nurtured by UC Berkeley played a crucial role in this remaking of me. This book draws heavily on my dissertation research, carried out under the supervision of a most inspiring dissertation committee, chaired by Raka Ray and composed of Michael Burawoy, Cihan Tugal, Saba Mahmood, and Norma Claire Morruzi. I am indebted to each of them for their rigorous critical engagement and invaluable support. The Iran that comes out of the pages of this book is in many ways different from the Iran that many readers imagine or know of. This is in huge part because this committee pushed me to bring to light complexities where simplicity seemed obvious, to not reproduce old tropes that conceal more than they reveal. I am particularly grateful to Raka for being a model meticulous and critical interlocutor who inspired and encouraged novel ways of looking and analyzing; to Michael for supporting me in developing my own voice, at my own pace, and for teaching me how to stay true to my own compass; to Cihan for helping me sharpen and tighten my analyses; and to Norma for critically engaging with this manuscript over and over again—I think we have both lost count of how many times—while providing me with endless emotional support. It pains me that Saba Mahmood will not be reading these lines. I hope that during our memorable walk on the corniche in Beirut in 2014 I managed to express my appreciation for her incisive critique, for being a feminist who never ceased to look critically at the very foundations on which she was standing, and for inspiring me to do the same.

At Berkeley I was part of Team Raka, otherwise known as the Berkeley Gender Group. This group met several times per year to exchange ideas, bounce arguments off each other, read different sections of each other's work, and relentlessly tear each other's work apart, only to help put it back together on a more solid foundation. Just the fact that I am able to list all these people as having been the early readers of my book fills me with immense warmth: Abigail Andrews, Jennifer Carlson, Kimberly Kay Hoang, Jordanna Matlon, Sarah Anne Minkin, Dawn Dow, Kate Mason, Katherine Maich, Kemi Balogun, and Katie Hasson, thank you for being part of this journey. I also want to take this opportunity to thank Tom Pessah, Siri Colom, Heidy Sarabia, Tanya Jones, Laleh Behbahanian, Kathryn Moller, and Sylvia Nam, who one way or another made my Berkeley years significant. Rana Mroue, your friendship has meant a lot. I cannot end this section without paying tribute to Kathy Rokni for embracing me for all those years with her warmth and friendship. That little white couch in her living room in Sunnyvale, California, was the adult equivalent of our childhood playground in Logan, Utah, decades ago.

Yasmeen Daifallah, Ana Villareal, and Hiba Bou Akar, we shared laughter and tears, insights and visions. Unique in your own ways, you showered me with kindness and sheer intellectual brilliance and constantly challenged me with your thirst for endless debates and discussions, from the very mundane to the very profound aspects of life. Together, my friends, we transformed what could be a lonesome experience into an exciting collective ride. We have come a long way!

At the Harvard Academy for International and Area Studies, I was surrounded by brilliant minds and thinkers. I am grateful to Michèle Lamont and the Harvard Academy Senior Scholars, particularly Timothy Colton and Steven Caton. Pascal Menoret and Timothy Nunan, thank you for the enthusiasm you showed for my work. As an Academy Scholar, I had the opportunity to organize an author's conference, a half-day workshop, at which Afsaneh Najmabadi, Farha Ghannam, Lynne Haney, Don Mitchell, and Arang Keshavarzian critically engaged with an earlier draft of this book and offered valuable feedback. Having been inspired by their works for years, I was incredibly appreciative for this opportunity.

During AY 2014–2015, I was the Mary Fox Whittlesey Chair and Visiting Assistant Professor of Sociology at the American University of Beirut, a veritable intellectual hub on the shores of the Mediterranean. I am, first and foremost, grateful to Sari Hanafi for providing me with all the intellectual, spatial, and financial resources that I needed to focus on teaching and writing. My students at AUB deserve their own line here. The classroom experience at AUB was close to ideal thanks to their eagerness to learn, ask questions, understand, and connect. During this time Lisa Hajjar was a great friend and mentor. I appreciated her intellectual rigor and political commitment, but also was impressed by how easily she trans-formed into a carefree soul, soaking in the little pleasures of life. Waleed Hazbun, Nadya Sbaiti, Omar Dewachi, and Hatim El-Hibri all offered valuable feedback on manuscript fragments I presented at AUB. Hatim also generously organized an unforgettable writing retreat in Shimlan, Lebanon. Last but most especially, I am thankful for all the moments shared and memories made with Anjali Nath and Samhita Sunya, whose intellectual input is present in my work and academic makeup.

Parts of this book were revised during my tenure at Syracuse University in New York. There, Carol Fadda-Conrey welcomed me into her family from day one. For me she embodies the ideals of feminist friendship and scholarship. Carol and Sean's house in Syracuse was a refuge on cold and lonesome winter days. I cherish their friendship, their open minds ready to discuss life and politics, and their read-iness to feed me with homemade Lebanese dishes or good old American BBQ. Sabina Schnell kept me company through sickness and health. Coming from dif-ferent disciplines, we learned how to think and write together and how to create our own moments of entertainment and amusement, as we frantically worked to send off books and articles. With Terrell Winder, we had many late-night work sessions, and our conversations in the earlier stages of my book proposal were invaluable. Farha Ternikar, thanks for extending a friendly hand and integrating me into your vast social and professional network in Syracuse. I am also grateful to Prema Kurien, Madonna Harrington Meyer, Cecilia Green, Gretchen Purser, and Amy Lutz at the department of sociology for their collegial support, for read-ily engaging with my work, and for patiently walking me through the first stages of my career. Jackie Orr, I appreciate your support, free spirit, and sparkling intellect. I am also thankful to Amy Kallander, who invited me to join the Humanities Cor-ridor Working Group on the theme of "Inclusion & Exclusion in the Modern Mid-dle East," which involved faculty from central New York colleges, namely Timur Hammond, Ziad Fahmy, and Kent F. Schull, who read and commented on por-tions of this book. Among the administrative staff, whose supportive role often remains unnoticed and unacknowledged, Janet Coria, Tara Slater, and Deborah Toole were extremely helpful in dealing with the exigencies of day-to-day work at Syracuse University; I am grateful to them for their support.

During my year at Lund University as a visiting researcher at the Center for Middle Eastern Studies, I was given the opportunity to refine the manuscript of this book. I am thankful to Dalia Abdelhady and all friends and colleagues at CMES who helped me get through the final stages of book writing. Malgorzata Kurjanska has been with me at UC Berkeley and then at the Harvard Academy of Scholars, but it was during my recurrent visits to Copenhagen that I came to greatly cherish her boundless intellectual energy, matched with her deep kindness. I am delighted that this book brought me all the way to Sweden and closer to her and her partner Wojtek and gave me the opportunity to savor their loyal friendship.

This book is the product of a long journey and represents the collective efforts of many, near and far, who deepened the pleasure of creation and lessened the despair of writing by enriching the content or facilitating the process. Asef Bayat, Rachel Rinaldo, Charles Kurzman, Deniz Kandiyoti, Behrooz Ghamari-Tabrizi, Frances Susan Hasso, Zakia Salime, Nadje Al-Ali, Azam Khatam, Naghmeh Sohrabi, Farideh Farhi, Ali Akbar Mahdi, Leslie Wang, Orit Avishai, and many others, including Ann Orloff, Rhacel Salazar Parrenas, Poulami Roychowdhury, Smitha Radhakrishnan, Jocelyn Viterna, Evren Savci, Marie E. Berry, Anna Korteweg, and Leslie Salzinger of the Gender and Power Research Network, have read or discussed various parts of this book. I am especially indebted to Eskandar Sadeghi-Boroujerdi for his willingness to read and comment on an earlier version of this book in a short notice. I am also grateful to people in Iran who have provided me with various levels of assistance during this project. Neda Habibollah generously helped with the archival work; Hamidreza Hosseini kindly shared his historical insights with me; Nahid Keshavarz has on several occasions offered her incisive account of the women's movements and activism in Iran; Parastoo Dokouhaki and Nasrin Afzali have always been readily available to discuss and answer my questions or help me locate sources; and Shirin Ahmadnia, Ebrahim Towfigh, and Karim Arghandehpour offered intellectual and/or institutional support at the earlier stages of this project, for which I am immensely grateful.

The research for this book was made possible by several grants, fellowships, and awards that I would like to acknowledge. First and foremost, I have been honored to receive the 2014 Mehrdad Mashayekhi Dissertation Award from the Association for Iranian Studies. The research for this book has also been supported by a Book Leave Fellowship from the Global Religion Research Initiative, a grant from the Program for the Advancement of Research on Conflict and Collaboration (PARCC) at Syracuse University, the American Association for University Women Dissertation Fellowship, the Woodrow Wilson Dissertation Fellowship in Women's Studies, the Dean's Normative Time Fellowship at UC Berkeley, a grant from the Al Falah Program at the Center for Middle Eastern Studies at UC Berkeley, and several mini grants, all too grand to mention. Portions of this book appear in the *Journal of Middle Eastern Women's Studies* and *Journal of Contemporary Ethnography*. An article from the research done for chapter 3 of this book, entitled "The Mothers' Paradise: Women-only Parks and the Dynamics of State Power in the Islamic Republic of Iran" (*Journal of Middle East Women's Studies* 10, no. 3 [2014]) won the Association for Middle East Women's Studies Best Graduate Paper Prize.

At the University of California Press, Naomi Schneider and Benjy Malings have been most considerate, and remarkably patient and reassuring as deadlines loomed closer and passed. I am very grateful for your support for and faith in this book.

After the submission of the manuscript, UCP copyeditor Sharon Langworthy has meticulously gone through the text to make it ready for publication.

I could not have written this work without the help of my copy editor, Allison Brown from Henry Street Editing, who joined me on this journey when this book was just an idea. She helped me transform an idea into a research proposal and then a book. I am sure she is as happy as I am to see this book, finally, in print. When Allison was consumed by her other projects, Jesse Nissim took the burden off my shoulders. I am grateful for her timely and discerning editorial services as well.

Spyros Sofos has been a dear companion, an avid research interlocutor, and a fabulous editor. In the final months of writing, he helped push the manuscript forward by judiciously engaging with the content; meticulously reworking the structure of my arguments; and patiently combing through the pages of this manuscript, masterfully taming the unruly words. I am indebted to him for all his self-less contributions throughout the process and for reminding me time and again, and in his own ways, that life is not exhausted within the limits of these pages, and that little things can be the source of massive happiness.

Away from the formalities of academic life, four childhood friends in Tehran—Masoomeh Niloufari, Mahboobeh Saberi, Nazli Alavi and Negar Karimi—have kept me grounded in, and connected to, everyday life in Iran by sharing with me much of what was theirs: their daily rhythms and routines, wants and aspirations, persuasions and provocations. Through their stories, Tehran remained a familiar and familial space, far away yet so close to my heart. They, along with Guity Shambayati, have provided coherence and continuity to the notion of home. I am also thankful to Mani Shahrir, who on several occasions acted like a first responder and came to my rescue with the required information to fill a gap in my narratives.

Present already before the outset of this intellectual journey, my family played a formative role in the product of this project and in much more. My father, Ahmad Shahrokni, did not live long enough to see me as a sociologist. As a professor of economics, he was an impassioned teacher. Our house, up until the moment he closed his eyes, was packed with his students, who were eager to share the vibrancy of his intellect and his passion. To me he remains a model of a committed researcher and an inspirational teacher. I can only hope to replicate that model in my own academic endeavors. My grandmother, "Papar," has enriched my life with her graceful presence. Quite often I find myself on a plane traveling from where I am, which keeps changing, to where she is: home. I keep coming back to her, and I sure hope to do so for many more years. Armin and Pardis, my brother and my sister-in-law, have also been companions in this long journey. Afarin, my sister, comes last, but there are no words to convey the indebtedness I have to her. Constantly there, thoughtful, caring, the sweetest sibling, she has, particularly in the past few years, carried most of the family weight on her shoulders, setting me free to read and write.

For years I have been rehearsing these last few lines, to express my gratitude to the person who has motivated me most, the force that has pushed me upward and forward: Shahla Shahriari has played so many roles over the years that I cannot do justice to the enormously important part she has played in my life. She has been my friend, my mentor, my teacher, my research assistant, my fan, and my audience. She has given me the conviction that anything is possible and the will to turn the possibility into reality. Shahla waited nine months to hold me in her hands, but more than nine years to see this book. It is to her, my mother, that I dedicate it with an unabated love.

The Politics of Gender Segregation in Iran

Long before it was concerned about Iran's possible access to the nuclear bomb, the Western media was concerned about the "chador bomb," Ayatollah Khomeini's call for women in Iran to wear the chador, the long black garment that covers the whole body, leaving only the face exposed (Jaynes 1979). The 1979 Islamic revolution was described as returning women to a shrouded life; "like a pearl in its shell," as the revolutionary slogan went, the woman was coated layer upon layer, shrouded not just by her veil but by walls, fences, and curtains installed across Tehran, and the rest of the country, as part of the state's gender segregation plan.

Upholding the Islamic identity of the state and inculcating that identity into society required prescribing and scrutinizing women's and men's bodily presentation. Whereas men were expected to refrain from certain practices such as wearing ties, short sleeves, and short pants, the focus on women's appearance carried additional weight, and transgression carried different connotations; women were positioned as the bearers of a redefined Islamic morality, and as such the possibility of a lapse necessitated protecting their chastity; "like cotton and fire," goes the proverb, "men and women should be kept separated," or else they could burn in a moment of unbridled attraction.[1] To prevent the "sin," the mixing of unrelated men and women, it was the woman's body that was more thoroughly inspected. Women had to pass through checkpoints installed at the entrances of universities, shopping malls, airports, theaters, and government buildings (Sciolino 1992). Stationed at each was a guard representing the state, her eyes scanning women's bodies in search of the "inappropriate": a few strands of hair sticking out of a scarf, the faded stains of lipstick, the broken traces of eyeliner, the color and length of the dress; every part, every gesture, my interviewees recalled, was scrutinized. Women who failed to pass the propriety test would be denied entry. These transformations were all part of the newly formed state's attempt to revolutionize the city, establishing an Islamic public order through the "moral purification" of public spaces and the institutionalization of "modesty." As the capital of the Islamic Republic of Iran, Tehran was to be transformed into an "Islamic city."[2]

Although much has been written about the 1979 Islamic revolution and its impact on life in Iran, the spatial policies and practices of the now forty-year-old regime remain curiously understudied. *Women in Place* is about the twists and turns of state policies regarding women's access to public spaces and what these changes signify in terms of state power. Through this approach, gender segregation provides a window into the transformations of and internal contradictions within the Iranian state and the changes in Iranian society over the past four decades.

Tehran in 2008, when I began conducting my fieldwork, was by all accounts very different from the Tehran of the 1980s. If the city were a movie, I would have said it had made a genre shift. In the Western media, Iran was now presented as Janus-faced: there it was, the Islamic Republic, included in the "axis of evil," posing a menacing threat to the world with its nuclear program, and there they were, the women of Iran, posing a menacing threat to the Islamic Republic from within.[3] Women were pitted against the state, both perceived to be engaged in a zero-sum game, the gains of one interpreted as the loss of the other. Women's bodies had once again come under the scrutiny of Western observers, who, like the government guards at the checkpoints, were searching for the "inappropriate"—length and color of scarves, slit overcoats, lipstick, nail polish, heel heights—only to label every "inappropriate" gesture "resistance," a sign of the state's fading authority, of its failing grip over women.[4] The "romance of resistance," to use Lila Abu-Lughod's (1990) phrase, took journalists and scholars alike to the "hidden" corners of Tehran. A new topography of Tehran, a veritable "city of lies" as Navai calls it (2014), extended from the "high-end coffee shops," where young women were smoking and mingling with young men (Erdbrink 2011), to the parties in the basements of villas in north Tehran—where "passionate uprisings" had been stirred up and Iranian youth danced, drank, and engaged in "unconventional" sexual activities (Mahdavi 2009)—and the "underground" world, where segregation was breached and "pleasures banned by the ayatollahs" could be freely explored (Khatib 2014).

But the truth is that one did not need to go all the way to the underground to find change. On the ground, too, change was tangible. In Tehran, the wearing of chadors had (mostly) decreased.[5] Women in colorful coats and scarves had become increasingly visible and vocal, public and mobile. They were "conquering enclosed public spaces," as Masserat Amir-Ebrahimi (2006) astutely points out. The conservatives in Iran attributed this trend to a "creeping liberalism." In a similar line of argumentation, scholars and journalists residing outside Iran attributed these transformations to the reformists coming to power in 1996, the overall loosening of social control in the postwar era, and the "mellowing down" of the clerics (Sciolino 2003).

Wearing of chadors had mostly gone down—true. But new walls were going up. Gender-segregated spaces were rapidly expanding. The roads and the rides were becoming increasingly segregated as newly launched women-only buses and taxis were providing women with exclusive rides across the city (Banakar and Payvar 2015). Away from the crowded streets, women could now spend their leisure time in one of the many women-only parks and entertainment hubs that were launched in Tehran and around the country to provide women with the incentive to exercise and take care of their health. And as Reuters reported, in May 2007 the city of Karaj, west of Tehran, saw the opening of the country's first women-only Internet café, with the conservative Mehr News Agency publicizing the fact that women could now "enjoy high-speed Internet and free computer lessons" from an all-female staff (Reuters, May 21, 2007). There were several women-only cafés and restaurants where women could get together with female friends and spend their money on food and drinks. In 2010 the state-owned Melli Bank opened its first women-only branch, alleging that this would make it easier for women to handle their own money.[6] Women-only businesses, encouraged by the state, were recognized as "the most lucrative spaces for income" and have continued to flourish in recent years (Bahramitash 2013). A reporter from the Iranian News Agency (IRNA, June 18, 2011) could not conceal his astonishment when describing the first women-only carwash, which was launched in northwest Tehran. At this carwash, an all-female staff provided various services for the customers. While the cars were being washed, the customers were directed to a waiting room, where they were served drinks and were offered psychological and self-help tips.[7]

Despite these developments, Tehran City Council member Elaheh Rastgoo stated in an interview in 2014 that Tehran's city spaces were still not optimal for women's use.[8] Among her suggestions was to increase the number of women-only spaces across the city—in effect to create a city within the city, a city of women. And indeed, as she was uttering these words, Tehran Municipality was already launching the women's city complexes (*Shahrbanu*), gigantic entertainment hubs organized in and around women-only parks.

As women became more public and visible and developed a sense of entitlement to city spaces and services, the state pursued a new gender segregation regime in the form of an expansion of women-only spaces. Some have argued that these attempts by the state to expand or reinforce gender segregation, which coincided with the coming to power of the conservatives and the eight-year presidency of Mahmood Ahmadinejad between 2005 and 2013, represent a conservative backlash against reformists' liberalism.[9] These concerns and controversies reached a peak when Ahmadinejad appointed Marzieh Vahid Dastjerdi, a conservative female politician and gynecologist who was considered the mastermind of gender-segregated health care, as the minister of health (Shahrokni 2009). In these accounts, the "renewed" interest in gender segregation and other "restrictive" policies during the 2000s is interpreted as the conservatives' way of getting back at the reformist faction. As a result, gender segregation is associated with conservatism and is presented as an exclusionary policy aimed at limiting women's presence and movement in public spaces and the public sphere, taking back the hard-won spaces to which women had come to feel entitled. However, none of these accounts addresses or explains the fact that gender segregation has remained a priority of the state agenda since 1979 and has been pursued under various administrations regardless of their ideological underpinnings.

What is the story of gender segregation policies in postrevolutionary Iran? How do various administrations justify their creation and expansion? Who uses gender-segregated spaces, and what meanings do they assign to them? And what does the transformation of gender-segregated spaces show us about the changing modalities of state power in Iran?

Women in Place offers a historicized and contextualized reading of gender-segregated spaces in Iran and seeks to answer these questions as it takes us on a historical tour of postrevolutionary Tehran by examining three illustrative sites of gender segregation: on city buses (chapter 2); inside the Mothers' Paradise, the first of the four women-only parks in the city (chapter 3); and outside the closed doors of Freedom Sports Stadium, where women are banned from attending men's sports matches (chapter 4).[10] Through these case studies, the book examines how the state establishes itself and retains its role as the ultimate arbiter of gender boundaries by regulating women's presence in public spaces. The tangibility and visibility of gender segregation practices have made the setting of gender boundaries central to the Islamic Republic's self-image and, effectively, authority; the state has thus attempted to solidify gender difference over several decades by creating physical and visible boundaries across the city. This drawing of gender boundaries was driven by ideological imperatives, the quest for legitimation, and practical exigencies and had no clear sense of direction, other than an undefined commitment to constructing Islamic spaces through segregation. In this not unambiguous process, Iranian women's increased public presence—even though partially enabled by state policy—has posed a challenge to state authority. The following chapters argue that the unsettling of the gender order caused by shifts in Iran's social, political, and economic environment prompted the Islamic state to develop a new regime of gender segregation, including strategies that would be flexible enough to address the need for women's increased use of public space while never relinquishing the state's authority as regulator.

As the case studies in this book indicate, in order for the state to address diverse and often conflicting interests, it had to adapt its policies to a shifting sociopolitical landscape. Thus, I contend, gender-segregated spaces shifted from functioning as *spaces of exclusion* aimed at restricting women's movements in the city to *spaces of inclusion* allegedly to facilitate their presence in urban public spaces. The shift from one regime of gender segregation to the other reflects, and is enabled by, a shift in the state's mode of regulation from *prohibition*—the disabling of undesired effects—to *provision*, the enabling of desired effects. The movement from prohibition to provision, I demonstrate, is accompanied by a discursive shift from protecting women's virtue and chastity in the name of *Islamic morality* to protecting women's rights and safety in the name of *secular liberal citizenship*.

Although the form and intensity of gender domination have varied over time, I argue that the changing balance in the state's modes of regulation—from prohibition to provision—is managed through the discourse of protection and is consistently accompanied by the characterization of the state as protector (Brown 1992, 3; Young 2003). This concept of protection, however, is not immutable but socially and historically defined. Indeed, the Islamic Republic, in its early stages, had already transformed the traditional Islamic notion of male guardianship into state protection and thus had effectively appropriated it. In subsequent years the impact of social change—in the form of an expanding middle class and the emergence of a client/consumer mentality (Alamdari 2005; Harris 2017; Keshavarzian 2007)—as well as the development of a bureaucratic logic, coupled with a liberal state understanding of protection as service provision rather than benevolent patronage, prompted further transformations. Thus, in order to tease out the complexity of policy change in Iran, a more nuanced reading of the abovementioned processes is required. Protection, I suggest, is flexible enough to accommodate multiple discursive regimes, including Islamic morality and liberal rights, thereby allowing the state to assert its authority in changing local and global contexts.

This book challenges the practice of reification of gender segregation by pointing out the differential degrees of prohibition and provision in the context of different regimes of gender segregation. Whereas *gender segregation* refers to a host of diverse modes of administering and ordering physical and social space and the position of gendered subjects therein, and while gender boundaries shift and remain open to contestation, the state's practice of that segregation acquires its unity at the level of representation, a representation that dissimulates the diversity of its forms and meanings. The constant (yet unsystematic and often wayward) partitioning of city spaces along gender lines, the habitual movement of bodies within these gendered spaces, and the state's endless (yet mostly futile) surveillance and supervision of these movements all help (re)create the idea and image of an Islamic city divided along gender lines. Therefore, I argue that the Islamic state is the producer of a gender-segregated spatial order, but at the same time it relies on that order to invent itself as precisely that: an Islamic state.

When it is regarded in this way, as a fluid and adaptable constant, gender segregation becomes a lens through which to view the broader workings of power and politics. But before delving into the case studies and what they tell us about the Islamic Republic, I look back at the longer history of how gender segregation has been practiced in Iran and consider the set of challenges the newly established revolutionary state faced when it tried to transform a practice that was historically upheld by society into a state project.

WOMEN AS SIGNS OF THE TIMES: A BRIEF HISTORY OF GENDER SEGREGATION IN IRAN

Under the Qajar dynasty (1796–1925), gender segregation and the occultation of women from the public eye were indicators of wealth, dignity, and status (Najmabadi 2005, 153).[11] While poor women and men mingled in city streets, wealthy women often had the bazaar merchant, the clothier, and the hairdresser come to them. They would also frequently be given exclusive access to select public baths and the streets leading to them at specific times (Khatib-Chahidi 1981; Varmaghani, Hossein, and Shani 2016). An affluent woman's place was at home, and even the home was divided into the inviolable private space of women (*andarooni*) and the semipublic space of men (*birooni*) (Hosseini et al. 2015). As Middle East historians have shown, the "depraved" classes did not have the means or the resources to compartmentalize their cramped households and replicate the deportment of the well-to-do (Boudagh and Ghaemmaghami 2011).[12]

For much of the nineteenth century public spaces remained men's territories, though toward the end of the Qajar dynasty women's confinement within the private space was for the first time problematized (Najmabadi 1991), and attempts were made to transform the public order by carving out women-only spaces, such as girls' schools, women-only theaters, and women's presses.[13] For example, in narrating the history of theater and cinema in Iran, Masood Mehrabi (1989) describes how during the nineteenth century young (male) Iranian students and diplomats who had been in Europe and had become infatuated with its cinematography decided upon their return to Iran to open private theaters to show European motion pictures. A few of these men—Ardashes Badmagerian (Ardeshir Khan), an Armenian Iranian merchant, together with Khanbaba Motazedi, the French-trained Iranian film entrepreneur, and Colonel Alinaqi Vasiri, a renowned musicologist and composer—paved the way for women's entrance into cinemas by opening Cinema Khorshid, Iran's first women-only theater in 1917 (Naficy 2012), an initiative that was to be emulated by the opening of many more such theaters. These women-only spaces, women's presses and reading circles in particular, contributed to the formation of a vibrant female public sphere, parallel to but not yet integrated with the male public sphere (Brookshaw 2013, 2014; McElrone 2005).[14]

Nevertheless, the encounters of Qajar shahs and officials with Europeans radically changed the ways in which they had come to understand their society's homosociality. Their fascination with the heterosocial Europe on the one hand, and the European travelers' disdainful accounts of Iranian homosocial relations on the other, led Qajar shahs and officials to see homosociality as a marker of difference and as something inferior to European heterosociality. Eventually, with the propagation of the discourse of modernity, homosociality became a key signifier of backwardness and subsequently a source of anxiety for Iranian statesmen (Naficy 2012; Najmabadi 2005). This recasting of homosociality prompted a "shift in the discourses and practices that set gender boundaries" (Thompson 2003). Thus, the modernizing tendency was to desegregate men and women and integrate women into the already established, male-dominated public sphere. In order for this "modern" heterosocial public space/sphere to emerge, new men and women were to be produced (Amin 2002; see also Abu-Lughod 1998). The new woman, in particular, had to break free and disengage from female bonds and spaces, which now signaled backwardness and vulgarity. The "modern" woman was to accompany her husband, educate her children, serve her nation, and be present and active in the male-dominated public spaces and spheres. She was pitted against her "traditional" counterpart, who was stuck in all-female spaces such as religious ceremonial gatherings and women's baths, holding on tight to her female bonds and companions (Najmabadi 1993). It could thus be argued that by espousing the "modern," women gained integration in public spaces through sacrificing other forms of agency associated with the homosocial interaction contexts that had developed over the course of the nineteenth century.

Accessing the male public sphere had become the "modern" woman's aspiration. This aspiration is beautifully portrayed in *Hall of Mirrors*, a novel written by renowned Iranian novelist Amir Hassan Cheheltan (1991). The story is set around the end of the Qajar period, during the time of Iran's Constitutional Revolution in 1906; the events are narrated by Mahrokhsar, whose father was Mirza, the founder and editor of a revolutionary weekly newspaper.[15] Mahrokhsar herself belongs to an all-female circle of revolutionaries; nevertheless, the novel is structured around her fascination with her father and his revolutionary circles and activities, all of which she witnesses through a keyhole that connects their world to hers. The novel shows how Mahrokhsar, her stepsister Mehrazam, and others were eventually recruited by Mirza and integrated into his circle of revolutionary comrades to distribute revolutionary pamphlets and newspapers.

Desegregation thus constituted a long and slow process, ridden with ambiguities. In early modernity women would be confined in the private domain, while public spaces would be the purview of men. Then came the institution of women-only public spaces such as theaters, women's presses, and reading circles, which, however, were seen as evidence of cultural backwardness by the westward-looking

Qajar monarchy and its bureaucracy. Timid moves toward desegregation, or rather the establishment of shared spaces, were "subverted" by informal segregation practices. For example, even where movie houses allowed women, segregation persisted, as women were separated from the men by a curtain or a divider erected in the middle. Even when an official barrier did not exist, it was not uncommon for women to sit on one side and men on the other (Naficy 2012). The more decisive push toward desegregation came under the reign of the Pahlavis.

Under the Pahlavis (1925–79) desegregation, along with deveiling, became official state policy. The Pahlavis adopted a modernizing discourse that focused on the emancipatory effects of heterosocialization and gender desegregation. For example, when one of the women-only theaters burned down in 1926, the fire was cited to highlight the necessity of having mixed theaters in a statement published in the Tehran daily newspaper *Nahid*: "When one remembers the pitiful incident in which many women and children, anxious and scared, desperately escaped the theater, one cannot but realize that, had they been accompanied by their husbands and brothers and (male) relatives, with the courage that one expects from the male sex, the men could have prevented this level of anxiety and instructed the women on how to patiently deal with danger—and that they would have ultimately rescued them from the fire" (quoted in Mehrabi 1989, 18). These justifications for the integration of women, like many other in that era, were anything but emancipatory, as they framed women as fully dependent on their men to think, respond, and act appropriately.

Through its desegregation policies, the Pahlavi regime sought to transform Iranian women into publicly visible modern citizens. Mandatory deveiling, experienced by many women as a violent process of prohibition, surveillance, and punishment, was also an attempt to modernize Iranian women—or rather, an attempt by the state to exhibit them as signifiers of Iran's modernity and have them perform its "progressive" political agenda. In order to signal modernity, in the 1960s, for example, Mohammad Reza Shah started showcasing young women in shorts and miniskirts in official celebrations, parades, and sporting events, and in welcoming foreign delegates. Through practices such as promoting attire that appealed to a Western male agenda, the identity of the state as "modern and progressive" came to be closely tied to women's dress and place. There was no longer status attached to invisibility and seclusion.

Unsurprisingly, modern urban design and spatial order in Tehran also copied European and American modern structures. Examples include the open kitchen layout inside homes (the bringing down of the wall and the symbolic boundary that separated the interior, private space reserved for women, known in the topography of the domestic space in Iran as *andarooni*, from the male-inhabited semi-public space, known as *birooni*); and the introduction of bars and cafés, shopping malls, and supermarkets.[16] Modernization brought about women's education and entrance into the workforce, the commercialization of products, the expansion of consumerism, and most important, the formation of an urban middle class. Women of the middle and upper classes eventually began to claim the streets, especially as the state, through its urban development plans, had made new spaces of consumption and education available. These developments reversed the traditional equation; women's mixing with men was no longer a signifier of backwardness but rather had become a marker of progress.

Nevertheless, as Nahid Yeganeh (1993, 15) argues, "The Pahlavi era had by no means succeeded in totally eradicating these practices [gender segregation and veiling]." In the final years of the Pahlavi regime, only 35 percent of women were literate; the majority of college students were men; and while women constituted around 14 percent of the workforce (Sansarian 1982), the job market remained mostly gender segregated. The jobs that state policies encouraged women to take were the so-called pink-collar jobs, those traditionally dominated by women and labeled as feminine, such as teaching and nursing.[17] Once on the job, women found it difficult to rise into leadership positions. That being said, the reforms did enable a small number of women to hold highly ranked positions. Aside from the fact that they were for the most part entrusted with responsibilities that were "appropriate" for women (for example, minister of education or minister of women's affairs), these women largely constituted exceptions, or token elites, in a male-dominated domain. Overall, Iranian society remained quite conservative with regard to male-female integration. Although men and women were officially encouraged to mix freely at work and in the public domain, women were still socially restricted by acceptable codes of behavior, dress, and speech.

After the overthrow of the shah Mohammad Reza Pahlavi, in 1979, the newly established Islamic state sought an alternative modernity that would do away with the moral and practical pitfalls of Western modernity, which had in part come to be represented by the Pahlavi policies of deveiling and desegregation. Reimagining the state entailed reimagining, first and foremost, the capital city: Tehran had to be reshaped in a way that would represent the state's "Islamic" vision through urban planning and regulating behaviors. Yet since Islamization was a process based on trial and error (discussed in more detail in chapter 2) and not on a fixed notion of Islamism, the shaping of this vision was mainly left in the hands of (male) state officials and their understanding of "Islam."

So the Islamic Republic resorted to a number of strategies to create a world after its own, uncertain, image. This process involved and to a large extent relied on undoing some of the previous regime's urban arrangements, including replacing symbols and images that evoked the ancient régime's "modernity" with alternative ones that referred to a revolutionary "Islamic" modernity, organizing public religious events in juxtaposition to the ones organized by the shah, rejecting the prerevolutionary secular dress codes and applying Islamic ones in their place, and implementing and formalizing gender segregation where the previous regime had introduced desegregation. In an early declarative action by the incoming regime, which simultaneously created a new public iconography in accordance with the values of an Islamic state, the Islamic Republic renamed major cityscapes. Thus, streets, squares, and major landmarks in Tehran and other cities across the country gained new names; in place of the names of the shahs and kings of the past appeared the names of Islam's saints and imams, and later those of the martyrs of the revolution and the Iran–Iraq War.[18]

In its attempt to build the "Islamic city," the state subsidized and promoted the production and expansion of "religious spaces" such as mosques and seminaries. According to one account, thirty-five years into the Islamic Republic, the number of mosques saw a ninefold increase (*Eghtesad-e Irani*, May 13, 2014).[19] Once again, the new public order required the production of new men and women. For men, ties and suits were replaced by loose, long-sleeved, button-down shirts. For women, even those from recognized religious minorities, veiling became compulsory, not just because it was a religious obligation but also because it symbolized the undoing of the Pahlavis' modernization project, which had been partially displayed in the deveiling of women.[20] Women were simultaneously subjects and symbols of Islamic morality; their bodies were both on stage and a stage upon which various politics and ideologies played out. Ayatollah Khomeini had in fact referred to the chador as the "flag of the revolution" (Sciolino 2003).

The dominant view was that in an Islamic public order, the home should be valorized as the woman's place unless the common good required women to step out to show their support for the new regime. In Tehran, several of my interviewees recall, many doors were shut in a woman's face, excluding her from the public life of the city. She was prohibited from going to public swimming pools and gymnasiums "until further notice," which meant until the government found the resources to launch women-only facilities. If jogging or stretching in the parks, she would be asked to stop, because the movement of her body was considered provocative and thus prohibited. If traveling alone, she would be left wandering the streets, as hotels were prohibited from accepting unaccompanied women (*Zan-e Rooz*, November 24, 1989). And since gender segregation was regarded as one of the defining principles of an Islamic city (Abu-Lughod 1987), the new state created a set of architectural and spatial imperatives to divide places along gender lines, marking them with visual screens—walls, fences, curtains, and signs—all of them demarcating the women's place.

The Islamic Republic of Iran likewise put its imprint on nature. In the north the Caspian Sea, a destination for tourists from across the country, was divided by thick curtains that kept men and women apart, not just on the seashore but in the sea as well (see figure 1).

FIGURE 1. A sea divided: barrier at the Caspian Sea. Photo from author's personal archive.

On hot summer days, men were free to cool down by taking a dip in the sea, anywhere, anytime; women were not. They had to search for designated segregated beaches, or secluded and unpopulated areas, to seek refuge from the heat. In the latter case, they had to do so with their clothes on to avoid the prying gaze of unknown men or of guards on the lookout for transgressors. At a higher altitude, in the Alborz mountain range, which stretches all the way from the northwest to the northeast of Iran, dazzling visitors with its snowy peaks, is Dizin, Iran's most popular ski resort. As travelers made their way up the mountains and into the resort, they would see ski slopes carefully divided into two separate areas by a fence. If a fence was ripped here or a curtain torn in the sea, it was the women rather than the men who would be banned from skiing down the slopes or swimming against the tides. Public indoor spaces that women had access to were likewise segregated. In the buses traversing the crowded streets of the cities, women were relegated to the smaller space in the back. Inside the university classrooms, students were spatially disciplined by the signs hanging on the walls directing "brothers" and "sisters" to sit in separate rows, to walk in separate hallways, and to eat in separate dining rooms.[21]

There were conflicts among the revolutionaries over how drastic the gender segregation measures should be. As a result, some walls were never erected. For example, once in power, Ayatollah Khomeini was faced with requests to bar women from attending his public sermons and lectures. He admitted that he had managed to "throw the shah out with these women" and that there was no way he could bar them from attending his lectures (quoted in Kurzman 2004, 151). Reportedly, when a group of conservative revolutionaries divided university classrooms by installing walls, Ayatollah Khomeini ordered their immediate dismantlement. Some walls were brought down as soon as they were built.[22]

Moreover, the state's prohibitive policies were often contested and never completed. The first round of protests occurred on March 8, 1979, when several thousand "bare-headed" women "dressed in blue jeans [and] jackets" marched out from Tehran University "through heavy snow and slush," raising their fists against mandatory veiling, "refusing religion-defined womanhood" (Jonathan 1979; see also Sadeghi-Boroujerdi 2013; Moghissi 2009; Tabari 1980). In Tehran, Shiraz, and other provincial cities (as discussed further in chapter 2), people resisted gender segregation on buses, causing delays and interruptions in its implementation (Paidar 1997). Complaints against the regime's constraining policies and discriminatory practices did not come only from those who opposed it. During the eight-year war with Iraq, war widows, sacralized through the state's war propaganda and empowered by its compensatory programs, were also at the forefront of many such protests, such as when they opposed the custody law according to which they had to give up the custody of their child(ren) if they remarried.[23] Furthermore, contestations were not always collective or organized. There were individual acts of disobedience, practices that would induce change without voicing protest. Asef Bayat (1997) labels such acts the "quiet encroachment of the ordinary"; for example, past universities' checkpoints, inside the restrooms (or even in the prayer rooms), women would redo their makeup; behind the wheel at night, in the dark, they would let their scarves slip; at dawn, before the guards would start their morning shift, they would gather in parks to jog and exercise. And higher up in the mountains, where the government's grip was looser, fences were torn and boundaries were breached—in winter by skiers and in summer by hikers. These spaces of prohibition were also spaces of contestation, fraught with tension and struggle, even if hidden.

Under the Islamic Republic, gender segregation was transformed from a social practice, upheld by the people, into a state project, and as the state sought to navigate different social, political, and economic challenges, gender segregation as a spatial practice took different forms. The first form of spatial segregation introduced has a temporal dimension. The practice of reserving the same space for men-only or women-only usage at different times has been seen as a practical way of conforming with the principles of gender segregation in instances when providing alternative facilities and infrastructures was deemed to be not feasible, such as in large public gymnasiums, public pools, and recently some water parks. The second form, which remains the dominant one, is the partitioning of a single space into separate areas for men and women. Examples include beaches and, as chapter 2 discusses in detail, city buses. These divided spaces have separate entrances for men and women and are often unequal in terms of both quantity and quality, though the state has moved toward the equalization of these separate spaces, as chapter 2 details. The third form is men-only spaces, access to which is limited or prohibited for women. Sports stadiums are a primary example, and chapter 4 tells the story of the political battles that have surrounded the question of women's access to Freedom Stadium, the largest and most important sports complex in Tehran.[24] A forth form of gender segregation is the creation of women-only spaces. Women still have access to mixed facilities, but these are "extra" spaces that are created exclusively for women and that men are prohibited from entering. Chapter 3 examines the Mothers' Paradise, the first women-only park in Tehran, and places it in the context of the city's rapid urbanization, the state's concern about a disaffected citizenry, the spread of a depoliticizing technocratic discourse on women's health, and the increasingly important role of municipal-level state organizations.

Each case study offers a particular account of the interests, both of civil society and of the state, that are bound up in gender-segregated spaces and often transcend gender. Each case thus exposes the ways that the state itself is often fraught with conflicting and contradictory interests, breaking down any notion of a singular, centralized state with a coherent project of Islamization, as I discuss further in the conclusion. Taken together, the three case studies allow me to tease out the various ways in which gender segregation policies have been implemented across time and space and to further disentangle the complex processes that make up gender politics in Iran.

READING GENDER SEGREGATION IN TEHRAN: CRITICAL APPROACHES

Gender segregation in Iran, but also elsewhere, needs to be seen in its complexity— recognizing the contradictions that are inherent in it and the social and political logics that underpin and drive it—yet that complexity and the intricacies of the state that implements such policies are frequently ignored.

Much of the literature on gender and Islam places emphasis on religion as a primary driver of gender segregation policies and practices. Adopting a rather ahistorical approach and turning a blind eye to the complex social dynamics at play, it attributes fixed religious meaning to the practice of gender segregation and to gender-segregated spaces. Such perspectives do not consider the notable diversity of gender segregation practices in the Muslim world, and indeed, in non-Muslim societies and communities.[25] By doing so, these approaches imply that there is an inextricable link between Islam and segregation and that the production of gender-segregated spaces is informed by some sort of Islamic blueprint that provides clear-cut methodologies and solutions to the complex problems that involve the structuring of public spaces. What is more, it is customary to approach gender segregation and the concomitant attempt to shape public space accordingly as a process that has exclusionary implications. Scholars often read gender segregation policies as exclusionary policies that limit and delineate women's access to and participation in public spaces and spheres. Such perspectives tend to rely on abstractions; gender-segregated spaces and the practices that imbue them with meaning are often decontextualized and presented as detached from the range of sociopolitical dynamics that shape their contours.

Indeed, some scholars have begun to problematize this religious lens, which has dominated much of the existing literature on gender segregation. Drawing on two Egyptian Salafi magazines, Aaron Rock-Singer (2016) challenges those who view gender segregation as a long-established religious principle and practice, instead stressing more current contexts of such practices and their significance, suggesting that gender segregation arose out of contemporary political calculations. Contemporary political exigencies and political competition indeed constitute a significant factor in the promotion and institutionalization of gender mixing and/or gender segregation. Roel Meijer (2010) also echoes this view in his recontextualization of gender segregation or mixing practices in Saudi Arabia through focusing on debates among the Saudi shaykhs.

In my attempt to address the inertia of prioritizing and reifying religion in the discussion of gender segregation, in this book I contend that we need to move away from an essentialized notion of an Islam that is invoked in these policies and that shapes these spaces. I argue that the Islamic character of these spaces is hardly fixed. It is itself the product of social and political struggles: a blueprint continually invented and revised at the same time as an elusive fuzzy destination, always in dialogue with the domestic and international challenges and opportunities the Islamic Republic faces. Contemporary political exigencies and political competition and calculations indeed constitute a significant factor in the promotion and institutionalization of gender mixing and/or gender segregation. A closer look into the political dynamics that mobilize or even (re)invent traditions or regimes of gender segregation can shed more light on gender segregation than poorly substantiated references to long-established, fixed religious traditions.

Through the three case studies examined here, I seek to challenge another widely held assumption that has almost acquired the status of conventional wisdom: the viewing of gender segregation as an invariably prohibitive and restrictive practice.[26] Physical gender segregation does not necessarily lead to the exclusion of women from public and political spheres. For example, in the Ottoman Empire, the central role played by women in protecting sovereign power and promoting its public culture of royal ceremonies, monument building, and patronage of the arts from behind the walls of the imperial harem indicates that women of the court were very much present in public life (Peirce 1993). This decoupling of physical segregation and social exclusion is also present in interpretations of the position of women in the classical era of Islam, who are said to have contributed to the production of the verbal texts of Islam (Ahmed 1992), delivered political sermons (Shariati 1971), participated in transmission of religious knowledge (Sayeed 2013), and been successful entrepreneurs (Koehler 2011). These examples reveal the nuances between various forms of visibility and suggests that even when women are "unseen" in public spaces, they are still very much present. Their voices, actions, and subjective experiences continue to affect and create the social world.

Similarly, in addition to historical evidence, more contemporary instances of gender segregation can complicate our understanding of its influence by highlighting their nonexclusionary effects. Gender segregation has meant that female micro entrepreneurs tend to remain invisible in countries such as Iran, yet women entrepreneurs are active and, as Bahramitash points out in her discussion of the connection between gender segregation and entrepreneurship, "gender segregation sells!" (2013).

Without underestimating the undeniably exclusive aspects of segregation, I am thus focusing on the ways in which such practices and policies may produce enabling contexts and generate a sense of security and gratification for those at their receiving end: women. Arguing that we need to take a more critical look at segregation and decouple physical segregation from social exclusion, I build on recent scholarship that has suggested that these spaces do not lead to exclusion per se. In fact, as my analysis shows, we should move away from the simple binary of exclusion versus inclusion and develop a more nuanced approach, premised on the contextualization of the implications of instances and regimes of gender segregation.

Gender-segregated spaces can create a feeling of comfort and security, as well as a sense of solidarity (Sehlikoglu 2016; Shahrokni 2014). They can also be empowering and can facilitate women's integration into male-dominated spaces such as universities (Rezai Rashti, Mehran, and Abdmolaei 2019). Far from being passive victims, women appropriate gender segregation and reproduce it daily, and on their own terms, by developing their own activities and discourses that are by women and for women (Le Renard 2008).[27]

Gender-segregated spaces embody, in differing degrees, logics of exclusion, prohibition, hierarchization and inclusion, integration, and empowerment. Accordingly, their study needs to be socially and historically situated, and the politics around their productions needs to be given due attention and analysis. *Islamic societies* alludes to commonalities premised on religion and practices guided by it, yet it is also a shorthand term that refers to a cluster of diverse, unevenly developed, and internally differentiated societies, characterized by hierarchies and stratification that result in similarly diverse, domestic conflicts over political and economic strategies and cultural identities (Kandiyoti and Poots

2019; Moghadam 2003; Osanloo 2009). Gender-segregated spaces are formed under various kinds of states and different forms of governance and are embedded in a full range of social relations, discourses, and practices that differ from state to state and society to society.

Building on and moving beyond these critical readings of gender segregation, *Women in Place* examines gender-segregated spaces as a fluid reality rather than a formulaic or fixed image. It explores the types of gender segregation and their various implications, and in doing so, opens up the space for crucial questions about the workings of power and the state. As stressed previously, the book does not discount the effects of Islamic ideologies on the Iranian state's gender segregation policies, but it does reject a unidimensional definition of gender segregation and contends that an exclusive focus on the religious aspect of gender segregation policies overlooks the effects of globalization, as well as key social, political, and economic developments at the national level.

As the subsequent chapters demonstrate, the Iranian state has proven itself to be a multifaceted institution that is racked by internal tensions and conflict, yet it has also shown itself capable of managing and, as Arang Keshavarzian (2005) has argued, even thriving on these conflicts. In treating the state, I have built on works that take this heterogeneity as their starting point and focus on the state's productive power—that is, on how it has incorporated previously autonomous social, political, and economic institutions such as the Tehran marketplace (Keshavarzian2007); how it has generated new demands and mobilized entire sectors of Iranian society, for example through its welfare policies (Harris 2017); and finally, how state regulations and production of new categories, such as "true transsexual," have led to the production of, for example, new spaces for non-normative living (Najmabadi 2013).

Rather than searching for the true essence of gender-segregated spaces in Islamic texts and treating them as enclosed and static entities, I approach these spaces as the producers and products of social meanings and processes (Massey 1994). As the subsequent chapters show, it is often at the intersection of political struggles over the interpretation of Islam (Ghamari-Tabrizi 2013; Mir-Hosseini 1999) and the state's negotiation of global and local pressures that the true story of gender-segregated spaces lies. These spaces and the meanings that are associated with them are never set. They are constantly in the making and thus acquire different meanings and identities across time. If we take the dynamism of social relations into account, then we must accept that this dynamism will be reflected in the physicality of spaces, which are at once producing and produced by these relations. Taking cues from critical and feminist geographers and their attention to the gendered dimensions of place production and place making, I argue that gender-segregated spaces should be studied as social processes that are never concluded, and that despite the façade of homogeneity and harmony, we should treat them as multivalent and full of internal conflicts (Lefebvre 2009; McDowell 1999). In this interpretation, what gives a place its specificity is the fact that "it is constructed out of a particular constellation of social relations, meeting and weaving together at a particular locus" (Massey 1994, 154).

In the case studies that follow, my goal is to reveal the porosity of gender boundaries and the continuously shifting form, content, and signification of gender-segregated spaces.[28] These shifts, I argue, become a matter of politics and bear the imprints of the power relations that characterize them, and as such they are to be recognized and explained rather than dismissed. Scholars have widely documented how power is enacted on space: power presents itself by assigning different individuals and institutions to particular spaces (Domosh and Seager 2001; Woodward 2002) by setting the rules for socially accepted forms of behavior within various spaces (Gardner 1995) and by unevenly distributing space and the access to it (Harvey 2000). Spaces are also shaped in particular ways that serve power, as Foucault's (1995) study of the panopticon and Gramsci's (1971) study of the factory under Fordism have shown. In these ways and many more, the modern state uses space in its efforts to control and regulate social relations among its constituencies (Lefebvre 2009; Crampton and Elden 2007).

Each new form of state and political power introduces its own spatial arrangement and its own administrative discourses about space, as well as the people populating it. Foucault notes this spatiality of power as he draws attention to the ways in which the state binds itself to space and thus suggests that "a whole history remains to be written of spaces—which would at the same time be the history of powers—from the great strategies of geopolitics to the little tactics of the habitat" (Foucault 1995).

In order to understand the politics of space, in this case gender-segregated spaces, we need to wed them to a broader exploration of the multifacetedness of state formation processes and their distributive, inclusionary, and exclusionary dimensions. As far as Iran is concerned, however, studies of state formation largely emphasize the state's religious dimension or its (trans)formation as a theocratic state (Arjomand 1988, 2009; Banuazizi 1994; Chehabi 1991; Moaddel 1986). In addition, most studies of the Iranian state focus on the state's negative, prohibitive, and repressive power. These studies characterize the Iranian state as an Islamist state that thrives on its anti-American and anti-Western rhetoric (Kraus 2010; Saghafi 2005), a patriarchal state that discriminates against women (Afshar 1985; Moallem 2001; Moghadam 1992; Shahidian 2002a, 2002b; Tohidi 2007), or an authoritarian state that curtails human rights (Miller 1996; Moghadam 2004). In these studies, the resilience of the Islamic Republic of Iran is attributed to its application of force, coercion, and repression. This emphasis on repression misses the nuanced character of state power and raises questions about why and how the state has survived in the forty years since the Iranian revolution. After all, "power would be a fragile thing if its only function were to repress, if it worked only through the mode of censorship, exclusion, blockage and repression, in the manner of a great Superego, exercising itself only in a negative way" (Foucault 1980, 59).

Overstating Iran's repressive power leads to the neglect of the various ways in which the state *enables* its desired effects, rather than (or alongside) disabling its undesired effects. Furthermore, I contend, an analysis of the Iranian state's gender policies and practices is not complete without an understanding of the various actors involved, the entanglement of diverse sets of interests, and the subsequent tensions and struggles that unfold in everyday spaces over the form in which and the intensity with which these policies are implemented. Gender segregation policies may be ideologically motivated and are clearly not devoid of symbolic violence, yet as I demonstrate in subsequent chapters, in order to be successfully implemented, they needed to incorporate a bureaucratic rhetoric of care and service provision provided by a state that was not immune to the global reach of liberal governmentality.

A TALE OF TWO REGIMES

In 1989, ten years after the revolution, a woman named Farideh submitted the following letter on behalf of "a group of [revolutionary] sister students in the holy city of Qom" to a women's weekly in Iran, complaining about the "numerous problems" they faced, among them limited access to public facilities:

> As you know, one of the most esteemed contributions of Hazrat Ayatollah al-Ozma Mar'ashi Najafi . . . is his public library in Qom.[29] Regretfully, however, this library is open only to brothers, and sisters cannot make use of it.[30] . . . Isn't it really upsetting that in the holy city of Qom . . . there is not a single library for women which could be accessed during different times of the day? Does it suffice for an Islamic government to every once in a while put up a show, in the form of a seminar, and praise the status of women, and not pay attention to the needs and demands of . . . half of the population? Shouldn't the educational, cultural and recreational facilities such as libraries [and] gymnasiums . . . be fairly and equally accessible to the public? Considering sisters' contribution to the victory of the revolution, their instrumental role in nurturing the martyrs, and their invaluable service behind the frontlines, which does not need a reminder or an elaboration, we expect that the regime's officials to genuinely work toward the fulfillment of sisters' needs, especially with regard to our access to the [aforementioned] library. (*Zan-e Rooz*, November 17, 1989)

This letter captures a moment in the life of the Islamic Republic of Iran when the *sisters* of the revolution, makers and sympathizers of the Islamic Republic, realizing that their revolution had reneged on its promise for new "fair" and "equal" brotherhood and sisterhood, were becoming vocal and more assertive in condemning discrimination imposed on them in the name of Islam and the revolution. The new state had promised the "sisters" of the revolution the restoration and protection of their dignity and respect through a life opposite the one that the "Western or Westoxicated Barbie dolls" lived (Moallem 2001). Barbie dolls they were no more, but they were surrounded by many symbolic, as well as concrete, walls and boundaries that signaled prohibition and contributed to their exclusion from the public space.

In 2009, thirty years after the revolution, I met with Mr. Reza Mostafavi, the director of social and cultural studies at Tehran Municipality, in hopes of designing and conducting a survey of women who use municipality-supervised, women-only spaces. Reluctant to permit such a survey, the director expressed his discomfort with how these spaces were being used:

> Once, during one of my nightly evaluation visits to public libraries, I saw a few women in the women's section. My God! I was shocked. You know that these libraries are open overnight. It was around midnight. "Don't they have fathers? Husbands? What are they doing here in the library at midnight?" I asked myself. So I approached one of them to figure out what she was doing in the library at midnight. It turned out that she was a doctor, a general practitioner. She wanted to take the medical specialty exams, but had two small children and with them at home she had no time or space to study for her exams. She told me that she was happy to have found that we had recently opened an overnight public library, with a designated space for women, in her neighborhood. She takes care of her children until her husband returns from work. They eat dinner together, after which she leaves the children with her husband and comes to the library to study for her exams.

The doctor—the wife, the mother of two—had left the home. And to the director's dismay, so had "a few" others. The night no longer belonged exclusively to men, as he thought it ought to.

Like Farideh and the "sisters" of the revolution of the 1980s, the women in the library in 2009, the "daughters" of the revolution, were also surrounded by walls, but whereas the earlier walls had signified prohibition and kept women from entering the libraries, these new walls signified provision of public spaces demarcated exclusively for women and facilitated their presence inside these spaces that previously had been reserved for the exclusive use of men. The doctor and the few other women who were inside the library at around midnight embraced these segregated spaces not simply because of some flat version of Islamic morality, but because of many practical and sometimes even non-Islamic concerns. These new walls enclosing women-only spaces had burgeoned in response to women's growing demand for access to public spaces. These segregated spaces were an act of provision, part of the state's attempt to facilitate women's presence in a hitherto inaccessible, masculine space, which simultaneously helped address women's increasingly vocal calls for their inclusion in Iran's intellectual and professional spheres.

Like the sisters of the revolution who had articulated their own claims to public space, the daughters of the revolution have been advocating for their right to those spaces. They have vocally and visibly claimed, and what is more, taken advantage of, the access to spaces provided for them. As the two examples provided here indicate, both sisters and daughters of the revolution did so by confronting brothers and sons of the revolution who had been hesitant to "grant" access to such spaces, either by not providing sufficient access (in 1989) or by disapproving of the impact that women's use of these spaces had on established hierarchies and sanctioned gender roles.

Leaving these commonalities aside, these two moments, one from 1989 and the other from 2009, point to two different regimes of gender segregation, characterized by distinct "gender logics," underlying modes of discourse, patterns of segregation, different methods of regulation, and shifting notions of female subjecthood.

Although gender segregation has remained in principle a central feature of the Islamic Republic, it is important to argue that the gender segregation regime of the 1980s was characterized by an emphasis on exclusion, closure, and prohibition, whereas the gender segregation regime of the 2000s is characterized by the prominence of inclusion, opening, and provision. In both cases, however, segregation is a means through which gender difference is activated and women's access to public space is regulated by the state. Specifically, I contend, for reasons that I elaborate on later, that gender-segregated spaces shifted from functioning as spaces of exclusion that restricted women's movements in the city to spaces of inclusion that facilitated, even if under male skepticism, their presence in urban public spaces. For example, as I demonstrate in chapter 3, while in the 1980s the state prohibited women's outdoor exercise by framing it as *makrūh* (religiously unacceptable), by the 2000s the state was providing women with outdoor exercise spaces in the form of women-only parks, as a solution to public health problems.

The predominance of one regime of gender segregation over the other is a reflection of, and enabled by, the shifting balance in the state's mode of regulation from prohibition to provision. Whereas the gender segregation regime of the 1980s was proactive in establishing a new gender order in accordance with Islamic predicates, the gender segregation regime of the 2000s was reactive and premised upon a recognition of new social forces and the continuously shifting gender order (see table 1). During the 1980s, the state promoted a gender order in which femininity was primarily associated with the private space, the family, the children, and the kitchen, and masculinity was associated with the public space of the streets, the workspace, and the city. Later, the state had to respond to a shifting gender order in which women were no longer homebound but were mobile and public, traversing the city in increasing numbers as students, workers, and shoppers. In many ways, the expansion of gender-segregated spaces in the 2000s was part of the state's

TABLE 1 Gender Segregation Regimes

Mode of . . .	1980s: Gender Segregation Regime I	2000s: Gender Segregation Regime II
Regulation	Prohibition	Provision
Female subjecthood	Moral subject	Citizen
Discourse	Islamic	Secular
Gender domination	Exclusion	Inclusion

attempt to accommodate—even if grudgingly—this increased presence while still regulating it by providing more "enclosed spaces."

Although provision prevailed as a mode of regulation, the days of prohibition were not over. In some cases, regulations oscillated between prohibition and permission. During my fieldwork I, along with a group of female friends, was once turned away from a bowling alley and another time let inside; we once played alongside our male companions but another time were asked to play in separate lanes. In other cases, prohibition was never lifted to begin with. For example, ever since the establishment of the Islamic Republic, women have been denied access to Freedom Stadium (more on this in chapter 4). Even in this case, however, state officials, faced with both domestic and international pressures, promised to provide women with a women-only sports stadium, adjacent to Freedom Stadium, and to look into possibilities for creating women-only sections inside Freedom Stadium itself. These promises, stated repeatedly since the mid-1990s, have not yet been fulfilled.

At the same time, and as chapters 3 and 4 show, prohibition is never absolute but continuously contested. As power is the product of continual negotiation, the perpetuation of state power depends for the most part on generating some degree of consent. The pragmatics of state power, combined with the articulation of societal demands, lead to different combinations of prohibition and provision. What is more, the Islamic state's views on gender are neither monolithic nor fixed or eternal; rather, there are different views across the state's various institutions, and views change as historical conditions shift. In order to comprehend these shifts, one must adopt a process-based sociology in which "analytic priority is given to describing the properties of a generative process or chain of events" (Lamont and Molnar 2002). Thus, in this book I focus on process rather than on conclusive outcomes; as a result, I address the many nuanced social meanings that arise from the study of these layered interactions among gender, space, and the state.

The movement from prohibition to provision is accompanied by a corollary discursive shift from protecting women's virtue to protecting their rights and choices. In the three case studies presented here, the state's discourse on gender segregation has shifted from one of Islamic morality to a more secular one of "masculinist protection," which frames women as vulnerable passengers on the buses (chapter 2), as unhealthy and sedentary citizens in need of exercise spaces (chapter 3), and as ill-treated spectators inside sports stadiums (chapter 4). In all instances, women need to be protected and provided for by the state. This shift in discourse might be said to index a withering away of the religious dimension of a state—as some would be quick to point out, with a celebratory tone—but what is more significant is how in all three cases, gender segregation is managed through a discourse of protection. By clinging to what Iris Marion Young refers to as the logic of masculinist protection, which is similar to Foucault's notion of pastoral power (Dreyfus and Rabinow 1982), the state aggrandizes itself and bolsters its relevance by presenting itself as the protector and by ultimately offering to protect the "fragile" bodies that are the very products of its earlier policies (Brown 1995; Foucault 2007; Young 2003).

As the state has progressively moved on, from a phase of revolutionary fervor in which it largely attempted to graft Islam onto most aspects of social life to a postrevolutionary phase that requires more negotiation with and responsiveness to an expanding middle class, it has adopted a new, liberal language that addresses and caters to women's rights and choices. I contend that this new discourse, which forms the basis of the state's hegemony, is reached through a long process of negotiation and trial and error, as the case studies, and particularly chapter 2's discussion of Tehran's buses, indicate. But before delving into Tehran Municipality's changing approaches to gender segregation on city buses, I address some of the methodological challenges of conducting fieldwork in the city that I call home.

AT HOME IN THE FIELD: METHODOLOGY

To research gender-segregated spaces and the Iranian state, I had to go back to Tehran, where I grew up, studied, and worked as a journalist from 1996 to 2002, prior to moving to the United States to begin a PhD program. This book is the result of more than nineteen months of systematic fieldwork in Tehran between 2008 and 2014. I collected data through participant observation and conducted 132 formal and informal interviews with women who use the spaces I focus on, as well as state and city officials. I have revisited my research sites frequently ever since. I also undertook archival research of over nine hundred newspaper reports from the Iranian Newspaper Archive Database at Ettelaat Institution, the archives of *Zanan* and *Zan-e Rooz* magazines, the online archives of various presses, municipal records at Tehran City Council, and parliamentary procedures on gender segregation from 1979 to 2014.

Turning my hometown into my research site had its own pearls and perils. The most obvious was the issue of language, both spoken language and body language. I am natively fluent in Farsi, and my body, too, has been socialized in Iran. The streets of Tehran are a familiar "stage" for me, to use Goffman's language (1959); the "scripts" for everyday interactions were all too familiar and everyday etiquette all too transparent. Or so I felt. This awareness made it easy for me to step into different "social roles" and enact different "parts" and "routines": the curious researcher; the desperate student; the dutiful daughter, friend, neighbor; the persistent ethnographer; and so on. On the bus, I had to be assertive but also friendly, trading my seat for a few minutes of someone's time, for example. When speaking with the Freedom Stadium security director, I was restrained but also quite good at letting noes fly over my head. Furthermore, I was comfortable slipping into various kinds of clothing; at the Iranian Parliament, I wore a long gray dress and a black *maghna'eh*, a nun-like cowl that covered all of my hair; during my daily rides on the bus, I dressed in my normal outfit of jeans, a short dress, and a colorful scarf loosely tied under my chin; and inside the women-only parks, I took off the dress and scarf and walked around with my interlocuters in T-shirts and pants.

Different spaces have different levels of clothing regulations. The change in clothing effects a change in attitude and manner, in how one carries one's body, and in how one presents oneself both physically and verbally. Being familiar with these guidelines and scripts enabled me to move fluently in and out of these spaces. I fit in and was less likely to attract unnecessary attention, and therefore I was able to form fruitful relations with various women; many older women assigned me "fictive kin" roles, calling me by terms such as *dokhtaram* (my girl/daughter).

During my fieldwork I also benefited from my access to a widespread network of former colleagues, friends, and relatives on which I could rely for collecting data, setting up interviews, social support, and the like.

Despite my familiarity and social network, things did not always go smoothly. The fact that my research site was also my home constituted the source of many problems. Along with the easy access to sites and informants my familiarity afforded me, at times it also made it harder for me to identify noteworthy data. For example, it was a foreign friend visiting me in Iran who pointed out that in most of our family gatherings, men and women would habitually cluster around one another, often on two opposite sides of the room. This was something that I had missed completely, although my eyes were otherwise trained to capture the subtleties of life. I also had to work against my own taken-for-granted understanding of respondents' statements and gestures, supposedly common cultural scripts, and my expectations and assumptions about my own city and its changing spaces. For example, one night, accompanied by a friend, I went to Vahdat Hall, a performing arts complex in Tehran, where a puppet opera of Rumi, a thirteenth-century Persian poet and Sufi mystic, was on stage. While my friend was looking for a parking spot, I walked toward the entrance, but since I did not see the "women's entrance" sign, I stepped back and went to the side street to look for it. When I came back I saw my friend waving at me at the entrance. "Where did you go?" she asked. "Looking for the women's entrance," I said, only to have her laugh at me.

"Seriously? This is it!" Then, pointing to the main entrance, she said jokingly, "After you M'lady!"

We were both the products of the system under which we had grown up. But having left Iran ten years before, I realized that like many other scholars, journalists, and activists living abroad, I was looking for rigid rules, while my interlocuters had grown accustomed to the flexibility, unpredictability, and inconsistency of the rules. Home, I then recognized, was something that I would have to discover anew. I also realized that the boundaries between my research site and my everyday living spaces were constantly blurred. A research opportunity could easily turn into a friendly gathering, and a gathering with friends could just as easily turn into a research opportunity.

The term *gender segregation* carries negative connotations in Iran, even among its backers, who kept encouraging me to "use other concepts that are not loaded with such negativity." The method of participant observation provided a chance for informal conversations with both men and women without explicitly using this stigmatized term. Nevertheless, my position as an Iranian American woman who grew up in Iran and had studied and worked both in Iran and in the United States affected how people interpreted my presence. As I observed my subjects, they were observing me, making sense of me through their own interpretative frameworks. For example, my interview with Rasool Khadem, a former wrestling world champion and a (conservative) member of Tehran City Council, almost came to an abrupt end when the discussion turned to women's access to sports stadiums. I had caught Khadem in the hallway of the city council building, and I noticed that he was accelerating his pace, as if readying to dismiss my interview request. Because I knew he was also pursuing a doctorate in sociology, I gave him my elevator pitch and uttered the magic words, "Just like you, I am a PhD student." The interview that followed went very well as we discussed parks and buses, two of the three sites in my study. I then asked about sports stadiums, where women are banned from attending men's sports matches, and he gave me the usual answers about the stadium space being inappropriate for women, about their safety being in danger, about the difficulties they have at all levels of power and also with the clerical establishment. When I did not simply accept these answers and asked follow-up questions, he became angry—really angry—turned off my recorder, and asked me to leave. Shocked, I asked, "What happened?" I could not figure out what had triggered this sudden anger. "I should have known you have come here with your feminist agenda," he replied. "After all you are studying in the US. I know what you want to hear, but you won't hear it from me."

The gaze was turned on me. And his was a suspicious gaze. He had a reading of my type—Iranian women studying abroad, working on women's issues—and that had suddenly unsettled him. There were certain tropes through which I could be read, and I could not prevent that. I was all too familiar for him, and his reaction was all too familiar for me. This familiarity kept me from giving up. I held my ground; I pointed out our similar positions as PhD students and the importance of research, stressing the fact that my being there was a sign that I was ready and willing to hear and document different voices. I reminded him of the moment when he became the world champion, of how many women might want to witness such moments and share the national pride with their fellow citizens inside the stadiums. This all, of course, required a thorough knowledge of my interviewee's background. I then slowly moved my hand toward the recorder, put my finger on the "record" button, and asked, "Shall we continue?" The interview lasted for another half an hour.

Sometimes my subjects' discomfort with the topic of gender-segregated spaces seemed to be a product of their reading of me as a young middle-class, loosely veiled woman studying in the United States.[31] "After all you are studying in the US. I know what you want to hear, but you won't hear it from me." This statement and its tone were engraved on my brain. Patricia Hill Collins (1986) talks about the outsider within the academy, but now I was an outsider in a place I called home. I was a potential suspect, and at times I had to define and defend myself to my interviewees, correct their assumptions, or ask them to stop reading me based on their narrow frameworks.

This encounter also prompted me to reflect on another aspect of the dynamics of my interaction with my interlocutors; My previous professional activity as an advocate of change/activist was making it difficult for me at times to differentiate or draw the line between being an objective researcher and being someone who is invested in a cause. In this instance, the tension with Rasool Khadem was partly the outcome of my effort not only to listen and probe in order to obtain information and insights, but also to convince him that women "should" be able to enter the stadium. Convincing, however, is not a researcher's job, despite one's personal engagement. My emphasis on persuading him about what constitutes women's rights altered the nature of our conversation; at the time I had not realized that his responses were exactly addressing why these rights could not be materialized. Confusing my roles in this interview, I was unable to take home its most valuable outcome: Khadem was indeed supporting that right but was trying to explain to me, albeit in subtle and indirect ways. the constraints that even well-meaning officials face within the corridors of power.

Instances of misreading, misunderstanding, and misrecognizing, however temporary and transient, were present throughout my research and required considerable effort to overcome or mitigate at the levels of my self-presentation, interaction with my interviewees, and reading the information that my encounters yielded. When I met Leila, a twenty-three-year-old hairdresser, in the Mothers' Paradise, she kept shifting between worrying about my judgment about her sense of comfort within the park and her disturbance at her own sense of comfort. She would constantly search for ways and words to justify her appreciation of these women-only parks: "I'm not traditional, you know. I am not backward. I already told you that on weekends I go hiking with my boyfriend. But you know things are different here." I did wonder whether Leila was in fact reacting to what she thought was my perception of gender-segregated spaces, especially since she seemed to go to the park of her own accord. "Would she have been so embarrassed if she had been with someone she perceived as understanding that enjoying the Mothers' Paradise didn't indicate backwardness?" I asked myself. It occurred to me that both Leila and Khadem had read me the same way. The only difference was that in positioning themselves vis-à-vis me, one attempted to appease me and the other to oppose me.

On a different occasion, I went to the office of Fahimeh, a college-educated woman in her late fifties with a long history in the publishing business. As a self-identified feminist writer and publisher, she very explicitly expressed her opposition to the expansion of these segregated spaces: "Nothing good can come out of it [gender segregation]. It's a pure form of discrimination against women." At the end of my interview I told her that I was meeting a friend at the Mothers' Paradise and asked if she would like to join me. Reluctantly, she agreed, saying "only because I want to see more of you!" Fahimeh, my friend Maryam, and I walked on one of the loop trails, ordered tea from the café, and sat on one of the benches to chat for a couple of hours. I noticed that Fahimeh had become more relaxed; with her veil on her shoulder and her coat unbuttoned, she stretched out on the grass. Later that day I asked Fahimeh if I could meet with her again to follow up on some of my questions. She smiled and said, "Only if we meet here in the park!" There was clearly a mismatch between her words, expressed in her office, and her bodily comfort, expressed through her relaxed movements and her desire to return to the park. Neither Leila nor Fahimeh was comfortable with the comfort they felt in the segregated park space. One appeared to be "embarrassed" by it; the other "denied" it. These stories point to my subjects' ambivalent attitudes toward these sites, which made me realize the complexity of my findings and the need for a sensitive, nuanced analysis of what I had heard and seen during my fieldwork.

Contradictory attitudes aside, most of my interviewees expressed interest in having more women-only spaces. Likewise, when I was browsing through various publications' letters to the editor about gender-segregated busing, I saw again and again how women had embraced, claimed, and then expanded these spaces. So rather than dismissing the voices that did not necessarily conform to my own values and expectations, I included them in my narrative and worked to interpret how their inclusion affected my understanding of the transformations of gender-segregated spaces and the politics around them.

While some voices might fall outside the stories that researchers tell because they do not fit within a framework that finds them relevant or intelligible (Avishai, Gerber and Randells 2012), others may fall off the radar because researchers choose the more convenient path of following a familiar cast of characters. The voices that are reflected in Iranian studies literature, especially those focusing on women's rights and issues, are largely either the voices of social movement activists or those of reformist politicians and officials. There are reasons for this tendency: scholars residing abroad are better connected to social movement activists and the reformist circles, most of whom work toward and welcome establishing transnational connections. Scholars may also tend to stay away from conservative officials out of fear that an interview request might bring them under the radar of the state, especially since addressing women's rights and gender equality is considered a subversive practice and recently, and in a number of cases, has been framed as a "threat to national security." I decided to forego access to the library of the Bus Company of Tehran after the company asked me to submit my written request through the Ministry of Science, Research, and Technology, fearing that this request might make me a suspect in the eyes of the state.

When I started my fieldwork, everything was calm, or as calm as the Iranian political climate could be. But the 2009 reelection of Mahmood Ahmadinejad, the conservative president who had the backing of Ayatollah Khamenei, the Supreme Leader, aroused suspicions of rigging. Allegations of fraud created turbulence, protesters' initially called for a recount of the vote, and the ousting of president-elect Ahmadinejad sparked several waves of protests—the Green Movement—that shook the country (see Harris 2012). Once the dust settled, I picked up the project where I had left off, contacting reformist officials, members of Parliament (MPs), and city council members first. But my requests for further interviews were often declined. One reformist official even had a secretary ask that I not contact that office again: "It's bad for both of us," the secretary said. The secretary then kindly added, "What were you thinking? We are all under attack and accused of having foreign ties, then you keep calling every day mentioning that you are a doctoral student in the US and want an appointment for an interview about women and the city?" Not wanting to endanger my subjects, and myself, and being behind schedule, I was forced to adapt my strategy to the new political landscape. Out of desperation I called the office of a female conservative MP. "Hold on, please," said the secretary for Laleh Eftekhari. Within a few minutes I had my first interview appointment set. I was emboldened, so I called Nafiseh Fayyazbakhsh, a conservative politician and former MP, then Maryam Behruzi, a conservative lawyer, former MP, and the founder of Zeinab Society, then Masoomeh Abad, a conservative member of Tehran City Council from 2007 to 2017, and many more. One after another, the conservatives accepted my requests for interviews. Their insights into what goes on in the corridors of power were valuable to my analysis of the state's positioning vis-à-vis gender issues, especially since they helped me tease out the internal conflicts and contradictions among the conservatives as well as those between various state organizations.

Part of the challenge I faced in securing cooperation was due to the way some scholars before me had broken their subjects' trust. Both a university professor and a former (reformist) minister expressed concern about working with me because they recalled two other Iranian scholars, one residing in the United States and the other in Europe, who had been loose in their translations and interpretations of people's statements and had made blanket generalizations about Iranian lives. These two scholars' unmindful treatment of their subjects prompted me to think carefully about the implications of the bonds we ethnographers form with our subjects during our fieldwork. It is important to recognize that when in the field, researchers' access and safety should not be taken for granted, for they are the products of the relationship between researchers and their subjects, the generosity and trust the latter afford the former. When researchers leave the field, it is important to extend their subjects the same thoughtfulness and respect in their writing, through considerate, accurate, and humane accounts of their stories. What if we made sure that our subjects had access to our published research? What if we all had to go back to our field sites with articles and books in hand and present our arguments publicly? What if we took the suspicious gazes from our suspects seriously? How would these considerations impact our writing? "We may have to write more circumspect ethnographies—a high price for any writer to pay," Scheper-Hughes (2000) states, "but also a small price to pay to guarantee responsibility and accountability."

What is not written in a text reveals as much about what goes on in the labyrinths of state power as what is written in explicit detail. "Could you pause the recorder, please?" was a common request during interviews. Often a lengthy conversation would follow, which entailed important information regarding the workings of the state, including details of "who said what" and "who did what." But it was all off the record. At some point the interview would resume—"Thanks, you can press the play button now"—but the "real" story was told during these "silent" pauses. To maintain honesty and integrity toward my subjects without losing all of the information shared between recordings, I have used various discursive techniques to mask the actors while still including the most crucial actions. For example, I have used passive voice to shift the focus away from the actor and toward the action of a sentence, as in: "The proposal was widely criticized." The person(s) critiquing remain blurry. At other times I have used pronouns with no antecedents, such as: "several officials" or "many of the clerics." My copy editor often inquired: "which ones? Clarify." Yet clarify was something that I could not do.

In addition to the aforementioned challenges of researching gender politics and policies in Iran, women's acts of resistance and hard-won but precarious victories and advances often presented an ethical dilemma. For example, when I was inside the House of Volleyball, a small stadium where major volleyball matches are held, a woman seated near me took my notebook away to read what I had written, then asked me to delete all the photographs on my camera. She accused me of disrespecting the privacy of the women attendees and overlooking their efforts to gain access to stadiums: "You say you are working on women's access to public spaces in Tehran! Well, by writing about our presence inside the House of Volleyball, you will actually jeopardize what we have gained and there might be no next time." She wanted to be able to watch the match without having to go through the daily struggles and negotiations with the guards at the entrance of the House of Volleyball, and my presence and writing "would ruin that," she said. They had promised the guard, who had let them in, "not to cause any trouble" by publicizing their presence inside the stadium. I decided not to include this story in my stadium chapter, but in 2013 a journalist reported on women's presence in the stadium and posted photographs of female fans cheering and clapping, generating much controversy among various factions of the state. As a result, and as the woman who read my notebook had forewarned, women were banned from attending men's volleyball matches. This encounter and the following events made me wonder: To whom should I be accountable? To my profession, which expects me to deliver an accurate description of the events, or to my subjects, who fear that my reporting might put, not them, but rather their choices and hard-fought-for momentary freedoms, however mundane and insignificant they might appear, at risk? Is it ethically right to include such stories, knowing that they might jeopardize women's future access to these stealthy moments of freedom? Whereas research ethical codes are very clear about the need to avoid engagement and interaction that might result in conventional notions of harm, they do not take into account the impact our ethnographic research may have on the right to temporary, fleeting moments of happiness our subjects might yearn for. Our quest for the larger picture often makes us disregard the little things that matter in people's lives (see Thrift 2000, 381 and 385). Ethnographers must face these dilemmas, "the underside of ethnographic work" (Fine 1993), which cannot be resolved but must be thoughtfully navigated.

A book is expected to provide a coherent argument that flows smoothly. It needs to be written in intelligible and clear language that can convey the cacophony of the disruptions and complications of daily life, as well as the ambiguities inherent in the interplay between power and resistance. Ultimately, "each ethnography is an attempt to fit a world into a genre. We make presentational choices" (Fine 1993). *Women in Place* is the outcome of my attempt to navigate the complex and uneven terrain of the messy world of Iranian gender politics and present the chart of my trail in a coherent piece.

Boundaries in Motion:
Sisters, Citizens, and Consumers
Get on the Bus

I arrive at the Qods Square bus stop in northeast Tehran at 7:00 a.m. and approach one of the drivers, who is sitting behind the wheel and cracking roasted watermelon seeds in his teeth as he waits for passengers to get on board. This is the beginning of the Qods-Resalat bus line, which runs from the northeast to the southeast of Tehran, and the bus will not take off until it is full. I say hello to the driver and get on board, at which point he stops cracking seeds and tells me that I have to use the back entrance. Surprised, I say, "Oh, I'm sorry, I thought women sit in front these days! I sat in the front section of a bus just yesterday!" He puts aside his pack of watermelon seeds and gets his cigarette pack out of his shirt pocket. Once he is done with what seems to be his daily morning ritual, he looks at me and says, "That was a BRT [Bus Rapid Transit] bus probably. Back or front what difference does it make?" He taps the top of his head: "*This* is your place! You [women] are the crown of our [men's] heads!" As I get off the bus to reenter at the back, a young woman wearing a khaki high school uniform bangs on the driver's window. He rolls down the window only to hear her shouting about the excess diesel emission: "Can't you see we are all suffocating at the bus stop? Turn off the engine sir! Or, excuse *me*, are you too busy cracking your [watermelon] seeds!" Instead of turning off the engine, he leaves the window open, lights up his cigarette, looks in the rearview mirror to see whether the bus is loaded or not, then urges the young woman to get on board as he is about to take off.

As we move down Shariati Avenue, which stretches from north to south and connects multiple commercial, medical, and educational hubs, the bus eventually becomes overcrowded with passengers. I look up and see the girl in the khaki uniform leaning on the metal bar, the divider that separates men from women. She is still complaining about the driver. The young boys next to her, but on the other side of the bar, laugh. One of them says, "Take it easy, *baba* [dude]! Look at mister driver! He is still rolling his eyes at you." Another boy mocks the driver. They all laugh. Transgression usually occurs where boundaries are erected. Or one might argue that it is only logical that the mingling happens where the separation begins; after all, that is the one zone of contact left on the bus. From this perspective, one can say that the separation remains incomplete.

Sitting in front of me are Narges and Shabnam, students of industrial engineering at 'Elm o San'at Technical University in Narmak, a neighborhood in east Tehran. Narges lives in Chizar, an old neighborhood in north Tehran. Shabnam lives in downtown Tehran but had stayed overnight with Narges to prepare for their exams. I ask them if they always go to university by bus. Shabnam is busy with her "last-minute review of the formula," so Narges responds:

> I used to drive to university until I noticed that it is much easier to go on these buses. Don't you think so? The traffic kills me. At least when I'm on the bus I don't need to worry about driving. It's a mess! Here [on the bus] gets messy too. But it's between us women. There's no *angoolak bazi* [groping]! Also, you know how it is, women get too close too fast! Once a woman entered the bus. There was no seat left. She asked me to scoot over so that she could sit next to me. Squeezed together, like one happy family!

"One happy family," indeed! By the time we reach the end of the line at Resalat, almost everyone knows me. I say good-bye to all, and we all go our separate ways.

On another visit, I take the same line back up to Qods. As the bus waits to depart, street vendors hop on, selling tablecloths, candies, cosmetics, and kitchen knives; "sometimes," one woman bus rider notes, "they even sell women's underwear, especially in the women-only compartments in the metro." Indeed, gender segregation is also enforced in the Metro, albeit only partially. Unlike with the compartmentalization of the city's buses, women Metro passengers have the option of either riding in one of the two women-only compartments or joining other travelers in mixed compartments. The majority of my interviewees expressed that they would rather ride in the women-only compartments.

I wonder what the vendors in the men's section sell, at which point I realize that these gender-segregated spaces are not just the product of the differences between the two genders. They (re)produce these differences as well. As the bus becomes crowded and as one moves away from the metal divider (see figure 2), one's understanding of the other's world lessens—that world appears to be inaccessible, different. This socially constructed difference simultaneously sets the two genders apart and pulls them together. It creates both distance and desire to overcome that distance.

A few weeks later, at the Khorasan Square bus stop, Fariba, a thirty-seven-year-old, stay-at-home mom, and I get to know each other. I tell her about my life in the United States and my research project, and she tells me about her marriage, her

FIGURE 2. A world apart: riding gender-segregated buses in Tehran.
Courtesy of Masoomeh Niloufari.

life, and "the complications of raising a twelve-year-old boy." Later, as we pass by
the cloth houses on Mowlavi Street, she tells me: "Here's a story for you." Pointing
to the "men's section," she continues:

> This past month, Ali [her twelve-year-old son] suddenly decided that he's become a
> man. One day at the bus stop, he refused to hold my hand [. . .] then when the bus
> came, he refused to get on the bus with me. "I'm a man!" he said. He ran and entered
> the "men's section" from the back. The worst ride ever! As far as I'm concerned, he is
> still a little boy. He doesn't even know the street names yet. I stayed near the divider
> the whole time and watched him. He, of course, refused to even make eye contact. I
> asked one of the [male] passengers to direct him to get off the bus when we reach[ed]
> the Moniriyeh bus stop.

Fariba has many stories to share about Ali. But this one in particular stays with me, as it demonstrates that for Ali, perhaps like many other boys his age, to become a man means distancing himself from his mother and from all that is associated with women and femininity. Fariba laughs and says: "Ali is *baba*'s boy now, walks with *baba*, eats with *baba*, talks with *baba*." What's particular in the Iranian case is the existence of a physical and visible boundary (the metal bar) between the two genders. For Ali, moving past the bus's metal bar and into the "men's section" was like a rite of passage that led him to manhood. Manhood for Ali is very much about where he is placed vis-à-vis his mother and other women. While in many other times and places these movements happen unconsciously and habitually, and as such remain invisible, here in Tehran, on the bus, the process of "becoming a man/woman" is a palpable one. The metal divider reproduces gender as a binary category and reconstructs gender difference on a daily basis.

Taking these bus rides provides me with the opportunity to meet with many women using Tehran's transport services, some eager to talk, some hesitant or demanding to be left alone. This time, on our way to Azadi terminal, Ms. Bagheri, a fifty-five-year-old domestic worker, is sitting next to me. She lives in a one-bedroom apartment in Narmak, a neighborhood in east Tehran, with her daughter, who is in college studying Arabic literature, and her son, who is a twenty-eight-year-old mechanic. "And your husband?" I ask. "He was a truck driver. He was killed in an accident fifteen years ago." Ms. Bagheri, who does not own a car, gets on different buses every day to reach the houses she has to clean. With tuition and fee increases in private colleges, she needs to work even longer hours to be able to keep her daughter in school: "I don't want her to end up like me!"[1] She takes her hands off her chador and lets it slip onto her shoulders. She then unknots her scarf, brings a small fan out of her purse, and fans herself, enjoying its breeze: "It's hot! Good that men can't see me here!" It *is* hot. The women's section is populated by female bus riders blocking the prying eyes of men, who are just on the other side of the metal bar, and since Ms. Bagheri is sitting at the far back, she trusts that no man will be able to see her uncovered hair. Zohreh, a sixty-three-year-old "housewife" sitting to my right, rolls her eyes and whispers: "C'mon! So they see your hair a little. What's the big deal?" She is in fact trying to scorn Ms. Bagheri for her religiosity, while making a point about her own disbelief in religious law. She leans in close to my ear and continues: "*This* is our problem, not the government," implying that the state succeeded in implementing mandatory veiling and other religious rules because it had the support of Ms. Bagheri and others like her.

The bus space is occupied by women of all classes and walks of life. Every day, the lives of women such as the schoolgirl in the khaki uniform, Narges and Shabnam, Zohreh, Fariba, Ms. Bagheri, and "mister driver" converge in the bus's interior, a fluid public sphere whose contours are always in the making.[2]

A bus is a mobile space, an ideology in motion. It moves from one neighborhood to the other, day after day, week after week, year after year. It is the same bus, but never the same space. Three decades ago, during the 1980s, the bus's interior was reshaped by a metal bar that divided it into two separate sections, signifying an Islamic public order. At that time women were conceived of merely as potential passengers, and not even ones deserving of equal space on the bus. They were relegated to the smaller section at the bus's back, while men took the more spacious front. Then, during the 2000s, the buses no longer represented a male space with token seats for women in the back. Women were allotted an equal, although still separate, bus space. On regular buses they still sat at the back; on BRT buses, however, they rode in front. For a short period of time they were also given the chance to steer the big wheel and drive the bus in and around the city. Today, the bus is the same bus, still divided, but what it signifies has changed; women's public presence, once considered an interruption of or an exception to public order, has become an integrated part of it, one requiring recognition and accommodation.[3]

How do we grasp the shifting contours of this space, the shifting reality of the metal bar that once signified an unequal distribution of bus space? How and why did the gender organization of the bus space—and the city it traverses—change over time? To answer these questions, we must look at the processes through which the project of bus segregation has been implemented. Far from being simply a practice of exclusion easily intelligible as an expression of the static patriarchy of the Islamic state, gender-segregated busing has changed with shifts in the sociopolitical context.

This chapter is both a case study of gender-segregated buses in Tehran and a history of the changing socioeconomic contexts in which the Iranian state has operated. As a chronological account, the chapter is structured around three periods: the decade after the revolution, which was also shaped by the long war with Iraq (1980–88); the postwar period of reconstruction, which was shaped by economic liberalization under the "cabinet of reconstruction" (1989–96) and the reformists (1997–2005); and the more recent period of (neo)liberalization, in which the state bus company was partially privatized. I demonstrate that gender-segregated spaces in a modern metropolis such as Tehran are shaped by, and reflect, a mixture of institutions, ideologies, and interests. These spaces gain their shape and meaning from a combination and coincidence of various historically embedded sociopolitical relations. In historically locating the state's production and regulation of gender-segregated buses, this chapter highlights the gradual expansion of women's access to the city, which has been accompanied by their discursive transformation from subjects of revolutionary Islamic morality ("sisters"), to rights-bearing citizens, and eventually, to consumers. To be clear, the periodization suggested here and this transition from moral sisterhood, to citizenry, to consumerism is not linear. Rather, it is disrupted by the fact that these three forms and modalities of subjecthood continue to be unevenly distributed and reproduced across state and society, dialectically interact, and transform one another in an open and unfolding process. Yet these qualifications notwithstanding, this threefold transition represents not negligible shifts in the way women have been perceived as, administered, provided for, and engaged with.

The deepening of gender segregation practices, then, signifies a gradual expansion—and not contraction—of women's access to the city. Discursively, whether women are regarded as sisters, citizens, or consumers, the state is able to position itself as their protector, protecting their chastity and their right to a comfortable ride. The metal bar remains on the bus as a sign of the state's regulatory authority. The state, as the arbiter of the gender boundary, is embodied in the metal bar that divides the bus into gendered halves.

MAKING SPACE FOR THE SISTERS

Ayatollah Khomeini was not just the leader of a revolutionary movement that aimed to end the fifty-four-year reign of the Pahlavi dynasty. To many in Iran, especially the "slum dwellers" whom he regularly addressed, Khomeini was a savior who had made social justice imaginable and an alternative future possible—a future "free from the clutches of the rich," wherein "serving the poor" stood above any other virtue (Abrahamian 2009).

On February 11, 1979, the revolutionaries triumphed, marking this day as the end of the Pahlavi monarchy. Yet for many in Iran (and beyond), it marked the first day of the future they had been promised, an opening, a beginning. Ayatollah Khomeini's devotees labeled him the Leader of the Dispossessed Masses of the World, and the revolution itself, although carried out by a diverse set of actors, came to be referred to as the "revolution of the "barefooted" (pa-berahneh).[4] The new government pledged to eliminate poverty, illiteracy, slums, and unemployment and to "provide [basic] services to every individual in the country."[5] In his first public speech upon his return to Iran in February 1979, Khomeini stated, "We are for Islam, not for capitalism . . . and Islam will eliminate class differences." (Abrahamian 2009). The new state promised the "dispossessed" free piped water, free electricity, and free public bus transportation.

Taking its concern for the poor to the street, the newly established state started questioning the way the city had been governed and regulated by the previous regime. In 1982 the Tehran Traffic Organization denounced "the monopoly of a large proportion of road space by a small proportion of the population, i.e., the car owners" as unfair: "It was not just for 800,000 private motor cars to endanger the environment of six million Tehrani citizens by subjecting them to the dangers from environmental pollution, accidents, and other related ailments" (Farahmand-Razavi 1994). Indeed, the previous regime had given priority to car owners and car ownership. "One Peykan [an Iranian-made car] for each Iranian" was a slogan that Amir Abbas Hoveyda, Iran's prime minister between 1965 and 1977, had occasionally used.[6] This slogan typifies the former regime's plans and policies to encourage private, individualized forms of mobility as opposed to collective and public transit ridership. To be sure, the Bus Company of Tehran (BCT) was established under the shah in 1956, and the need for an efficient public transportation structure was mentioned in the Tehran Comprehensive Plan, which was published by the Tehran Traffic Organization in 1969 (Farahmand-Razavi 1994). Nevertheless, rather than investing in the expansion of public transportation, Iran under the Pahlavis developed a significant automotive industry. The first Paykan was assembled in 1967 by Iran National (Iran Khodro), the leading vehicle manufacturer, founded in 1962 under the supervision of Chrysler Europe. Within a decade, Iran National had started full-scale manufacturing of the car, except for the engine, and was producing 100,000 Paykans each year.[7] Hoveyda claimed that with the growth of the automobile industry, Iran's gross national product (GNP) enjoyed "an 8 to 10 percent 'cruising speed'" (Meyer 2003, 134).

In the Islamic Republic, this privileging of private car ownership and the consequent disregard for public transportation were interpreted as part of "an agenda that was aimed at pulling down the disadvantaged even further into the dark abyss of dependency" (*Zan-e Rooz*, August 8, 1981). To lend a hand to the disadvantaged and to provide them with fresh air, the new regime adopted a policy of car restraint. The eventual investor flight from Iran following the revolution meant that by the mid-1980s the expansion of the car market had come to a halt; foreign consultants, investors, and professionals had left, creating a vacuum that brought the domestic production of cars to a trickle. The import of foreign cars had also come to a standstill. In addition, the government restricted vehicle access to the nineteen square kilometers comprising the inner central business district, which was marked as a restricted traffic zone.[8] This created demand for better quality as well as a larger quantity of buses (Keshavarzian 2007, 181).

The state was quick, and quite successful, in limiting private car usage, but it was unable to provide acceptable levels of bus service to an increasingly displeased public. Then, with the dust of the revolution not yet settled, Iran was hit by two major political storms. First, on November 4, 1979, members of the Muslim Student Followers of the Imam's Line climbed over the walls of the US embassy, which Khomeini had deemed the "American spy den in Tehran," and took as hostages sixty-six US diplomats and citizens. Four hundred and forty-four days later, the hostages were set free. For Americans, the hostage crisis ended there. Iranians, however, were hit by the backlash. In response to the hostage taking, President Jimmy Carter issued an executive order freezing $12 billion in Iranian assets, and the United States has kept tightening the economic sanctions on Iran ever since. Second, on September 22, 1980, the Iraqi army, led by Saddam Hussein, invaded

Iran via air and land, initiating what came to be known as the twentieth century's longest conventional war, an eight-year war that significantly impacted Iranian society. The war, along with the 1985 collapse of oil prices, created a tight budget situation. The economy was crumbling.

The revolution and the war drew more and more people to Tehran, which was labeled the main migrant-receiving province. The streets of the capital witnessed the arrival of newcomers, *les misérables* hit by war and inspired by revolutionary promises. In one decade, between 1976 and 1986, the urban population of Iran soared by 72 percent (Bayat 2011). In Tehran, the urban population rose from 4,947,876 in 1976 to 7,222,190 in 1986. The villager seeking a better life, the displaced in search of a roof, the unemployed looking for better prospects, all came to Tehran, more so than other big cities, perceiving it as the promised land wherein the "future free from the clutches of the rich" would be realized. Tehran grew in size and in population. In 1979, at the advent of the revolution, Tehran had nearly 5 million inhabitants; within a decade they increased to around 9 million. By the time the war ended, the land area of Tehran, at six hundred square kilometers, was three times larger than what it had been in 1970 (Bayat 2010). The future looked bleak.

The ever-increasing population, including the influx of war refugees from the southern cities, had put new levels of pressure on the transportation system. Buses were worn-out and were regularly taken out of service. Passengers faced long delays and frequent disruptions to service. They waited in long lines before they could get on a bus, and many complained that they felt like "sheep being herded into a small space" (*Zan-e Rooz*, November 17, 1984). The regime faced increasing demands to equip the bus lines with more and better buses, or at least to refurbish the old ones. It was time for the newly established state to deliver the promised services. Yet what was left in the treasury was mainly spent on the war.[9] Furthermore, with the foreign professionals gone, the BCT required some time to readjust, make policies, and train experts (Farahmand-Razavi 1994). Demand was high, and supply was low, so the timeworn buses were put back on the streets. Exhausted were both the buses and their passengers.

The transportation problems were even worse for women. Women had been driving in Iran since the 1940s, but their access to private cars was limited. Up until recent decades, and despite Hoveyda's slogan, car ownership had been limited mostly to men of the upper classes. Buses, on the other hand, were "poor transit for the poor." Thus women, especially women from the working classes, had to rely on public transportation for their commutes. During the first years of the Islamic Republic, buses were, as Jaleh, a sixty-eight-year-old retired nurse, recalled, "men's territories." According to Jaleh and a few other interviewees, "The buses looked more like sardine cans." Under such circumstances, Jaleh added, "the few women who did ride the buses felt sandwiched in between men." The letters to the editor of *Zan-e Rooz* magazine, Iran's oldest women's weekly, provide a window onto women's anxiety about the unwarranted physical contact between men and women on the buses. For instance, in a letter to the editor in 1981, a woman named Parivash wrote, "As a woman I cannot bear the idea of standing in close physical contact with these men." She explained that men, whether "brothers" (Islamists) or "comrades" (secular leftists), continued to harass women on the buses (*Zan-e Rooz*, June 20, 1981). Whereas Parivash complained about sexual harassment and emphasized that for her, discomfort had nothing to do with religious ethics, religious women were concerned about their chastity and religious purity. These letters also capture the concern that some men, particularly religious men, had with protecting their "sisters'" propriety, as indicated in the words of a male bus rider in 1981:

> Due to the congestion inside the buses, some of our sisters, who would have to stand in the close proximity of unrelated men, are extremely uncomfortable (due to the pressures coming from the crowd) and they sometimes consider their ridership haram. Regardless, they are bound to use the buses. (*Zan-e Rooz*, August 8, 1981)

Since in Islam the unnecessary mingling of, and physical contact between, unrelated men and women is religiously forbidden, the crowded bus space of the Islamic Republic, within which men and women would constantly fall over each other at every bus stop, undermined the "Islamic" public order. Some, like M. D. (the letter writer used only her initials), who rode the bus to and from work, suggested that the BCT, now a public agency operating under Tehran Municipality and by extension the Ministry of Interior, should either "increase the number of buses in each bus line" or alternatively "segregate the bus space into a women's and a men's section" (*Zan-e Rooz*, March 13, 1987).

As early as 1981, the BCT issued statements declaring that it would "seek to find the most appropriate method to guarantee that Islamic rules and ethics are respected by all bus passengers and that dear citizens, especially observant Muslim sisters, are not troubled" (*Zan-e Rooz*, August 29, 1981). Nevertheless, the chaotic situation on the buses persisted, an indication of the state's failure to deliver the dignified life it had promised for women. Lacking sufficient funds to add new buses to the city bus lines, the BCT attempted to experiment with a new plan: gender segregation on the buses. Valiollah Chahpoor, then the director of the BCT, stated in an interview:

> Since we are an Islamic republic we have to make sure that our deeds follow the rules of an Islamic republic. Our deeds have to be in harmony with our mottos, and thus we had to do something about women's presence in society and the protection in public transportation of our sisters and their hijab. What I mean is that when our *sisters* are obliged to observe the hijab in the streets, we cannot let them be under pressure on the buses.... We are Muslims and believe in Islam. The Qur'an says when an unrelated man and woman are in a room, the door should be left open....

All these instructions have been given to prevent moral corruption. We follow the Islamic rules. (*Zan-e Rooz*, January 20, 1988)

According to various statements published by BCT officials, separating men from women would not make the bus more spacious, but it would at least make the bus space more Islamic. The BCT was put in charge of administering and supervising the segregation project, which, as the following sections illustrate, was based on improvisation and experimentation.

GENDER SEGREGATION ON THE DOUBLE-DECKER BUSES

The 1980s were the years of the double-decker buses, giant ship-like, blue and orange buses with two floors.[10] Gender segregation on these buses was easy, or so it seemed; the first floor was assigned to "sisters" and the second floor to "brothers." The use of "sisters" and "brothers" as opposed to "women" and "men" points to the dominance of an Islamic and a revolutionary discourse and ethics. But as the giant bus traversed the city, its first floor remained partially empty. "Brothers" were crowded on the second floor, while there were not that many "sisters" to fill in the first-floor space. The plan did not appear feasible. Thus, the BCT developed a new plan. This time, the second floor and part of the first floor were given to men. In order to reduce physical contact between the two genders, women were asked to use a rear entrance, tear their own tickets, and throw them in a metal box installed by the door. Men's tickets would be collected at the front door by the driver's assistant. Moreover, explained the director of the BCT in a 1988 interview, the bus company installed movable dividers on the first floor "so that depending on the number of passengers [they] could be moved back and forth, giving more space to brothers and sisters respectively" (*Zan-e Rooz*, January 20, 1988). In effect, however, as buses were always overloaded with passengers, the metal bar was fixed in a way that women could only use one-third of the bus space on the first floor.

The double-decker buses were eventually removed from the streets. A few were kept at Jannat Abad parking to be eventually exhibited at what was supposed to become the bus museum. The streets of Tehran had become jam-packed, leaving no space for these giant buses to travel between neighborhoods.

GENDER SEGREGATION ON THE REGULAR BUSES

Alongside the double-decker buses were the regular one-floor buses. The BCT had a difficult time coming up with a viable plan to segregate these buses, partially because unlike the double-decker buses, the regular buses of the early 1980s had only one door, in front. At first they decided to allocate one bus to women and one to men. "It was a ridiculous plan!" says Tahereh, one of my interviewees. According to Tahereh, who is in her late sixties, this plan created a lot of problems for families who wanted to reach the same destination but had to wait for different buses. At the time, bus riders made their complaints public by writing to various newspapers and magazines about cases in which, for example, "couples had been forced to take separate buses when going shopping, a mother accompanying her sick son to hospital had been forced to travel on a separate bus and so on" (Paidar 1997). Moreover, as reports published in various magazines indicate, the partially empty women-only buses that passed by the bus stops filled with male passengers left the men frustrated and angry, aggravating rather than remedying the transportation chaos. Men complained that it did not make sense for them to stand in line while a bus gave rides to only a few women (*Zan-e Rooz*, November 10, 1989). Bus drivers reported that every time they reached the beginning of a bus line, they would inevitably get involved in a fight with the impatient male passengers, who could not accept the idea of women-only buses. Soon the BCT gave up the idea of women-only buses.

The importation of two-door buses made it possible to replace this plan with a system in which "where possible, men would use the front door and therefore occupy the front space of the bus and women would use the back door" (*Zan-e Rooz*, October 15, 1982). And thus, on the bus's exterior, "brothers" was written next to the front door and "sisters" next to the back door. The newly imported buses did not have a metal divider, so there were no boundaries between the men's and women's sections. Ahmad Ziyaee Boroojani, the BCT director at the time, stated: "If there [were] more sisters, they [would] take up more space, and if there [were] more brothers, they would take up more space." As far as the BCT was concerned, "the problem was solved." For the bus riders, however, the problem persisted. "Who pays attention to the signs on the outside of the bus?" wrote a reader in a 1984 letter to the editor of *Zan-e Rooz*.

In the late 1980s the BCT launched a new fleet of buses that also had metal bars like the ones that had proved to be successful on the double-decker buses, as well as on regular buses in the two provincial cities of Isfahan and Tabriz.[11] In these buses with the dividers, women would get on the bus through the front door and men through the back door, a reversal of the system on the double-decker buses. "It was all messed up," remembered Fatemeh, a fifty-one-year-old mother of two. "I did not have a car back then and had to use the bus on a daily basis." She explained to me that bus riders would often find themselves clueless about which door they should use, how much space they could take up, whether women-only buses still existed, and whether they should tear their own tickets or give them to the driver's assistant. "Every day there was a fight at the bus stop among the passengers and the driver and among the passengers themselves," she recounted.

The BCT kept experimenting with different plans. Eventually it settled on a unified plan across all bus lines and in all cities. The BCT relegated women to the back third of the bus and sent men up to the more spacious front, separating them by a divider. The new buses had two doors, which also made it possible for women to use the back door and for men to use the front. Along with this change, the BCT issued the following statement:

> In order to respect our valued passengers and abide by the holy boundaries inside the buses and in order to prevent some moral problems, with the efforts of officials and with full capacity we have undertaken to implement the gender segregation plan inside the buses to promote the appropriate Islamic ethics. This plan is still in effect; however, since no plan could be successfully implemented without the active and widespread participation of the people, we expect the hezbollah nation to stand by our colleagues in the gender segregation campaign and cooperate.[12] While using the buses, sisters use the back door and brothers the front door, and so in this way each citizen will play their part in this valuable Islamic move. (*Zan-e Rooz*, December 13, 1991)

Despite occasional complaints by the bus riders about the "inconsistency" of the gender segregation plans, sporadic reports of vandalism (i.e., breaking the metal divider), and the BCT's statements about "Tehranis' lack of cooperation," the plan succeeded (*Zan-e Rooz*, October 15, 1982). With physical contact between men and women bus riders reduced to a minimum, the bus space was finally "Islamized." The metal bar signified the Islamization of the bus space; the unequal distribution of the bus space reflected the established gender order, according to which women were primarily associated with home and domesticity and therefore required less space in public.

But this gender order was about to change as women were becoming more mobile. Ironically, their mobility outside the home, and across the city, was partially enabled by the initial gender segregation plans in the 1980s.[13] According to several of my respondents, gender segregation of the bus space facilitated their movement. They pointed out that the separate bus space removed not only the "fear of committing sin" but also the "hassle of competition with men." In Iran, at least until shortly before this change was made, people waiting to board a bus would frequently form a disorderly line, and thus eventually it would become difficult to figure out what the initial order had been. Upon the bus's arrival, men and women would then run toward the bus door. "Under these circumstances," Zahra Sadr-Azam Nouri, a former (female) district mayor in Tehran, explained to me:

> The gender segregation plan came as a blessing. Women have to make sure that their chador or head-scarf is not falling off; sometimes they carry a bag, a bunch of books, or their grocery shopping, or a child—or even two. It is difficult to compete with men. So perhaps the initial planners of gender segregation did not have this in mind,

but what I find significant is that with segregation, women had to compete with women and *that* was a blessing. I am talking from experience!

With the "Islamization" of the bus space, many women who had been hesitant to ride the buses started using them. For example, Neda, whose family lives in Tarasht, a working-class neighborhood in west Tehran, explained to me that without the allocation of distinct spaces to men and women, her mother would have been confined within the house and would have only gone out with Neda's father or in a relative's car: "Her movement was limited. She would have perhaps just walked across the neighborhood to buy groceries." Neda's mother is extremely observant, Neda explains, and rarely talks to strange men—"except the bakers and the grocers," she adds, "who are not 'strangers' anymore!" For the past fifteen years, however, Neda's mother has been getting on the bus, traveling from the southern part of the city to the center to help Neda with child care. Gender segregation has made it possible for women like Neda's mother to feel comfortable and proper riding buses—and for men like Neda's father to permit this movement. In 1989, after the implementation of an earlier version of the gender segregation plan, BCT director Valiollah Chahpoor had also remarked on how the partitioned space for women had brought a new female ridership:

> After the implementation of the gender segregation plan, we noticed that we gained new passengers, meaning that those of our sisters who had never used the buses were added to our bus passengers. In Baharestan Square, I myself witnessed this situation: I saw sisters who were getting on the bus who told me that they had never ridden a bus before. This is very valuable for us, as we realize that we have managed to give transportation services, however minor, to our sisters. (*Zan-e Rooz*, January 20, 1989)

By the second half of the 1980s, women had increasingly found their way into public spaces and spheres. The "veiled sisters," initially addressed as morale boosters for their "warrior brothers," were now being recruited as revolutionary guards and mobilized into the Basij (Mobilization of the Disinherited), the Construction Struggle and Literacy Campaign, and Medical Aid (Moallem 2005). As the war continued, they were even asked to be prepared to take up arms in defense of Islam. The Basiji women were already demanding from their peers the same level of respect and acknowledgment that they were receiving from the "Imam"[14] (Paidar 1997). The veiled sisters had gained a voice and were demanding to be heard. Their demands began to crack the pillars of the existing gender order, and these cracks were about to grow wider.

In 1983 one of the male members of the Iranian Parliament, concerned about the "threat" of women's work, stated: "In Islamic society woman's upkeep is the responsibility of her husband and she should not have to work. . . . If this changes, everything will change; there will be no submission by women" (Paidar 1997, 323).

In the years that followed, the masculinized public space of the earlier postrevolutionary years gave way to a more feminized one. And with that, to the deputy's dismay, "everything changed."

CITIZENS' RIGHT TO SAFE RIDES

During the 1990s Tehran's landscape began to look different. Women were gradually being included in public spaces—albeit segregated ones—as shifts in social, political, and economic imperatives slowly but surely drove women into the spaces of work, education, and consumption, demonstrating the failure of "the ideology of domesticity" promoted by the Islamic Republic (Moghadam 1988). Several factors contributed to this shift. As the war continued, the "warrior brothers" turned into "martyr brothers" in increasing numbers (Moallem 2005). The number of those gone missing or taken captive was also on the rise (Kurzman 2004). Wounded by the war, and mourning the loss of their fathers, husbands, and brothers, many women found themselves the new heads of their households. They could no longer rely on men to do public tasks or earn an income. They had to look outside the confines of their homes for their livelihood.

In the meantime, "the populist considerations of the Islamic state, the religious ideal of charity, the Iran-Iraq war, and the US-led economic sanctions led to the emergence of a welfare state" that provided state-funded social services in different areas, including but not limited to health and education. All these services induced changes in the size, structure, and social functions of the family (Ladier-Fouladi 2002). The fertility rate decreased from 5.15 children per woman in 1989 to 2.21 in 2000, the age of first marriage increased, and following the successful state-funded family-planning program, the annual population growth rate declined from 3.4 percent in 1986 to 1.5 percent in 1996 (Hoodfar and Assadpour 2000).[15] These demographic shifts further facilitated women's entrance into the public spaces of the city. In addition, the relative growth in the rate of divorce and the lagging number of new marriages left many women in charge of their own lives, further necessitating their entrance into the city.[16] It was not just women without men who were put in charge of their own lives. With soaring inflation and low salaries, women who years earlier could rely on the income of their husbands or fathers had to leave their homes and take whatever employment they could find. There was also a growing desire among women to go to work and be considered productive laborers.

Thus, with the gradual weakening of women's ties to the domestic sphere, along with the expansion of spaces of education, work, leisure, and consumption, during the 1990s women emerged out of their homes and entered jobs and schools. In addition, with the end of the war in 1988, President Hashemi Rafsanjani's (1989–1997) developmentalist agenda, whose main priority was Iran's reintegration into the global economy, opened the door to International Monetary Fund (IMF) and World Bank involvement in the reconstruction effort and inspired free market–oriented structural adjustment policies. Rafsanjani's government drafted the First Development Plan (1989–1993),which embraced free market economic principles and aimed at galvanizing the industrial sector and partially privatizing some of the state organizations. The discrepancy between ideological prescriptions and economic imperatives, or what some refer to as "market fundamentalism," led to an increased demand for women's employment, which in effect turned "sisters" into productive laborers (Bahramitash 2003a). Whereas in 1976, three years prior to the establishment of the Islamic Republic, 70 percent of women were "housewives," by 1996 the percentage had declined to 59 percent, which considering the population growth, means that a large number of women were released into public spaces (Shaditalab 2005). From dipping, after the revolution, to a low of 8.90 percent in 1986–87, according to World Bank data, women's participation in Iran's labor force rose in the 1990s, from 10.44 percent of the total labor force at the beginning of the decade to 15.60 percent by 2000.[17] Needless to say, official data underestimate women's participation in the labor market, as many women are active in informal, home-based, or "invisible" sectors of the economy, for which there is not sufficient information. Nevertheless, reflecting patterns throughout the Middle East, women's share of public- and service-sector employment increased rapidly, reaching 47.40 percent in 1996 (Alaedini and Razavi 2005, 62). In terms of education, although a wide disparity between men and women had persisted since the 1970s, literacy rates among women rose substantially in both rural and urban areas, reaching near parity in 1996/97 (Alaedini and Razavi 2005). In 1998, for the first time in Iranian history women outnumbered men by over 2 percent among newly admitted university students. Since then their share of higher education has been continuously on the rise (Shahrokni 2019, 84–102; also see Rezai Rashti 2015; Shavarini 2005; Shirazi 2019). These trends have been accompanied by the development of a "feminist consciousness" among the youth, especially women, which has shaped many of their demands and activities (Kurzman 2004).

These circumstances, along with the initial gender segregation plans, led to an increase in women's use of the public bus system, to the point that the number of women on a bus was closer to the number of men and had become equal during rush hours. Thus, the 1990s could be called the decade of the gradual feminization of public spaces as martyrs' wives, university students, single and working mothers, single women, and married women all found reasons to get out and about in the city, especially as the city was becoming more vibrant and giving.

Quantitative developments brought with them qualitative transformations. As women rode the buses in increasing numbers and made their way around the city, a new notion of femininity emerged, one that was no longer associated with domesticity and that demanded recognition in the city. That small section at the back of the bus had made women's rides religiously pure and physically safe, encouraging them to lay claim to it as a space of their own. The (segregated) bus space shifted from being a feminine space to a "feminist" space; as women developed a sense of entitlement to their (separate) section on the bus, the metal bar came to embody the unjust distribution of bus space, prompting them to demand a larger share of the bus space and, perhaps more important, equal access to it.

"From the back seat in Iran," wrote Elaine Sciolino for the *New York Times* on April 23, 1992, "murmurs of unrest could be heard." The complaints expressed in letters to the editor of *Zan-e Rooz* were no longer about the unwarranted and illegitimate physical contact with "brothers," but about men crossing the boundaries and taking over women's seats. Women passengers were no longer primarily concerned with men treating them as passive targets of daily harassment but with their entitlement to a space that was at first denied to them and later only conditionally theirs. For instance, in 1996 a female government employee wrote to the magazine:

> When we manage to get on the bus we see men sitting in *our* sections and they do not even get up [to give their seats away to women], and so women, in a section that's *theirs*, have to stand on their feet. (Emphasis added.)

By the late 1990s, not only had women developed a sense of entitlement to these segregated spaces, but they also had formulated men's intrusion as a violation of women's rights. Men's presence in these spaces now represented a threat not to women's purity or safety, but rather to their sense of entitlement. Another woman, who regularly rode the bus line to al-Zahra University, a women's university, wrote:

> I am a regular on the Valiasr–al-Zahra University bus line. There are many girls' schools on this bus line and at the end of the line we have al-Zahra University. It is obvious that women are the main passengers on this line. . . . I can say with certainty that in most of the hours, only women ride this line. In light of this, the number of seats allocated to women is extremely unfair. Men have six or seven rows, and women have only two rows. The main problem is not that there are not enough seats. The main problem is that there is little space for women and therefore on many occasions women cannot get on the bus while the seats in the men's section remain empty. (*Zan-e Rooz*, August 3, 1996)

Consequently, the BCT officials realized that they had to provide women with more bus space. In order to expand women's share of the bus space, the BCT followed two strategies: equal division, where possible, of the existing bus space between the two genders, and the provision of women-only buses. Reacting to a shifting gender order, the BCT had to re-place the bar, redraw the gender boundary, and move it to create an equal bus for women. The bar was the same bar, but its repositioning signified a shifting gender order to both the officials charged with addressing women's demands and the practicalities underlying them and the women passengers themselves. In this order, women "deserved" and demanded a larger space on the buses. The other strategy was for the BCT to launch women-only buses. In 2003 Mohammad Sarafian, the director of the BCT at the time, went as far as announcing that in response to women's needs and demands, the BCT would "allocate 10 to 20 percent of the buses in different districts of Tehran to women so that they can ride the buses more comfortably" (*Zan-e Rooz*, September 13, 2003). Launching women-only buses was not a new initiative. As early as 1992, and in response to the growing presence of women in public, one of the local branches of the BCT had tested the waters and during "women's week" had temporarily hired six women bus drivers to "demonstrate women's ability in driving buses" (*Jomhoori Islami*, December 28, 1992).[18] This symbolic move was frowned upon by many people, who raised their concerns about its impropriety, as a letter from a *Zan-e Rooz* (September 13, 2003) reader illustrates:

> This act is not respectful to women's esteemed position in our society—exactly the opposite: it is discourteous to them and overlooks their respected position. . . . This act does not demonstrate women's ability in carrying out social affairs, but on the contrary crushes their social and emotional character by imposing on them a difficult task. . . . Islamic Iran is not a blank page that can be turned into a copy of the decadent West.

Ultimately, the local branch's initiative to launch women-only buses was suspended, and the BCT failed to put women on the roads as bus drivers.

For similar reasons, and due to the BCT's own internal institutional conflicts in the early 2000s, Safarian's suggestion did not materialize. Nevertheless, the BCT did acknowledge the need to expand women's share of the bus space as passengers.

Later in 2003 Sarafian stated that the limited space at the back of the bus was no longer sufficient for women and thus, as "bus segregation is to accommodate women and provide them with more comfort," the BCT had decided that in each bus line, every thirty minutes one bus would transfer only women (*Zan-e Rooz*, December 5, 2003). This plan was still impractical, given how the gender composition of the bus passengers would change with the time of day and neighborhood. Nonetheless, the BCT officials acknowledged women's right to comfortable, secure spaces and stated that their demands and needs had to be accommodated. The place of the body became the center of women's needs. This marked the boundary between self and the other in a social as much as a physical sense and became a defining element of the female self. The carving out of women's personal space and its contours were to be defined, drawn by the state, and this shift in discourse indicates how the state, as represented by BCT officials, evolved and situated itself as the protector of women's personal space.

By the second half of the 2000s even official language had shifted to highlight women's right to a separate, comfortable, safe, and religiously pure space. The state was now protecting women's space from men's intrusion. Crossing the boundary or neglecting the metal bar was now both about disrespecting the authority of the state and about denigrating women's rights. For instance, in 2006 Mohammad Ahmadi Bafandeh, then director of the BCT, stated (*Etemad*, December 17, 2006):

> Unfortunately, a number of men who do not respect women's rights and are indifferent about the existing rules create problems for women and other passengers by taking seats from the women's section.

During the Islamic Republic's early years, public space had been marked as masculine, and women's presence in it was only grudgingly tolerated through the creation of small, segregated, women-only spaces. In this initial phase of segregation during the 1980s, the state had defined women as moral subjects and framed gender-segregated busing as part of the state's Islamization project and the maintenance of traditional gender norms. In the second phase of segregation during the early 2000s, the state defined women as citizens with rights of access to a safe and comfortable journey through the public spaces of the city. Officials spoke of women as having a right to (segregated) bus spaces and of men's intrusion into these spaces as a violation of their rights. "Respecting" women required that the state accommodate not only Islamic gender norms but also women's need for comfortable and harassment-free rides. Economic necessities made mobility imperative, and gender-segregated busing produced a new, particularly feminine space that allowed mobility to be viewed as appropriately—and even deservedly—feminine. The BCT had unknowingly contributed to the transformation of the very social order on the basis of which the initial gender segregation plans had been carried out. Though it was initially an exception to the rule, by carving out a distinct feminized space within the masculine public space, the state enabled women to expand the area within which their movement took place, in effect making the "exception" of women's presence less and less exceptional. The state had to accommodate women's needs, protect their personal space, and respect their rights of access to (bus) space.

WOMEN'S MOBILITY AS PROFITABLE

Once again, citizens demanded an extended high-quality transportation system and expected a response. At the same time, the state was grappling with a literal impasse in the capital. Tehran of the 2000s, with its gridlocked traffic, was likened to an oversized parking lot, where the more than four million cars attempting to transit the city were stalled on the roads for hours. To make matters worse, this "oversized parking lot" was cloaked by an eye-stinging brown cloud of dust and air pollution, which reportedly choked more than three thousand people per month—a "collective suicide," it has been called (Erdbrink 2013).

The looming of this cloud and the severity of air pollution had on many occasions forced the government to announce "smog holidays," during which government offices and schools were shut down, costing Iran 350 millions of dollars.[19] The smog was partially caused by substandard gasoline produced domestically after trade sanctions limited Iran's access to high-quality gasoline. The sanctions also squeezed the state's capacity to supply its growing car market with catalytic converters, a standard engine feature that reduces the emission of harmful gases.

Concurrently, the car restraint policies of the earlier years were either reversed or relaxed. First of all, access to the restricted traffic zone could now be purchased in the form of single-day, weeklong, or annual passes. Moreover, since the early 2000s automobile production in Iran had grown exponentially, making Iran the fifth fastest growing automaker in the world and the largest in the Middle East, with the annual production of more than 1.6 million cars (Dubowitz and Ottolenghi 2013). There were now over twenty-five automakers in Iran, which were in joint ventures with popular international automakers. At the same time, due to the postwar liberalization of the economy pursued under the presidencies of both Rafsanjani (1989–97) and Mohammad Khatami (1997–2005), car imports were steadily on the rise (Wilman and Bax 2015). This trend indicates a renewed consideration of the middle and upper classes as opposed to the "barefooted." Available data suggest that car ownership and usage in the Tehran region had been rising rapidly between the mid-1990s and 2000. Indeed, the number of private cars owned by Tehranis increased at a staggering pace, from 95 cars per 1,000 inhabitants in 1995 to 138 per 1,000 inhabitants in 2003 (Ataian 2011, 99). But this increase in car ownership had an additional story to tell, that of a persisting urban divide. The figures throw into sharp relief a capital city region split along the lines of the historical pattern of north-south socioeconomic urban divide and suggest that the increase in car ownership has been uneven in geographical terms. Thus, car ownership in the poor southern districts reached only 69 per 1,000 inhabitants in 2003, while in the northern, more affluent, districts car ownership was just under five times higher, at 314 cars per 1,000 inhabitants (Ataian 2011, 100).[20]

But in addition to this geographical and socioeconomic divide, Tehran faced additional challenges in terms of the urgent need to develop a transportation infrastructure fit for purpose. In 1980 Tehran Municipality started undergoing a series of changes that related to both the scope of its services and the area of jurisdiction. This transformation of the city was to continue for decades to come. In a recognition of the de facto expansion of the space the capital occupied, 120 villages and 2 cities were incorporated into the area of the municipal authority, increasing Tehran's area from an original 225 square kilometers to 520. Yet the city's rapid physical growth was coupled with the unplanned, uncontrolled, and uncoordinated development of its districts and exacerbated the anarchy characterizing the mix of land uses in the city. The urban sprawl of Tehran faced severe transportation problems, as the need for the population to be "on the road" and cover the long distances separating their localities of residence, work, education, and leisure had resulted in the rapid development of roads and highways traversing the city (Roshan et al. 2010).

The challenge faced by city and transportation planners and the politicians entrusted with the running of the capital was thus twofold: to mitigate the north-south inequalities in the already established urban fabric and to integrate the districts of the expanded metropolis through the development of an efficient transit infrastructure. Alas, not only was there a lack of coherent urban planning logic to address these challenges, but also the expansion of Tehran's metropolitan area was not accompanied by a comprehensive development plan for mass transportation. By the 2000s the lack of investment in public transportation and its inefficient organization meant that the city was not delivering acceptable levels of service to an increasingly mobile public. The bus service had deteriorated; in the absence of efficient public transportation provision or a coherent blueprint thereof, numbers of car trips went up, passenger numbers dropped, congestion and air pollution problems intensified, and the quantity of complaints shot up. The state was once again failing to fulfill its mission as a provider.

The BCT, as a state agent, had to undertake to expand and improve the bus space and in the process, the women's share of it. In view of the inefficient and overly large public sector on the one hand, and on the other the neoliberal logic dominating the global financial and technical assistance institutions toward which Iran was turning for help at the time, the solution was to look outside the state, to the private sector. President Khatami had been openly critical of the economic situation, calling the economy "sick,"; in mid-1998 he announced that his government was considering "structural changes" to address the state's dysfunctions. Indeed, on the first anniversary of his inauguration (August 2, 1998), Khatami presented his much-anticipated economic program. His administration's Economic Recovery Plan, finalized in consultation with the IMF and implemented in 1998, and the subsequent launching of the third Five-Year (Development) Plan in 2000, facilitated this transition, as the core objectives of both plans revolved around the concepts of privatization, deregulation, reduction of government size, and liberalization. In line with IMF advice, Khatami identified as the keys to economic recovery the mobilization of domestic capital and the creation of an environment free of state interference in and control over the market, which would reassure and attract foreign investors.[21]

Thus, the early 2000s saw the beginning of a long process through which Tehran adopted a policy agenda geared toward the privatization of the BCT in order to respond to the growing demands of its female population and to improve its quality of service, accessibility, and efficiency for all. Tehran Municipality took the steps needed to attract private sector partnership in operating the city's public transport services. This policy agenda was in line with principle 44 of the Constitution of the Islamic Republic of Iran, which encourages the "increase [of] the share of the private and cooperative sectors in the national economy" and the "decrease [of] the financial and managerial responsibilities of the government in managing economic activity." According to this principle, first the state had to "strengthen the private and cooperative sectors to prepare them for widespread economic activities" and, in this case, for "expanding and upgrading national standards" in the transport network. Then it could rely on the private sector to take over functions or responsibilities that had come to be regarded as properly within the state's purview. Finally, the state would "supervise and support the relevant authorities after the transfer in order to realize the goals of the transfer."

It is within this new reality of "rolling back the state" from the provision of everyday services and the entry of the private sector into the transportation provision game that the state started working on a transport master plan for Tehran, as well as the rest of Iran. Adhering to the technocratic logic of the Economic Recovery Plan and the Five-Year (Development) Plan, the fleshing out of Tehran's transport blueprint needed to meet the growing mobility needs and expectations of Tehranis, relying largely on outside consultants—transportation experts who worked closely with consultants from the World Bank and United Nations Human Settlements Programme (UN-Habitat)—and private investment. Whereas during the 1980s the economy had evolved around the notion of "(religious and political) loyalty (taa'hod) being more important than expertise (takhassos)," during the 2000s market logic prevailed, experts were celebrated (see Farahmand-Razavi 1994), and there was a spike in "customer satisfaction" research.

Although the privatization of the BCT provoked opposition and protest among the bus drivers, who as state employees were apprehensive about the prospects of this process for their livelihood and employment status, both the state and Tehran Municipality pushed for the plan to work. As Heather Allen (2013, 9) points out, "In less than three years the total share of private sector in annual trips reached to more than forty percent." By 2013 more than 70 percent of Tehran's Bus Company was privatized, and eighteen private companies assisted the state in providing transportation services that conformed with the international standards set forth by the World Bank, UN-Habitat, and World Health Organization (WHO) (see table 2).

The BCT started looking to this new phase as a way to make transportation profitable. The ever-increasing population of female bus riders was seen as "potentially the most profitable category," said Maziar, one of the city experts at the BCT.[22] Thus in 2006, twenty-four years after its first failed attempt to establish women-only buses, the BCT once again launched women-only buses, for which it hired women bus drivers. In April of that year, Mohammad Ahmadi Bafandeh, then the BCT director, announced that

TABLE 2 Privatization of the City's Bus Lines and Buses

Year	Publicly Operated Lines	Privately Operated Lines	Publicly Owned and Operated Buses	Privately Owned and Operated Buses	Percent of Privately Owned and Operated Buses
2007	294	107	6,071	1,319	18
2008	249	127	5,644	2,209	28
2009	200	159	4,490	2,675	37
2010	178	165	3,919	3,102	44

SOURCE: Based on Allen (2013).

the hiring of women drivers for vans and minibuses is now on the agenda, and effective in June, women will be able to use women-only public transportation vehicles into which no man has the right to enter.... We have published the call-for-drivers announcement. We aim to provide women with a feeling of security. I am asking people who have the ability to establish private transportation companies to do so and use women drivers in routes many women take. (*Sharq*, April 10, 2006)

Safarali Ghazian, the BCT's public affairs director, described the plan to hire women drivers as an attempt to have women participate in and partially take responsibility for the transportation of women. Ghazian encouraged women to apply for these positions and added:

Women's participation in this plan would provide us with the incentive to quickly launch these transportation lines.... We should wait and see if women have the courage and the guts to do so or not. (*Sharq*, April 10, 2006)

As Ghazian's remarks indicate, by the latter half of the 2000s, BCT officials were referring to women both as citizens with rights and civic responsibilities and as profit-making workers who could "serve the female population." In a way, the hiring of women drivers was basically a way to get more publicity, as well as a marketing tactic to court women passengers.

The privatization plan was complemented by Bus Rapid Transit, a high-quality, bus-based transit system that delivers fast and comfortable services. Introduced in Tehran in 2007 after municipal officials visited the TransMilenio BRT operation in Bogota, Colombia, the BRT lines generated much controversy. First of all, the BCT reintroduced the concept of women-only buses, intended to provide female passengers with extra bus space during rush hours (*Kanoon-e Zanan-e Irani*, January 4, 2007). They also hired thirty women bus drivers to drive the regular BRT buses on BRT Line 1, which goes all the way from Tehranpars, in east Tehran, to Azadi bus terminal, in west Tehran. One of the city experts at the BCT told me that it was only natural for the municipality to think about profit. "But they also create opportunities for women," he added. The (male) bus drivers that I interviewed believed that this was merely a "show to encourage people to use these newly launched services." Davood, a (male) bus driver who spoke to me during his "tea-break," said, "It's a changed world! *We* [men] don't have job security, then ..." before slurping his tea. He was in fact expressing his concern about the new roles women were taking up in society, in this case driving buses.

The plan, the launching of the BRT and the hiring of female bus drivers, was successful in that it found its way to the reports published by international organizations such as UN-Habitat, which praised Tehran's mayor, Mohammad Baqir Qalibaf, for his efforts in expanding the BRT and for the ways in which the BRT had contributed to "gender balance":

> The opportunities created for women as BRT bus drivers go well beyond just a job, but bring them respect in the community as well as the fact that they seem to be able to effectively carry out their duties outperforming some of their male colleagues! This in turn helps provide social equity and clearly demonstrates that formal public transport not only provides sustainable transport choices but they can also increase equal opportunity for the creation and retention of green jobs. (Allen 2013)

Nevertheless, this initiative was not welcomed by the more conservative section of the population. Conservative bloggers criticized the municipality for "pushing women into masculine territories" and held it responsible for "motherless homes" and "men's indifference toward their breadwinning roles." Female BRT drivers also faced some resistance from both their husbands at home and their (male) colleagues at work, as one of them who had turned to driving a taxi told me. Soon they were all removed from behind the big wheel and were sent back to the BCT offices for clerical work, except those who, like Afsaneh, preferred to go back on the road to drive taxis: "Once on the road and behind the wheel, I'm my own boss!"

The BRT buses offered yet another controversial feature: the rapid-transit buses reversed the position of the women's and men's sections, with men sitting in the back and women sitting in front. Maziar, the city expert at the BCT, told me that "not only had women complained about having to sit at the back of the bus, but it had also come into question from the international community." He was quick to add with a smirk: "I personally don't understand what the difference is. Why is the front space a better space? But anyhow, that has changed now! Rest in peace that on the BRTs men sit at the back." This time, it was the men whose murmurs of unrest could be heard from the back seats. A male blogger who writes for the so-called Men's Rights Association, a self-described "group of lawyers and concerned citizens who aim to counter the spread of feminist ideas," outlined the problematic changes introduced by the BRTs in a blog post:[23]

1. The equal bus space for men and women on the BRTs: if you measure from the back of the bus to the metal divider and from the metal divider to the

driver's seat you realize that the space is divided into two equal halves. However, there are twenty seats in the men's section as opposed to the eighteen seats in the women's section. Thus you realize that the men's space is actually tighter.

2. Because the engine is continuously working, there is a lot of noise in the back: considering the fact that in public and work spaces, men are given the heavy tasks and women are given the light clerical/administrative duties we expected that the front space be given to men as they carry the heavy burden of responsibilities and this could have facilitated their peaceful commute between home and work place.

3. One door for men and two doors for women: the women's section is usually crowded only during the rush hours and especially when the offices close (around 3:30 to 7 p.m.) but the men's section is crowded all day. It is therefore surprising that women have the better space with two doors, and men have the space with only one door.

Indeed, new initiatives aimed to expand the municipality's transport service provision, such as the launching of various BRT lines, created some uproar. The mistrust toward the hitherto inefficient public transport and its limited capacity could not be easily overcome. When Line 2 was about to be launched, for example, the municipality faced strong opposition from local businesses. The main reason, one of the shopkeepers told me, was the fear that the introduction of the new line and the infrastructure (such as the introduction of traffic management measures in the form of dedicated bus lanes) that was required, instead of leading to better access for shoppers, might affect the market adversely, as Line 2 runs through a major shopping center on Mowlavi Avenue, southeast of Tehran where the cloth and curtain bazaars are located. Business owners were concerned that because there would be a dedicated traffic lane for the bus, the launching of a BRT line would damage their businesses because access by car would be limited. However, in time these fears proved to be based on the incorrect assumption that economic activity relied on "men behind wheels." Concerns soon dissipated, as the launching of Line 2 actually contributed significantly to the growth of local businesses; in a shop owner's words, "Women found the BRT a very convenient way to do their shopping." Indeed, about 35 percent of BRT passengers, many of them women, had never used the corresponding ordinary bus system (Montazeri and Hashemi 2009). Increased mobility for women and autonomy in their transit through the city's districts made it easier for them to participate more actively, and more visibly, in the city's economic life, as shoppers and consumers.

It was not just women as consumers who found the BRT convenient. My interviews with women bus riders reveal that professional women were also increasingly turning to the BRT. As stated in a report published for UN-Habitat in 2013:

Prior to 2007, bus transport was seen as being "poor transit for the poor" but the success of the BRT and market research surveys show that BRT is an attractive service to the middle and professional classes. As these are the people that are more likely to also own a car, this is the target group that is the most important to persuade to use public transport, but it can be difficult to attract them to regular bus services. Research carried out by the municipality showed that of the BRT passengers, 44 percent had university degrees; 24 percent high-school diplomas; 11 percent associate degrees; 13 percent no diploma; and 8 percent graduate degrees. (Allen 2013)

Sima, a project manager at a pharmaceutical company, for example, stated that she no longer uses her private car for her work commutes "because of the traffic." She emphasized that "BRT buses are faster and cleaner, and are good for the environment." In fact, Sima was so "happy" with these services that she had started to "encourage [her] colleagues" to use them as well. The irony here is that with Sima's informal "advertising," we have an indication that (professional, middle-class) women are in effect promoting the state's (gender-segregated) bus services. While the shift in the way women have seen their access to public transport from a concession to a right is undeniable, it is hard to ignore the fact that through the idiom of convenience, women turn from protesters against, to promoters of and participants in, the state's project of administering gender and space.

Overall, and despite the controversies, the majority of the people eventually came to see the BRTs as a relief; they could get to their destinations faster, and the new buses were cleaner, more comfortable, and air-conditioned. The success of the BRTs soon became translatable in performance and financial terms: the first year of operation of the new bus lines saw an increase of a stunning 77 percent in the number of daily passengers. Soon the BRT was rolled out in other routes in the city, reducing travel times and improving the travel experience, as my interviewees attested. Today the BRT consists of ten lines that span the city and collectively carry 1.8 million passengers daily, an indication of the popularity of the system.[24]

THE CUSTOMER IS ALWAYS RIGHT

During the 1980s the politics of mobility was driven by both Islamic morality, which required the separation of men and women, and a concern for the popular classes, the "barefooted." Today, a market logic governs the BCT, as it attempts to make buses profitable and seeks to reclaim the city for the middle and upper classes. Buses have turned into mobile billboards that carry giant pictures of Sony and Samsung products; life-sized portraits of celebrities and movie posters; and images of various commodities, such as detergents, ice cream, frozen foods, pots, and pans. Bus shelters are also adorned with images of flowers and birds, as part of beautification projects, or are covered with advertisements of Hamrahe Aval Internet services, Irancell mobiles, private language institutions, or the bonuses and promotions that various banks offer their customers. These advertisements and their messages are directed toward citizens-as-customers and not citizens-as-subjects-of-Islamic-morality.

This shift toward a more consumer-oriented service is not devoid of particular choices. The faster and cleaner transit system came at a price. Higher fares brought about a two-tier system and introduced differential experiences of traveling in the city; it produced two different versions of Tehran with distinct geographies and a choice of trajectories. The BCT has in effect produced a two-tier bus system, wherein the fare for the private buses is ten times the fare for the public buses. While fare increases may not be an issue for middle-class women, they do matter for women of lower classes. The BRT service introduction constituted a break with the older philosophy of public transport service as "poor transit for poor people." The experience of traveling in comfort and in less time was reserved to the middle class and professionals, as the new bus fares were out of reach for poorer passengers. These passengers remained at the bus stops left behind by the new services, waiting for the slower, older, congested services; for them, their destinations remained as remote as before. Female passengers also experienced urban transit differently depending on their socioeconomic status. Being able to afford the better services meant they had more and higher quality bus space at their disposal while benefiting from shorter travel times. On the other end of the spectrum, public transport usage for poorer women remained an ordeal on the older, cheaper lines with more restricted women's sections, longer waiting times, and the need to have pre-bought tickets to board the services as opposed to being able to buy tickets on board the BRT services. Their travel had to be carefully planned to minimize cost and reduce transit times, as their time was less valued given they could not afford a better service. Benefiting from the new service-centered mentality of the BCT depended on where one found oneself in class, gender, and movement in the city nexus.

During one of my bus rides I took note of a lone woman at the bus stop. Her chador was shabby and dusty, as were her purse and her shoes. Her face was gloomy and her eyes anxious, an anxiety that guided the rhythm of her restless movement from one side of the bus stop to the other. She had a ticket in her hand waiting for the bus to come and take her to Mofid Children Hospital. As we waited at the bus stop, she explained to me that she was from Saveh, a city located about one hundred kilometers southwest of Tehran. Her child's "incurable disease" had brought her to Tehran. As the bus arrived, we both ran toward the door. I went up the steps. The driver asked me for 250 tomans, the price for one single ride. As soon as she noticed this exchange with the driver, she stepped off the bus. I told her that she should get on, as this bus would take her to the hospital. She showed me her ticket and said, "But this is not a ticket bus!" She got off the bus, neither because she was out of cash nor because she could not afford the fare, but because the fare difference was so significant that she would rather wait for the public bus than pay it. As the bus pulled away from the curb, the image of the woman in her shabby chador eventually faded away. She was left behind, the forgotten "beneficiary" of the republic.

The fare increase on private buses had other, unexpected implications as well. People started acting like customers with a right to sit where they please. Since these buses were ten times more expensive than the regular public buses, individual men and women felt they should be able to sit, so if they found their section full they would often cross into the other section to find an available seat. Sarah, a thirty-two-year-old journalist, told me: "I pay for my ticket and so I am entitled to that empty seat regardless of the section within which it is located." In other words, passengers such as Sarah have started mobilizing a market logic that gives them the right to take advantage of goods and services as consumers.

The pages of conservative newspapers such as *Jomhoori Islami* and *Kayhan*, along with magazines of the 2000s such as *Zan-e Rooz*, are filled with complaints about a "creeping feminism" that demoralizes the bus space. Some began to worry that private buses were turning into a stage for "Satan to dance" as unrelated men and women mingled (*Zan-e Rooz*, December 24, 2006). One of the city experts at the BCT emphasized that these "irregularities" happen only on the private buses, outside the purview of the state. As it turned out, it was not just the services that were outsourced, but the "irregularities" as well; rolling back the state in the area of urban transportation meant that blame could now be directed away from the state and onto the private sector. Nevertheless, the expert insisted that they [the BCT officials] are still committed to the principle of gender segregation and that the buses will remain divided by a metal bar.

The experience of gender segregation in public transportation, therefore, has been informed not only by religious morality, but also by a host of other significant factors, such as redefinitions of citizenship and rights, consumer and service provision ideologies, and of course their interplay at different points in time. The partition, the metal bar in the bus that separates the men's and women's sections, has moved across time as the state has tried to negotiate an increase of women in public space and navigate through the exigencies of a changing economic and social reality. The expansion of women's physical space on buses, as represented by the 2006 launch of the women-only buses, and the expansion of women's discursive space, as registered in women's invocation of rights, do not represent an erosion of state power. The state responds to changing material realities and prevailing discourses with a certain level of flexibility, but such flexibility should be understood as one understands the moving divider: there may be more or less space, more or less inclusion—that is, where the boundary is erected may move—but the state continues to act as arbitrator of the gender boundary and through the very act of such arbitration (re)asserts its authority.

Happy and Healthy in Mothers' Paradise

Women-Only Parks and the Expansion of the State

Up on the Abbas Abad hills in northeast Tehran is the Mothers' Paradise, one of the city's 2,135 parks and the first of its four women-only parks. Founded in 2007, the Mothers' Paradise spreads over an area of about thirty-seven acres. Women are not banned from entering mixed parks, but their presence in these parks—as in all other public spaces—is conditioned upon their donning the veil.[1] The park is reserved exclusively for women every day except Friday, when it is "open to families," meaning that on Fridays women-only parks are considered mixed spaces, which are open to all people regardless of age or gender.[2] In the Mothers' Paradise, in the absence of men, women are allowed to take off their veils and wear the clothing of their choice. They may come in groups or as individuals. Everyone finds a way to amuse themselves in the Mothers' Paradise. The park is equipped with fitness machines, a day-care center, a playground, a three-mile bike trail, a library, a health center, picnic areas, and chess tables. An all-female staff of more than seventy employees runs the park. These women landscape and garden, collect trash and clean, rent out bikes, conduct group exercises, and maintain and manage the grounds. Female guards hired by the Iranian police department maintain security inside the park, and two male guards monitor the entrance to ensure that no man enters the park or harasses women outside the entrance. The manager of the park tells me that park usage is high "and the number of visitors is increasing." Schools treat the park as a space for extracurricular activities, while district municipalities and government organizations occasionally use the park to treat their female staff to picnics and exercise retreats.[3]

In the public space of the park, women form temporary bonds across class and social status. For example, on a visit to the sports club in the park, I find it difficult to figure out who is who. The "boss," the "secretary," and the "janitor" are all sitting around a table having tea while discussing the upcoming presidential elections and whether or not they should vote, and if so, which of the candidates would have women's backs. As I start inspecting the announcements on the wall, their conversation shifts from the presidential elections to child care. "I left Golnar [her daughter] with my mom this morning. She's been sick for the past few days!" says one. Another woman, getting up to fetch the sugar, says in response, "*Azizam*, this is just the beginning. Within four days after sending Arman [her son] to day care, he came back with a severe cold, and this happened several times since then." I ask for a bike. The woman sitting on the chair in front of me says to the woman who has gone to get the sugar, "This woman wants a bike, could you rent out one to her?" I ask the woman sitting on the chair in front of me about their tennis classes. She points to the woman who just gave me the bike and says, "She's the boss here. Ask her!" It is only when I need more specific information that I figure out who the official boss is. While class is still a visible category through which one can distinguish both visitors and staff, the park provides a space wherein women of various classes can come together and engage with one another in a meaningful way. This temporary permeability of class boundaries shows a significant shift from the social conventions and indicates how the rules that normally govern lives in Iran are relaxed or bent in most women-only spaces. While class and status do not cease functioning as markers of difference, these spaces bring women together as "women" in a city dominated by men. These spaces provide frameworks of interaction revolving around common concerns and thus are conducive to the transformation of women in individual terms to women in collective terms.

There are other ways in which the public space of the park offers a relative sense of freedom, another kind of retreat, wherein social regulations are temporarily suspended. On another visit to the Mothers' Paradise, I see young schoolgirls enthusiastically climbing trees, their pink school uniforms and white headscarves hung on the branches. They remind me of the scene in the American musical drama *The Sound of Music* (1965) in which the retired naval officer and widower, Captain Von Trapp, returns from a trip with his fiancée and finds his children swinging from branches on a tree-lined street, singing and screaming with joy— an expression of physical release from the captain's authoritative parenting and strict military discipline.

On the other side of the park, a few meters from the monument that commemorates women martyrs of the Iran–Iraq War (1980–88), a group of high school girls are celebrating their friend's birthday. After enjoying cake, the girls bring the world to their private corner with the help of a cell phone. They turn on the phone's MP3 player, and the sound of Los Angeles–produced Persian pop music (formally banned in Iran) fills the air: "*Khanum del beh to bastam / del-e hama ro shekastam.*"[4] The schoolgirls dance to all the prohibited tunes. Then the female guards, the only women who—as state representatives—are still covered in their Islamic hijab, approach the party. I worry that they will confiscate the girls' cell phones, that they might give the girls a sharp warning, or that they might ruin the birthday party. My fears, rooted in my own childhood experiences of growing up in Iran in the 1980s, appear to be baseless; the guards pass by them without so much as a glance. "The guards in the women-only parks are there to provide women with security, with protection," one of the guards tells me. The guards represent the state as the provider of protection for women. "Protecting women from what?" I ask. "From men's intrusion," she says, pointing out that some of them are trained in martial arts and emphasizing that it is not their job to "tell these girls to dance or not to dance."[5]

The park space is not used just for leisure and entertainment. It has at times been transformed into a space for activism. In an interview I did with a member of the feminist group The One Million Signature Campaign, which at the time was collecting signatures to demand changes to the discriminatory laws, the woman stated that they had gone to women-only parks to collect more signatures and to educate women about their rights.[6] She said that every time they organized a workshop or a meeting, they were faced with pressure from the police and security forces. In this way, too, the women-only parks were "a blessing." The activists could meet and talk face to face with women without first having to bring them all together. Ironically, because the state treats these spaces as "feminine" and thus "apolitical," there are no hostile police or security authorities interfering with women's organizing efforts or intimidating would-be supporters.[7]

It appeared to me that the Mothers' Paradise and similar women-only parks have come to stand for more than mere entertainment, health, or exercise spaces; they have turned into what Nancy Fraser (1990) calls "alternative or distinct public spheres"; in other words, alternative spheres of citizenship. Public spaces become "public spheres" (Habermas 1989), not because the municipality designed them as such, but because of the practices of the individuals who occupy them.

Not everyone, however, is into dancing, entertainment, or political activism. Some women use the park space for other kinds of informal gatherings. During one of my visits I see a group of retired high school teachers who are sitting in a circle on the grass next to the fountains, listening to an older woman recite poems by Hafez. Next to them, a group of middle-aged housewives have spread a large picnic rug. One of the latter, Mrs. Akbari, tells me that she and her friends and neighbors come here often. "With no man around," she tells me, "this park *is* a paradise!" They spread their picnic rugs on the grass and stay there for hours. "We do different things: talk, gossip, sleep, exercise. I sometimes even chop and rinse herbs (*sabzi pak kardan*) here!" Activities usually considered within the domestic realm are lived out in public (Hayden 1981). Mrs. Akbari brings her "house"—her household duties—to the park, because her children—a son and a daughter—are "old enough" and "are busy with their own lives," and her husband "spends most of his time at work," so she easily gets bored at home. "It's a small house, you know!"

In fact, the situation of Mrs. Akbari and her like is one of the many factors that has prompted Tehran Municipality to launch women-only parks. Mr. Mostafavi, a senior official at Tehran Municipality, explained:

> When we decided to open women-only parks, we were thinking of housewives stuck in small apartments all day, putting up with their children, cooking and cleaning. This could make women get depressed, anxious, and impatient. So when the poor husband returns from work, she has no patience and would easily pick on him or start a quarrel.

The motivation for opening women-only parks, as Mr. Mostafavi's statements indicate, was to create "angels of the home" (McDowell 1999, 75–80), under whose wings men could rest in peace. Nevertheless, some of the discussions generated inside and about the park extended to the private spaces of homes, transforming the power dynamics within them and thus disrupting the "peace." Azam, a fifty-nine-year-old housewife, explained to me that several of her neighbors had circulated a petition opposing the designation of "the best park in the neighborhood" exclusively to women:

> That night our dinner turned into something like the presidential debates you see on T.V.[8] We were discussing the petition. My husband was upset because he used to go to this park in the mornings. My two sons, twenty and twenty-eight, took their father's side. I told them: "Would you like to have a depressed crippled mother at home? Or would you rather I go out, get some fresh air, walk a bit, inhale some oxygen and live longer?" I told them you have the whole city to yourself. Leave this park for me.

Echoing Virginia Woolf, who argued in 1929 that for a woman's creativity and freedom to flourish, she should have "a room of her own," this Iranian Woolf demanded not a room, but a park of one's own, or her share of the city.

Azam's comment echoed the statements of the city and government officials who had stressed that the state provided parks to women out of a concern for women's health problems that arose from lack of fresh air and exercise. Yet in the early 1980s, while the Islamic Republic consolidated its political rule at home and fought a territorial war on the international front, leisure sports and exercise came to be considered unnecessary and un-Islamic. Hassan Ghafourifard, the former governor of Tehran, recalled in a 1986 interview that in that atmosphere, someone had called and asked him if playing volleyball was *haram* (religiously forbidden). "Sports were considered haram or at best a form of boisterous carousing," he added (*Zan-e Rooz*, March 7, 1986). Women's exercise and leisure-time activities especially were seen as morally decadent and thus prohibited. The regime's main concern with regard to women was to craft pious and educated mothers (as evidenced in both pronatalist and education policies of the 1980s); the question of women's leisure and physical exercise was addressed in a prohibitive way, by determining where women could not go and what they could not do.[9] In fact, several state officials were quoted in news reports referring to women's outdoor exercise as *makruh*, an Islamic term to describe an act that is not forbidden but is strongly discouraged. Shahla Habibi, Iran's presidential adviser on women's affairs in the 1990s, recalled in her interview with me how difficult it was to get officials to support women's sports and make them less taboo by speaking in public about them.

Issues of *Zan-e Rooz* magazine, one of the oldest women's weeklies in Iran, from that period provide a window onto the atmosphere of public parks in those days. The magazine's reports suggest that under existing circumstances, women's outdoor exercise in the parks had become a stressful activity. The news of a potential ban on women's outdoor exercise in the parks had made women anxious. One of the male instructors had asked women to "respect the authorities" and "conduct their exercises indoors" in the gyms (*Zan-e Rooz*, October 21, 1989). Indeed, Ghafourifard (1986) had also suggested that new social restrictions made it necessary for the state to build indoor exercise and sports facilities for women: "In general three tasks should be carried out before women are able to exercise: (1) erase the negative image of women's sports which has been inherited from the previous regime, (2) avoid extremist behavior [fundamentalism], (3) provide women with necessary sports facilities." But women could not wait until these three conditions were fulfilled, and as the national budget was spent mostly on the war with Iraq, there was little indication that these tasks would be completed any time soon. Women wanted "fresh air" and not the "smelly" environment of the Hijab Complex (the only women's indoor sports complex in the early 1980s). Nevertheless, the ban, or the threat of it, had discouraged many women from going to the parks to run and exercise, whether alone or with groups of friends. In a 1989 *Zan-e Rooz* article, one of the exercise instructors pointed out that over the three-year period from 1985 to 1988, the number of women attending his sessions had increased from zero to 150. "However," he stated, "over a period of three days, since the newspapers spread the rumor of the ban, one hundred of them [had] opted out" (*Zan-e Rooz*, October 21, 1989).

During this time of prohibition, women's outdoor exercise didn't completely disappear; it just retreated to the stealthy corners of outdoor spaces. Thus, despite frequent warnings and interruptions from the guards, those women who were enthusiastic about outdoor group exercise, although still few in number in the 1980s, went to parks or enclosed public areas, such as the green spaces of large residential complexes, to silently and discreetly perform their morning exercises. Bahar, a forty-four-year-old architect, recalled how she and her friends, "both male and female," would get together in the green space of Parc de Princes Apartments in Shiraz Avenue to play volleyball, something they could not do in public parks. "After all, the government guards could not be in all places all the time," stated Zahra, one of my interviewees, who has since 1989 lived in Ekbatan, a sprawling high-rise community in western Tehran, with its own exclusive facilities and green space. These comments evidence both the costly and limiting nature of the prohibitive measures.

Zan-e Rooz's portrayal of women's outdoor exercise in the 1980s is grey and gloomy. Members of the self-titled 1980s generation (*daheh-ye Shasti-ha*) recall how in those years "the government criminalized public displays of happiness" (Behrouzan 2016). This stands in sharp contrast to my observations in the late 2000s both in women-only parks such as the Mothers' Paradise and in mixed parks such as Mellat Park, in north Tehran, and Laleh Park, in the downtown area. What was noticeable in these parks was the concentrated effort of the municipality to create joyful and colorful spaces wherein people could socialize, exercise, and entertain themselves. Whereas after the revolution the state viewed women's outdoor exercise as a moral problem, today, not only does it coordinate women's group exercises in mixed parks, but it also provides women with a green space of their own in the form of women-only parks. In order to better make sense of the nature of and reasons for this change, one needs to pay attention to a host of factors that are often ignored in the analysis of the complex and continually evolving relationship between women, state, and society in Iran. Tehran's rapid urbanization has had a significant impact on the change of focus and emphasis of state policies and priorities, as has the state's increasing concern about its continued legitimacy in the eyes of a disaffected citizenry. Other significant factors that should not be overlooked are the ongoing spread of a technocratic discourse on health and the increasingly important role of the municipality as a unit of governance and a locus for mobilization and articulation of demands and grievances. Rather than interpret the reopening of space for women as the state's capitulation to civil society, in this chapter I examine how the park's success reflects a structural deepening of the state at the municipal and submunicipal levels, as well as a maturing of the state's productive capacity to enable desired behaviors and practices among its citizens by redrawing the gender boundary.

UNDER PRESSURE: URBAN RENEWAL
IN POSTWAR TEHRAN

If the 1980s were marked by the rapid and unplanned horizontal expansion of the city, as discussed in the previous chapter, the 1990s marked its rapid and planned vertical expansion. In 1990 one of the founders of the Executives of Construction Party led by President Rafsanjani, Gholamhossein Karbaschi, was appointed mayor of Tehran. Karbaschi had an entrepreneurial approach to city building and looked at it as a profit-making machine. His goal was to make Tehran Municipality self-sufficient and debt free. During his term, the city embarked on a path to growth and development (Adelkhah 2000).

According to Tehran Municipality's Center for Budget and Statistics, the city's development budget, as a percentage of total budget, jumped from 28 percent in 1989 to 63 percent in 1991, and to 83 percent in 1996.[10] Thus, the political-economic context of the 1990s could be described as one of urbanization run amok. The shortage of funds brought about by an overhaul of the central government's financial transfers structure in 1985 left Tehran Municipality with no choice but to diversify its funding sources. A new strategy, devised by the city's mayoral office, headed by Karbaschi, instituted a break with the past and involved an ambitious yet controversial program of urban renewal. The new strategy aspired to be more inclusive and to pursue more actively the integration of Tehran's fragmented and disillusioned population (Ehsani 1999). Yet this not uncontroversial attempt to transform the city involved engaging the private sector, notably a speculative and entrepreneurial urban middle class that was invited to finance Karbaschi's ambitious program. From 1990 to 1998 the sale of residential permits in explicit violation of zoning laws, which exempted developers from zoning regulations by allowing them to both subdivide plots and build high-rises well above the permitted norm, led to the expansion and acceleration of speculative apartment building in both the poorer and more affluent districts of Tehran and the mushrooming of high-rises and Soviet-style apartment buildings (Ehsani 2009, 23). As I argue later in this chapter, the resulting reduction in the average size of a Tehran dwelling by half (to 646 square feet; Ehsani 2009, 19–20), had a significant impact on the lifestyles of urban dwellers, with the majority of women, in particular, being more affected due to their closer association with the rapidly shrinking domestic space (see figure 3).

Prior to the vertical expansion of Tehran and the change in the city's landscape in the 1990s, women treated their neighborhood streets as their front lawns. As several of my interviewees recalled, they used to gather in the afternoons to catch up on the "neighborhood news." These gatherings usually took place on the street or on their front porches. The younger generation would occupy the backyards, jumping rope and playing hopscotch or other street games. As the years passed and most neighborhoods expanded vertically, backyards disappeared or were replaced by a single green space shared by the many families who lived in the apartment complexes that were built in place of the one- and two-story houses. The narrow streets of the old neighborhoods were now filled with huge apartment complexes, most of whose units ranged in size from 430 to 1,000 square feet— which, according to Sahba, one of my interviewees, "could be suffocating, if you have two children running around all the time." The streets were packed with cars and populated by "strangers," that is, new neighbors, who were no longer known to the whole neighborhood. The most visible casualty of this profound urban and social transformation brought about by the underregulated construction of the new apartment buildings and the high-rises that altered the city fabric in the 1990s

FIGURE 3. Tehran's shrinking living space. Courtesy of Afarin Shahrokni.

was the eradication or marginalization of the neighborhood networks and intimate traditional spaces in which they thrived.

Yet the contraction of dwelling spaces coexisted with the expansion of urban public spaces and the changing of their appearance. As a city, Tehran had mourned for eight years over its soldiers' corpses; it was a city with a background music of jets, sirens, and explosions, a city populated by black-cloaked *depress* (Persianized term for depressed) citizens (Behrouzan 2016). A postrevolution population spike, which had peaked in the 1980s, meant that there was an enormous baby boom generation coming of age. For this younger population, the revolution and the war were nothing but vague memories captured in family albums and movies. Karbaschi, the new mayor of Tehran was well aware of the fact that with the diminishing of revolutionary zeal in the postwar reconstruction era, something other than the revolution and war monuments was needed for the citizenry to develop a sense of belonging to the city. Having consolidated its power at the national level over the Iranian territory at large, the state eventually developed policies that focused on the "local." The emphasis of state apparatuses shifted to the consolidation of state power at the level of the locality. But achieving control at the municipal level entailed building a new hegemonic project, establishing connections, responding to needs and aspirations, and providing services. The state was under pressure to provide for a population that had been traumatized by war and squeezed by inflation and that now demanded a better life. To accomplish this the state initiated a process of devolution of power and delegated some of its responsibilities to local and municipal organizations. In Tehran, under Karbaschi the city gradually transformed into a city of parks and flowers, of festivals and fountains. Municipality-led beautification programs aimed at rejuvenating cityscapes. Many of the wartime murals that had glorified martyrdom and death on the battlefield were replaced with more hopeful visual motifs, such as doves, flowers, and butterflies.[11]

Through the municipality's efforts, both the appearance of the city and its relationship to its inhabitants were transformed. The mayor used the slogan, "Our City, Our Home!" to generate a sense of belonging to, respect for, and entitlement to the city. The cult of urban citizenship and "the right to the city" were promoted. Our city, like our home, had to be made comfortable for all the members of the big family of Tehranis, the city's citizens. The mayor ordered that fences and walls around the parks be removed, making parks accessible and available to all. Between 1989 and 1995 alone, the number of parks leaped from 184 to 680, and the amount of green space available on a per capita level jumped from 2 to 11 square meters, despite a rapidly growing population (Shams 2014). Praising Karbaschi for his efforts in expanding public parks, Fariba Adelkhah (2000) describes the public mixed-gender parks as an extension of the street and the familiar traditional spaces, where families could gather and spend their evenings—as many in fact did. Indeed, these new green spaces became a refuge for elderly retired men playing backgammon or chess and elderly women knitting and chatting. Family picnics became a familiar sight, with the familial space in each case demarcated by the contours of the rugs families or other groups of park visitors would spread underneath them, earmarking personal or more intimate segments out of these public spaces and treating them as their dining rooms.

But beyond the idyllic ambience of the parks, the horizon was lined with menacing clouds, as the tensions and conflicts within and between different state apparatuses were hard to conceal.[12] The post-Khomeini era provided a framework for different, hitherto largely restrained voices and interests to be expressed in the corridors of power. Preexisting divides that had up to then remained latent as the revolutionary state strove to consolidate its hold over Iranian society and its position internationally became visible, and public debate was marked by the deepening of the ideological and political divides between the conservative and reformist factions that had emerged in the course of revolutionary power struggles (Arjomand 2009).[13] These political rifts did not and do not relate only to politics writ large, and they did not exhaust themselves at the national level. They had and still have implications for the "little things," for how life is organized at the local level or at the level of the everyday. They affect the structure of everyday spaces in which urban life unfolds in terms of both shape and content. In his 1996 report about Tehran's "tree-loving mayor," Robert Fisk (1996), writing for the *Independent*, sheds light on this tension. He points to the opening of the unisex cycle tracks in Tehran's Chitgar Park and the space they provide for the city's teenagers "to meet outside the suffocating rules" of the morality patrols. Yet he is quick to note a sign erected on the cycle path that reads: "Women are forbidden to ride bicycles on the path. . . . Violators will be prosecuted." While the municipality, with the backing of Rafsanjani as the president, leaned toward the application of productive measures by opening up the urban space to different sectors of society (by 1998, Tehran Municipality boasted 628 parks and had opened 128 cultural houses), the conservative faction of the state continued to push for prohibitive measures. Ironically, and to the conservatives' annoyance, it was mostly the women, especially younger women, who welcomed the municipality's rejuvenation and beautification projects and formed the majority of those using the newly established cultural centers and parks (Ehsani 1999; Shams 2014).

Women were using these newly opened spaces of leisure and consumption in increasing numbers, and their bodies could no longer be contained within the private sphere. The shrinking of domestic space and the loss of traditional outdoor social spaces, along with the limitations set on women's movement in public, had pushed women to carve out these "breathing spaces" (to use the words of an interviewee) for themselves, outside the reach of the state. A couple of my interviewees recalled, just like Zahra and Bahar, how during the early 1990s, when they were still teenagers, they would use the semipublic green spaces of their residential complexes or the less visible corners of public parks to play volleyball, badminton, or dodgeball, if they could gather a larger group. The state soon saw these spaces as a challenge to its control of gender boundaries, forcing it to renegotiate where the boundary is drawn. We must consider these spaces as the background against which the women-only parks emerged.

WOMEN'S OUTDOOR EXERCISE, FROM PROBLEM TO SOLUTION

Women's parks emerged as a solution first to a problem of disaffection ("bad citizens") and the lure of Western "cultural invasion," and later to women's mental and physical health problems. The state's redrawing of the gender boundary, I argue, also serves as a larger problem-solving effort in response to changes in the political economy.

Under Rafsanjani's developmentalist cabinet (1989–1997), the state had to manage several contradictions. While local governments were preoccupied with citizens' attachment to the city, the central government was busy planning a turn toward a free market economy. Following World Bank–inspired structural adjustment policies and advocating a free market economy might have been helpful in temporarily saving Iran from a postwar economic crisis, but like many other state projects and policies, it produced undesired effects as well. Opening the domestic market to consumer imports as part of the liberalization of the economy—and as a salve to a war-deprived population—also brought unintended consequences along the lines of what Ayatollah Khamenei, the leader of the Islamic Republic, labeled "cultural invasion" (Arjomand 2009, 177–178).

Western (cultural) products had "invaded" the domestic market through widespread informal and black market networks. The global commercialization of Western leisure products and practices had put Iran in a disadvantageous position vis-à-vis the West in what was termed the "cultural war," undermining the Islamic Republic's efforts to maintain the "Islamic" features of its cities and citizens.[14] The loosening attachment to the revolutionary and religious ideals and values thus became one of the greatest concerns of the state. "Bad hijabs," a term referring to women who were lax in maintaining their Islamic hijab, came to be seen as a sign of this detachment, or so it was interpreted by the state, foreign observers, and even social science scholars. These "alarming" social developments, these "pathologies," generated a sense of urgency among some state officials to advocate for the expansion of public spaces and spheres. Official governmental reports listed factors responsible for the expansion of "morally corrupt networks": unemployment; the "marriage crisis"; and the lack of cultural, sports, and entertainment spaces and facilities (Public Culture Council 2011).[15] Some realized that the state could no longer rely merely on prohibition and the banning of Western cultural products. New technologies, such as the development of the modern Internet, the launching of satellite radio and television, the release of compact discs for audio and video recordings, and data storage, had made it difficult and costly to monitor every individual. These officials advocated that instead, the state should produce alternative cultural products and spaces.

It was at this time that the idea of women-only parks first came into being. In 1993 the Presidential Center of Women's Affairs and Participation, led by Shahla Habibi, pushed Tehran Municipality to convert the seventy-five-acre Taleghani Park into a women-only park so that "women could exercise in open air with their gym clothes and without the veil" (*Zan-e Rooz*, June 11, 1993). The municipality offered the rationale that providing alternative spaces for leisure and exercise would help direct attention away from the infiltrating Western cultural goods and prevent the consumption patterns and behaviors associated with such goods by what they considered to be "susceptible" groups of the population such as youth and women. "Since the Western countries do everything in their capacity to corrupt [our] youth," said Habibi in an interview with *Zan-e Rooz*, "the lack of [morally] healthy entertainment hubs and spaces could have dangerous [moral] implications" for susceptible and vulnerable population groups such as "women," and "the youth" (June 11, 1993). Here we see the emergence of a discourse that frames women's exercise and entertainment not as a problem, but as a solution to the problems associated with the "Western cultural invasion." The importance of exercise for women's physical and mental health is only raised as an afterthought. In the same interview, Habibi referred to the opening of women-only parks and similar acts as a necessity; she highlighted the implications of such acts for the mental and physical health of the population and invited women to show their support for such projects by attending the park and using its facilities.

But as Habibi explained in my 2009 interview with her, the project initially suffered from poor advertising and a lack of cooperation and support from other state organizations. The municipality did not fully convert the park into a women-only park; instead it implemented the necessary security measures to reserve the park exclusively for women only on Saturdays, Mondays, and Wednesdays from 6:00 a.m. to 4:00 p.m.[16] Despite Habibi's call, women showed little interest in using the space provided for them at Taleghani Park. The project was a failure partially because the state failed to truly invest in the project of women's parks, as illustrated by the limited way it converted the park space and the lack of investment in publicizing it. But other factors also contributed to the failure of this project: the park was neither centrally located nor easily accessible by public transportation; furthermore, the obsession with fitness and weight loss was not yet widespread. Thus, Taleghani Park was deserted on women-only days. Soon the empty space was reclaimed by men, leaving the park as an example of the state's failed attempt to create a women-only park in the early 1990s.

Nevertheless, during the same period Habibi proposed that the parks in all districts in Tehran should allocate specific spaces for women's sports and exercise activities, and this call resulted in a chain of political activities. District municipalities created women's sports offices, which were mostly responsible for organizing and coordinating women's morning and group exercises, now conducted under the supervision of female instructors in public parks, where women, still observing their hijab, could do aerobics and stretching exercises—something unimaginable a decade earlier. This was important, as it paved the way for women's increased ability to claim their own space of authority in the years that followed.

In a personal interview with me, one of these female instructors indicated that the women who attended these events were initially mostly "middle-aged housewives," but the women's sports offices successfully promoted group exercise in the parks for women of all walks of life. During my visit to three women's sports offices, I had the chance to review the annual reports produced by the office directors; these were invariably replete with extensive lists of the promotional events and outreach programs that they administered. Similarly, interviews with four female instructors in the sports offices confirmed the commitment and excitement of the staff regarding promoting women's exercise as well as a more practical concern with protecting and maintaining their jobs through demonstrating their productivity and listing in detail all the initiatives they had come up with for women in the district under their supervision.

By the end of the 1990s the outdoor exercise sessions organized by district municipalities had become elaborate events, often accompanied by competitions, prize drawings, food, and other festivities. Women's morning exercises and competitions in public parks were no longer policed by the state, but rather organized and regulated by it. Women's outdoor exercise, previously carried out in stealth, was now approvingly carried out under the gaze of female instructors. In other words, the state managed to bring into the light and under its wing that part of everyday life that had flourished outside the permitted zones. It might be easy for onlookers to see these changes as improvements to women's quality of life, yet while that may be true, the state has also used these improvements to expand its reach into the previously unregulated areas of women's lives.

The end of the 1990s marked the beginning of the so-called reform era. This period was characterized by the state's move toward social and political liberalization, as opposed to the economic liberalization of the previous era.[17] Khatami was less interested in economic policy, but since that was still controlled by other political factions, economic liberalization continued, as did the problems associated with it. Nevertheless, the major issue in this era was the deepening of political rivalry between the conservatives and the reformists, which hindered the smooth functioning and collaboration of various state apparatuses. The conservatives swiftly criticized the Khatami administration's focus on political and social liberalism. Cries of "creeping liberalism" were raised against Khatami's reformist agenda. In 1998 these tensions reached their peak, leading to the arrest of Karbaschi, the mayor of Tehran and a key ally of the reformist president. Karbaschi was arrested on embezzlement charges, tried, convicted, and eventually imprisoned in what was widely seen as a politically motivated attack by the conservative judiciary on the reformist government. Local politics, and the everyday spaces in which it unfolded, became the field where conservatives chose to fight their reformist opponents. With Karbaschi removed from the Tehran Municipality, the city entered a period of turmoil. Between 1999 and 2003 Tehran saw the coming and going of three mayors, all of whom were removed for political reasons.[18]

Despite these disruptions and political frictions, different state factions acknowledged the need for the provision of alternative spaces, even if in the name of "cultural defense." After years of unsuccessful attempts to reinforce bans on Western (cultural) products, they unanimously agreed on the cause: a lack of conviviality, entertainment, and sports facilities.[19] Policy-making institutions and organizations with different political affiliations passed bills or designed proposals demanding the allocation of sufficient funds and resources for the organization and facilitation of leisure-time activities for both women and youth.[20] Despite their agreement about the source of the problem, they held different ideas about how to respond. For example, although the reformists and the conservatives agreed that it was necessary to expand women-only spaces, the reformists saw this as a way to "expand" women's spaces, while the conservatives saw it as the "regulation" of women's access to public space. Different intentions and motivations notwithstanding, the outcome was the same: there would be an expansion of exercise and entertainment spaces. Within this atmosphere, the idea of women-only parks was revived.

In 2000 the "social and cultural experts" of the Education and Training Organization of Tehran (ETO), a subdivision of Tehran's Department of Education, published a report that contained information about schoolgirls' poor health conditions.[21] The report suggested that due to their lack of access to sports facilities and thus their lack of physical activity, schoolgirls were suffering from various bone and joint diseases. This, the report suggested, was partially the outcome of the state's earlier project of urban development and partially caused by women's obligation to veil and cover their bodies in public. It also suggested that the covering, which is required by law, had caused a lack of exposure to sunlight, which in turn caused hair loss. One of the main recommendations listed in the ETO report was that the city facilitate the expansion of space for schoolgirls' sports by creating women-only parks. While in earlier decades women's exercise had been framed as an antidote to the "Western cultural invasion"—with considerations for women's health added as an afterthought—now the health of women was brought to the fore, and women-only parks were presented as a solution to public health problems. Here we see how the initial concern about the moral health of women, and by extension the society, was translated into concern about the physical health of individual women.

The report identified two main factors as responsible for women's health problems: urban development and compulsory veiling. This was not the first time that Khatami's administration had tacitly presented the veil as a health hazard. In fact, earlier that same year the Ministry of Education had issued a directive stating that "elementary students [could] wear bright, happy colors such as light blue, beige, pink, light green and yellow in school." The directive suggested that this move would "brighten the mood and raise hope among students, and preserve their psychological health" (*Hurriyet Daily News* 2000). Women's veiled bodies, which had once symbolized the state's properly Islamic identity, had turned into "unhealthy" bodies symbolizing the state's failure to provide and care for its subjects. That the connection between vitamin D deficiency and women's hijab was a publicly discussed problem only two decades after the founding of the Islamic Republic of Iran shows how the Islamic Republic was able to draw upon the authority of medical discourse in the modern world, despite its own strong ideological commitment to mandatory veiling as a principal symbol of its sovereign identity. In this context, the Iranian state had to acknowledge the medical discourse of deprivation and respond to it through the provision of the women-only parks. As a result, the Iranian state was caught in the contradictions of its own identity as a modern Islamic nation. In a fine balancing act, the report made the expression of criticisms against (mandatory) veiling possible and opened a space for them at the official level, while at the same time depoliticizing these criticisms by presenting them as part of a health problem and not as a rejection of the principle of veiling per se. It thus finessed the problem by continuing to require mandatory veiling not just as a religious obligation, but as a solution to contemporary women's objectification through the male gaze, while encouraging segregated unveiling as a solution to contemporary bodies' deprivations.

Turning the recommendations of the ETO into a national policy, the Ministry of Interior (of Khatami's administration) sent a directive to all of the provincial governors asking them "to consult with the women's affairs offices and munici-palities to locate a space of at least 107,000 square feet, which could immediately be purchased and transformed into a cultural and entertainment hub for women" (quoted in *Iran*, July 1, 2007).

In 2003 the newly elected conservative mayor of Tehran, Mahmoud Ahmadine-jad, demanded that the Tehran Parks and Green Space Organization locate ideal spots across Tehran and convert them, whether partially or in their entirety, to women-only parks.[22] Four parks from among the 1,357 existing parks were chosen. The official reports and interviews released by the city council and the municipality demonstrate that these four spots were chosen based on the following three criteria:

1. *Visual security*: In order to satisfy the clerics that the uncovered women inside the park were protected from the prying eyes of men, the parks had to be built either on heights (see figure 4) or in places that could be easily partitioned off by trees and/or walls. These were ironically deemed "Wuthering Heights" by one of my interviewees.[23]

2. *Accessibility*: The parks had to be built in places that were easily accessible by public transportation so that women would have no difficulty reaching them.

3. *Social justice*: The authorities wanted to make sure that the green space and the sports and entertainment facilities were evenly distributed across the city and available to women of varying classes (see figure 5).

These criteria suggest that the state, in responding to what it had formulated as "women's need," had to take into account the religious as well as the popular demands and concerns of and about women.

Meanwhile, Mayor Ahmadinejad tried to push for the construction of the first women-only park in Tehran, but his attempts failed, partly because of the political opposition he received from the Presidential Center for Women's Affairs and Par-ticipation, headed by the reformist Zahra Shojaee. In an interview with *Sharq*

FIGURE 4. "Wuthering Heights," the Mothers' Paradise on Abbas
Abad Hills, Tehran. Courtesy of Masoomeh Niloofari.

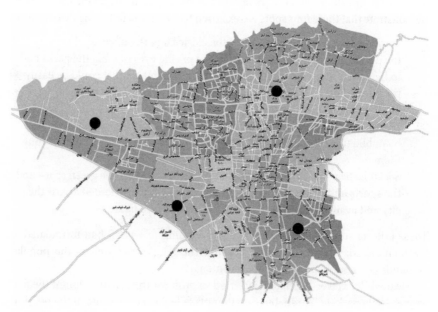

FIGURE 5. The distribution of women-only parks across Tehran. Courtesy of Mahboobeh
Saberi.

(December 6, 2003), she claimed that women's main demand was not entertainment but rather employment. Shojaee allegedly also blocked the budget allocated for the creation of such parks, and although she denied this in my interview with her, the claim itself points to the continuous rifts within the state and between different state factions.

By this point the state was totally fragmented insofar as the forces that controlled its different apparatuses were concerned. The administration and Parliament were in the hands of the reformist faction, while the Tehran City Council and Tehran Municipality were in the hands of the conservatives. Thus, although the push for the creation of women-only parks had originally come in 2002 from the reformist-led administration, the Presidential Center for Women's Affairs and Participation obstructed the municipality's formation of these parks, due to the reformists' political rivalry with the conservatives in Tehran's municipal government and their competing visions about women's provisions. In her 2009 interview with me, Fereshteh Alimohammadi, the city expert who had prepared the final proposal for the Tehran City Council, claimed that the tensions had nothing to do with the parks per se but were about "who delivers" and "who gets the credit for such provision." Regardless, by this time both factions within the state had realized that their legitimacy and popularity depended on how well they provided for the population. Alimohammadi's words echo the words of Reza, one of the male guards at the entrance of the park, whom I interviewed during one of my visits to the Mothers' Paradise. He said: "Do you think they really care about you [women]? Wishful thinking! All they cared about was to get this board up there that says 'The Mothers' Paradise.'" Reza implied that the opening of the park was a mere show to demonstrate that the state treats women well. This cynical but all-too-familiar remark about many of the state's initiatives points to the Iranian state's use of women and "women's rights" as a screen on which to project a positive self-image for Iranians and the rest of the world to see.

In 2004 it was the Tehran City Council, led by the conservatives, that passed a bill permitting the municipality to pursue the creation of women-only parks:

> With respect to mothers' constructive position, their role in the growth of society, their emotional and educational centrality within the family, and their effective role in the process of human cultivation and reduction of social pathologies, and with the aim of boosting their mental and physical capabilities, directing their leisure time, and providing them with appropriate opportunities for healthy entertainment in Tehran, the municipality is obliged to provide and allocate proper spaces in the existing parks. Furthermore, it will design and establish exclusive spaces in Tehran to be called "Mothers' Parks." (Tehran City Council, October 5, 2004)

Note the transformation of the official language: women go from being "schoolgirls," mentioned in the 2002 report by ETO, to being "mothers," reinforcing the notion that although a woman may have rights and needs as an individual, she may claim them only as a family member. This use of familial language also has an additional effect: it constitutes an attempt by the state to desexualize public space and regulate sexuality in public. Yet ironically, the state's gender boundary drawing and the practices of mandatory veiling and gender segregation are heteronormative policies that reproduce sexual(ized) bodies by admitting that these require regulating.

These contradictions inherent in state policies have also prompted the state agencies and their political superiors to articulate in official discourse their concern over, and intention to mitigate, the problems earlier policies have brought about. This is clearly reflected in the way state institutions represent the raison d'être of women-only parks. According to the bill passed by the city council in 2004, women-only parks are multidimensional in purpose, redressing a variety of pressures that crowded urban living has created for women:

> The expansion of apartment living and the increase in the frequency of everyday frictions and tensions and the lack of sports spaces have led to irreparable consequences, such as limited movement capabilities and heightened physical—and consequently mental and emotional—disorders, especially for women. These problems are two hundred times more for mothers because they have to deal with pregnancy complications, childcare problems, and housework duties. The mothers' parks, by creating natural spaces and providing proper facilities and offering entertaining programs, could offer a venue for a variety of sports activities which suit different age cohorts within the target population.

The flouting of regulations that had led to the anarchic development of Tehran and other Iranian cities, the complicity of state authorities in this, and the failure of the legal system to comprehensively address the problems and requirements of urban life had indeed given rise to a host of psychological and social problems among urban inhabitants. In the absence of shared spaces conducive to interaction and the development of social bonds, neighbors, despite their proximity, often found themselves disconnected from each other in an inimical, densely built environment. In the case of Tehran, what was once called the City of Green and Trees could be likened to a congested urban desert.

With the passage of this bill, what was once considered luxurious and unnecessary was reframed and presented as "women's needs."

In 2005 Ahmadinejad became Iran's president, and Mohammad Baqir Qalibaf, another conservative, replaced Ahmadinejad as mayor of Tehran. Upon assuming the mayorship, Qalibaf announced that he would not launch new projects but would instead finish what his predecessor had left unfinished, including the creation of women-only parks. With a conservative heading the municipality and a conservative now in the presidential office, there was no political opposition to the project. Instead, there was a dovetailing of structural consolidation and a lifting of partisan deadlock. Thus, in 2007 the Mothers' Paradise was opened in the northeast of Tehran, and in 2008 the Women's Paradise park was opened in the southeast section of the city. At the time of my fieldwork, the two other women-only parks were under construction.

Reaffirming the vision of the 2002 bill, these parks were designed to fulfill women's need for exercise and leisure. It is not surprising that officials formulated the construction of women-only parks in terms of women's need for exercise and not in terms of the requirements of an Islamic morality if we take into account that, according to "data from two values surveys conducted by researchers from the University of Tehran, Iran" in 2000 and 2005, "the stress on the Islamic identity of the nation [by the Iranian state]" has begotten "oppositional responses from Iranians" (Moaddel 2010). Referring to these surveys, Moaddel argues that among the Iranian population there is both a shift toward "social individualism, liberal democracy, [and] gender equality" (2010, 535) and an increasing demand on the state to "take more responsibility for meeting citizens' needs" (542). To maintain its legitimacy under such circumstances, the Islamic Republic of Iran had to tone down its prohibitive measures and instead highlight its role as providing for and protecting its citizens.

Furthermore, women-only parks provided an opportunity for the Iranian state to refashion its global image by presenting itself as a caring state, a provider and protector—rather than a violator—of women's rights. Ahmadinejad's coming to presidential power heightened animosity from the United States and its allies, but the construction of women-only parks in 2007 earned considerable praise. Ayatollah Safi Golpayegani, an eminent conservative cleric, characteristically stated that the establishment of women-only parks was a significant development, while another leading conservative member of the clergy, Ayatollah Makarem Shirazi, focused on the international acclaim that such initiatives could bring to the Iranian Republic.[24] Indeed, not only conservative clerics in Qom commented, but also foreign observers such as an Agence France-Presse reporter, who was amused to see Iranian women in "spaghetti strap vests and lycra shorts" (*Agence-France Presse*, June 17, 2008). In January 2008 Qalibaf was acknowledged and awarded for his efforts as the mayor of Tehran by the City Mayors Foundation, an international think tank dedicated to urban affairs.

Ironically, women's outdoor exercise in public parks, which was once characterized as unnecessary and un-Islamic, was now highly encouraged and promoted by the state. The language used in the officials' interviews and reports on women-only parks highlights the shift in the state's attitude toward women's leisure activities and exercise. Women were now recognized as both mothers of the nation and citizens (with needs), whose health was in danger and who therefore had to be "served" by the state. "As citizens, they have paid their dues during the revolution and the war," wrote 175 MPs in a letter, stating that "it is now the state's obligation to serve them" (*Resalat*, May 17, 2006). In various interviews with the press, Rasool Khadem, the conservative head of the Social and Cultural Commission of the City Council of Tehran; Fereshteh Alimohammadi, the legal adviser to the commission; and Soheila Jelodarzadeh, a reformist MP, all emphasized that as citizens, women have the right to freely and comfortably exercise in public—a right that, as they all said, had long been forgotten. Khadem pointed out that "women always complain about the considerable restrictions that they face. . . . They always tell me 'Men are free to run and play in the streets, to enjoy the sun and the nature whenever they want. Women must be provided with the same conditions!'" (*Iran*, October 27, 2004). Emphasizing the responsibilities of the state toward its citizens, Zahra Moshir, the head of the Women's Office of Tehran Municipality and also Mayor Qalibaf's wife, pointed to the results of a survey of Tehrani women that was conducted in 2006: "The survey showed that access to sports and entertainment hubs was ranked first among women's requests of the municipality. Thus, we decided to seriously pursue the project of constructing women-only parks" (*Ettelaat*, May 15, 2008). Mokhtari, the head of the Parks and Green Space Organization of Tehran Municipality, also stated: "If, because of our religious and moral beliefs, we impose specific codes of conduct on women, then we have to provide them with a space where they can enjoy the green space peacefully and securely" (*Etemad-e Melli* July 29, 2008). The meaning could not be clearer: the state no longer merely expected women to follow imposed rules and codes of conduct but was itself expected to meet women's expectations.

In what seemed to be a coordinated effort, several state officials, Tehran city councilors, and MPs from various political factions praised the opening of the Mothers' Paradise and pointed out that since women bear the burden of religion and must be covered all the time, it is necessary that they be provided with sports and entertainment facilities where they could take off their veils, wear the clothing of their choice, and freely exercise. Thus, in their statements about the opening of the Mothers' Paradise, state officials and city councilors managed to shift attention away from state-imposed compulsory veiling toward the optional unveiling in select spaces provided by the government. As a result, perhaps inadvertently in these statements, the focus shifted from the association of veiling with lack of freedom to the association of unveiling with freedom—and most important, with the freedom being provided by the state. Here once again, the intricate mechanisms of state power lay hidden from sight while the world saw the liberal mandate of individual choice. Instead of presenting itself as the prohibiter or curtailer of freedom, the state now presented itself as the provider upon whom subjects could rely.

The park was welcomed by most of the women who populated it on a daily basis. However, there were a few objections. Some women, including feminist activists and the outspoken film director Tahmineh Milani, expressed concerns about the expansion of gender-segregated spaces and their long-term effects on the relationships between the opposite sexes. A group of neighborhood men who had lost access to their favorite park also signed a petition and held a small protest during the inauguration ceremony. Speaking to the protesters, Qalibaf argued that as women account for half the city's population, their needs should be met (Sinaiee 2008).

In 2008 the Mothers' Paradise, the first park of its kind in Tehran, hosted more than a thousand women per day (*Abrar*, November 13, 2008). Although as early as the late 1980s some state officials had expressed concerns over the lack of exercise space for women and its negative impact on their mental and physical health, the first attempt to establish a women-only park in 1993 had failed partly because women, as the potential users of this space, did not see the merits of the project and showed little interest in using such spaces. The success of this new emphasis on the discourse of "women's health" and its appeal to women can only be understood in the context of the increasing importance of municipal and submunicipal divisions in promoting women-only parks and their importance for women's health. Now nations across the globe proudly focus on cultivating healthy bodies through proper nutrition and sufficient exercise. Iran is no exception. As an example, in the early 1990s the Jane Fonda workout videos were found only in well-to-do houses, but by the 2000s there were thousands of yoga and aerobics classes across the country, including in religious cities such as Mashhad, Isfahan, and even Qom.[25]

Mansoureh, one of the female exercise instructors of Tehran Municipality, stated in her interview with me that the municipality aims to "provide" women with one women-only park in each district of Tehran. "Women want more of these parks," Mansoureh claimed. When I shared this news with a group of women in the Mothers' Paradise, they all welcomed the "much-delayed" initiative. Women want more of what the state wants them to want. In the process, the line between "interest at the level of the consciousness of each individual" and "interest considered as the interest of the population" becomes blurry.[26] However, there is more at stake here than internalizing the norms of the Islamic Republic. As Moruzzi and Sadeghi (2006) point out, "The decline of formal traditionalism has meant that gender inequality has evolved into specifically modern forms: sexual harassment on the street, gender discrimination in the workplace." In their interviews with young women across the religious spectrum, they found that many complained of "the sexual saturation of the youth public sphere, including the real spaces of parks and shopping areas." Thus, there is a small step from this reality to the state posing as women's protector.

The convergence of individual women's interests with state interests completes the process through which, in dealing with women's outdoor exercise and activities, the Iranian state shifted from relying on prohibition to renegotiating the gender boundary and redrawing it in a way that accommodates women's increased presence in public spaces and facilitates the production of "healthy bodies." Instead of prohibiting outdoor exercise in the name of Islam, it produces new spaces and "rationalizes" and "justifies" the need for these segregated spaces through secular authoritative concepts and discourses of public health. In doing so, the state ultimately enables its desired behaviors and practices, such as women exercising separately from men, not through coercion and prohibition but through protection and provision.

But what does this process entail? How does the state ultimately succeed in promoting women-only parks? The answer, I argue, lies in what I call scaling-down and the municipalization of health, the key mechanisms through which the state successfully negotiates and redraws the gender boundary to expand women's access to public green and exercise spaces.

SCALING DOWN AND REACHING OUT: THE MUNICIPALITY AT WORK

The story of the Mothers' Paradise, far from merely exploring the politics of gender segregation as this is implemented through the development of women-only parks, helps trace the ebbs and flows of the state building projects. In its second decade, the Islamic Republic of Iran found itself caught up in a web of unexpected consequences resulting from its earlier policies of compulsory veiling and urban development. Tehran had become a jam-packed, polluted, and depressed city of more than eight million. Women's reported mental and physical health problems, which were associated with veiling and the depressive, confined lifestyle promoted by the state, pointed to the failures of a system that had promised to bring women dignity and integrity. On the other hand, the spread of the "bad hijab" phenomenon and women's disregard of the bans on women's exercise in public places, as well as their continuous presence in mixed-gender parks, pointed to the ineffectiveness of the state's prohibitive and disciplinary measures (Bayat 2010, 2007). In addition, with the globalization of cultural and political products and practices, Iran found itself in a disadvantageous position vis-à-vis the West, in which the banning of Western products was no longer feasible. Within this environment, far too many things were escaping the state's regulatory authority. It was against this background that the Iranian state reconfigured its mode of regulation to what seemed to be a more effective and productive form: provision of exclusive exercise and green spaces for women. By seizing upon the problems it had created, the state invested in its own failures as opportunities to shape a problem space in which it could offer a solution.

The Mothers' Paradise stands on top of the Abbas Abad hills as a sign of the productivity of state power. Rather than being the product of the state's vertical (top-down) initiative, founded on religious justifications or the discourse of cultural invasion, this park is the product of a state's initiative that draws on a medicalizing discourse, which is of a piece with popular discourses on health and depression and as such permeates the boundaries of "state" and "society." The success of the Mothers' Paradise as a state project could be partially attributed to the conservatives' rise to power, which put an end to the deadlock caused by political rivalries between conservative and reformist factions. However, the political deadlock is secondary, and the real story is about the state's increasingly sophisticated ability to coordinate across scales and reach into everyday life. The Mothers' Paradise illustrates how the state facilitated provision by "scaling down." The scaling down, through municipalization, enabled a redrawing of the gender boundary in a way to expand women's (separate) exercise spaces, a transformation that was achieved by reorganizing everyday life through a discourse of health.

But what was significant about the discourse of health? In her groundbreaking work on mental health in Iran, Orkideh Behrouzan (2016) shows how during the 1990s a state-sanctioned discourse about mental health (*salamt-e ravani*) developed, and the term *depression* was normalized as it became one way to deal with ruptured pasts;unstable presents marred by ambiguity, anxiety, and confusion; and uncertain futures. In this context, problems that had previously been confined to the universe of the undiscussed because of their political "quality" could now be articulated. Behrouzan (2016) cites unpublished statistics from the Iranian Ministry of Health and Medical Education that revealed an explosion in antidepressant prescriptions between 1997 and 2008, suggesting that the medicalization of grievances and frustrations became at the time a vehicle of dealing with them.

As social issues and solutions to essentially social problems were mediated or translated through the use of the language of medicine, local authorities started responding accordingly. In 2005 Tehran Municipality launched its Department of Health and hired several doctors and physicians as health experts, with the objective of promoting urban health by increasing Tehranis' participation in active leisure pursuits and incidental activity. This initiative was also partially funded and encouraged by the new urban health policies and projects of WHO, in which the international organization categorized and ranked neighborhoods based on "health" indexes that it provided. Furthermore, as part of WHO's emphasis on increasing physical activity, countries such as Iran developed new public health campaigns aimed at reducing the prevalence of lifestyle diseases, such as atherosclerosis, heart disease, obesity, and diabetes.

Dr. Mohammad Golmakani, head of the Department of Health, told me during a 2010 interview that "all doctors, my colleagues here in the Department of Health [will] need to act like caring parents." His colleagues included the doctors, experts, and instructors who were recruited to "serve the citizens" in one of the four hundred Health Houses at various sites that go all the way down to the neighborhood level.

Dr. Golmakani was calling on the doctors to "win the hearts, minds, and trust of the citizens" by incorporating the empathetic, compassionate demeanor of a caring parent—or in other words, to be pastoral rather than disciplinary or repressive. In fact, these health experts, along with the exercise instructors of the Women's Sports Offices, were charged with "shepherding" the population's health and happiness (Rose 2001). They were consequential to mediating the shift from one mode of regulation, prohibition, to another, provision.

Health experts were employed to promote an understanding of health as a subjective, embodied experience, underpinned by a notion of gratification and pleasure. To make exercise pleasurable on a daily basis, they organized collective events such as hiking, marathons, yoga, aerobics, or simple stretching exercises, both in women-only parks and in the separate spaces in mixed-gender parks. For example, during one of the events organized by the municipality's Department of Health and Women's Sports Offices to mark the naming of October 20 as the national day of Iranian women's health by the municipality, the then minister of health, Marzieh Vahid Dastjerdi, exercised alongside the other female participants to highlight the importance of exercise for women's health. This might have just been arranged as a photo op, but that itself shows how state officials at the national level realized the importance of everyday spaces and activities. In another event organized by Tehran Municipality, around seven thousand senior citizens, including thousands of women, gathered in Velayat Park in southern Tehran to mark health week. Such work facilitates the interpellation of women into particular ways of being "good" (that is, modest) and healthy, active citizens at the same time; through the provision of health-promoting activities in segregated spaces, women are enjoined to constitute themselves as particular subjects embodying both the moral/modest subjecthood required by "Islamic" morality and the ideal of an active and healthy citizen promoted by international health organizations as well as more liberal politicians.

As the state started to redraw the gender boundary and reshape the public space to facilitate women's presence, it simultaneously increased its grip on previously unregulated spaces of everyday life. In this way, the state exercised a more effective form of power that was focused more on regulation than prohibition and was more concerned with the enabling of desired practices than with the disabling of undesired ones. The story of the gradual (re)opening of the space for women, therefore, is the story of the gradual (re)orientation of state power. Yet the expansion of the state's scope of power constitutes part of a more complex picture. The fact that any perceived gains for women are provisional and at the discretion of the state, which can act in its prohibitory or regulatory mode when it so chooses, should not obscure the inextricable coupling of power with resistance. The walls that embrace the Mothers' Paradise, just like the metal bars that divide the bus space, signify the undeniable fact of the state's enduring authority. However, these walls and the metal bars, just like the gates of the Freedom Stadium, discussed in the next chapter, can be and in fact are sites of contestation and negotiation of state power.

Soccer Goals and Political Points

The Gendered Politics of Stadium Access

"The city of Melbourne glitters in the early evening as the MCG [Melbourne Cricket Ground] prepares to host Australia's most important football [soccer] match in four years, to be played out in the country's biggest sporting arena, a colossal venue for a colossal game. It is Australia versus Iran, the second and final leg of a two-legged contest which began in the courtroom of Azadi [Freedom] Stadium in Tehran a week ago. Now Australia will provide its own courtroom, a full house of 98,000 people roaring in full voice as the Socceroos [the official nickname of the Australian national team] attempt to make history" (Murray 1997).[1]

These were the opening remarks of Les Murray, Australian soccer analyst, broadcasting live from Melbourne on November 29, 1997. Thirty-one of the thirty-two spots available in the 1998 FIFA World Cup, the world championship for men's national association soccer teams, had already been claimed by the qualifying teams. The winner of this match would take the last spot on the list, ensuring it a trip to Paris for the final tournament. As the head referee blew his whistle to signal the start of the game, Les Murray claimed that Australia was "just ninety minutes away from being among soccer's elites in the World Cup finals" (Murray 1997).[2]

Indeed, as the minutes passed by, Australia got closer and closer to soccer's most elite club. Seventy-six minutes into the game, Australia still had a 2–0 lead against Iran. Then, as a global audience of more than one billion followed the match, Iran scored its first goal. But Australia still led the game. Players continued to furiously tackle each other. Attackers constantly attempted to score another goal, Australians aimed to secure their lead, Iranians hoping for a 2–2 tie, which would automatically give Iran the lead according to away-goals rules, which dictate that "any goals scored at the ground of the opposing team will count as double."[3] The ball kept rolling. Players were panting. The clock was ticking. The ball traveled across the soccer field and more than one billion pairs of eyes traveled with it. There were only ten minutes left before the referee blew his whistle three times, signaling the end of the game. The countdown began. Les Murray and Johnny Warren, the popular Australian soccer player who had played in Australia's first and last World Cup appearance in 1974, anxiously got ready to cheer Australia's entry in the World Cup after twenty-four years.

But these last ten minutes were a game-changer, and as the adage goes, "It ain't over 'til it's over." Against all expectations, Iran made a comeback. In the blink of an eye, Ali Daei, a world-renowned center-forward, passed the ball to Khodadad Azizi, who was named the Asian Player of the Year just a few months before. Azizi flew toward the goal with the ball glued to his feet, out-sprinted the Australian defense, and on a breakaway, chipped the ball over the goalkeeper, and knocked it into the goal to end the game at a 2–2 draw. "Disaster for Australia!" shouted Murray, clearly distraught. Warren, openly weeping on the air, said: "In boxing terms they are knocked out!" Australia was denied a place in the finals. Iran made it to the World Cup after twenty years.

The flapping of Azizi's wings in Melbourne caused a tsunami of ecstasy in Tehran, 7,845 miles away. An icon of "disaster" for Australians, Azizi became a legend on the other side of the globe. Iranians, frenzied and jubilant, poured into the streets, screaming for joy and waving the national flag. Some were distributing candy and cookies, some blowing their plastic horns, some dancing to a song in their hearts only they could hear, some impersonating Azizi's final moves, and some just enthusiastically observing the outburst of emotions that had long been suppressed. Men and women, together, reclaimed the streets of Tehran, turning the city into a gigantic stage for national glory and solidarity. The police, themselves flabbergasted by the magnificent performance of the national team, did not intervene.

Tehran was restless that night. Hours after midnight one could hear people honking horns, shouting Azizi's name, singing patriotic songs, and playing loud music. National glory had created a liminal space in which the rule of law was temporarily suspended, allowing people to display their happiness publicly through songs and dances, activities that were inconceivable just a few days before. The national team had helped bring together a nation, squeezed by the postrevolutionary upheavals, the war, US-led sanctions, tight social control, and political tensions. Men and women, the people and the police, the secular and the religious, the conservatives and the reformists, young and old and with diverse ethnic backgrounds, were stitched together by the threads of a national victory.

The next morning the "heroes of the nation" were on their way back to Iran. As the city woke up, the government made an announcement demanding that the people of Iran not populate the airport and inviting them to instead attend the welcoming ceremony to be held at the Freedom Stadium, the biggest sports complex in Iran, located in Tehran. As soon as the announcement was concluded, the stitches that had held the nation together were torn apart. Ever since the Islamic Republic of Iran was established in 1979, women had been banned from entering sports stadiums, including the stadium where the ceremony was being held. Although no actual law specifically prohibited women's spectatorship of men's matches, the stadium's practice of denying women entry had hardly been publicly questioned.

By setting up Freedom Stadium as a stage where national glory and solidarity could be celebrated, but without women, the state had inadvertently drawn attention to a hitherto imperceptible scar: the ban on women's sports spectatorship. In other words, the state unknowingly facilitated the translation of what was at best a private trouble into a notable public issue (Mills 1959). The ban became a national problem overnight. The stakes were high: top-level state officials from fifty-five Islamic countries had convened in Tehran for the Eighth Islamic Summit; many women, in groups or as families, were already on their way to Tehran from the surrounding towns, eager to welcome the soccer players; and Mohammad Khatami, who had been elected president of Iran on May 23, 1997, just six months before the game, had run on a platform of liberalization and reform. And the whole world was watching. All of this worked in favor of women. The ban was lifted.

As the gates of Freedom Stadium opened, between three and five thousand women surged in. Women were assigned to a special section. The rest of the stadium was populated by more than ninety thousand men. Together in harmony, the nation was ready to rise as the soccer players were brought into the stadium in a helicopter that landed on the green grass of Freedom soccer field. As the players got off the helicopter, it became difficult to differentiate men's voices from women's as they shouted with joy, "Iran, Iran, Iran!" This "horizontal comradeship" had, for a moment, made the nation imaginable (Anderson 1983). Nevertheless, this sense of inclusive comradeship was merely an exception, a fleeting, frustrated glimpse of the potential for change. The morning after, the ban was reinstated, and women were denied access to Freedom once again.

The shot that Azizi directed toward the Australian goal had had a butterfly effect, setting in motion a chain of events that transformed the already complex political scene in Iran in terms of alliances and possibilities. This chapter offers a historical narrative about the developments in the ban on women's sports spectatorship and examines the different historical moments in which the ban was constructed as a national problem. The gender boundary regulating women's access to sports stadiums has been drawn and redrawn several times over the past four decades, and each redrawing has offered a space for political contestation between various political players at the national and international levels. In chronicling the strategies that various groups adopted, I highlight how each group mobilized the terms of gender, (trans)national politics, and religion to promote or oppose women's right to sports spectatorship.

Whereas those clerics who supported the ban drew on their religious authority and emphasized the religious/moral aspect of the ban (i.e., looking at the half-naked bodies of sportsmen is religiously forbidden), some state actors, such as the police, upheld the ban in the name of protecting women as citizens and pointed to the unfeasibility of lifting the ban due to the loutish—and thus not women-friendly—atmosphere of sports stadiums. President Khatami, as well as his successors, Presidents Ahmadinejad and, more recently, Hassan Rouhani, as well as the Tehran Sports Organization, have supported the opening of the stadium to women, albeit in the form of separate and exclusive sections. At the international level, the Fédération Internationale de Football Association (FIFA) and the Asian Football Confederation (AFC) have supported women's access in terms of gender equality. On the other hand, women have consistently found themselves caught up in a political game that has been fought in their name and on their own bodies, as both domestic and international political players have been using women's issues to strategically reshape their political alliances and secure or enhance their political authority. Women, in turn, have navigated these political games and invested in the opportunity structures created by infighting between different state actors and factions as well as international pressure from FIFA and AFC. This chapter traces and examines the factors at play at different junctures when women's rights activists teamed up with various actors to press for the removal of the ban. It is important to note at this point that the term *women* as used in this chapter, as in the entire book, refers not only to women as a category, subjected to structures of domination, but also to women as a part of the population whose lived experience of, and responses to, this domination is diverse, inflected in terms of class, education, generation, and location.

An analysis of the developments around women's sports spectatorship requires that we account for the internal and external dynamics of political struggles. Instead of reducing the ban on women's sports spectatorship to a crude Islamism, I argue that it is more fruitful and theoretically constructive to look at this case as a microcosm of broader developments in political contestations and state fragmentation. Approaching sporting events (here soccer matches) as an arena in which political contestations are played out (Frey and Eitzen 1991), this chapter looks in particular at the gender boundary that regulates access to such events as a site of heightened contention. I demonstrate how different political entities and state and societal actors rally around various gendered discourses of protection to allegedly guard women as moral subjects (protecting their chastity in the name of Islam), secure them as citizens (protecting their physical safety as vulnerable citizens), and defend them as liberal subjects of a global governance (protecting their freedom and autonomy). Taking cues from Partha Chatterjee (1993), I demonstrate how women, their rights, and their bodies are used to assert and reconstitute the state's regulatory authority but also to challenge the state's authority or claims to political power. More than trying to locate who prohibits or who permits women's access to the stadiums—indeed, assorted domestic and international actors have been involved in such decisions and displayed considerable inconsistency over time in their positions—what this chapter seeks to do is to uncover how gender segregation has become an instrument in the pursuit of power, of the assertion of ultimate sovereignty. Consequently, gender segregation constitutes a means of circumscribing the boundaries of the political itself.

WARMING UP: EMBRACING SOCCER AS A GATEWAY TO THE WORLD

In 1978, a year before the Islamic revolution, the Iranian national soccer team made its first appearance in the World Cup, and Iranian sports were gaining momentum in international competitions. In 1979, with the shah gone and Ayatollah Khomeini in his place, a new approach to sports and international competition was adopted. Pursuing a foreign policy motto of "neither East, nor West," Iran withdrew from the international community and put an end to its participation in most international competitions. Women's sports were suspended. Men's sports did not fare well, either. Suspicion toward the sport as a Western cultural product with the potential to erode the authority of the revolutionary state reinforced the tendency toward abstention. For much of the 1980s, Iranian sportsmen and sportswomen were "riding the pine"—sitting on the bench, never getting into a game.

In the early 1990s the Islamic state switched gears. It was during the 1990 World Cup that Iranian officials discovered soccer's potential for constructing a nation anew. This revelation came after an earthquake with a magnitude of 7.4 turned the densely populated areas of Manjil and Rudbar into rubble, leaving around 40,000 killed, an estimated 100,00 injured, and 500,000 homeless. The country was just emerging from the destruction wrought in the south and southwest by the eight-year war with Iraq when the earthquake hit and shook its northwestern cities. Soccer provided a space for national recovery. Jurgen Klinsmann, West Germany's captain, who had led his team to championship, offered sympathy over the earthquake tragedy, which put Iran in the international media for something other than revolution, war, and extremism. Soccer diplomacy, some officials figured, could play in the Iranian state's favor. Moreover, the state officials, realizing the need to expand spaces of entertainment for the population or at least to ameliorate the pain caused by their losses, discovered a new opportunity in soccer and international sporting events. In *Life, and Nothing More* (1992), the acclaimed Iranian director Abbas Kiarostami drives through areas devastated by the earthquake, depicting how those who survived continue to live and endure. In one of the most effective scenes, we see the director's son, a kid from Tehran obsessed with the World Cup, ecstatic to find out that people of a nearby village, most of whom are now living in tents, are lifting an antenna that will allow them to watch the World Cup finals. Amid the rubble, villagers come together to watch soccer. Their miseries are temporarily forgotten.

State officials recognized and acknowledged the importance of sports in both their entertaining and competitive aspects. In 1993 Iran's supreme leader Ayatollah Khamenei lent his weight to those voices who supported the rehabilitation of sports as a national resource. In a statement stressing the importance of professional sports, he emphasized the impact of professional and champion athletes on Iran's international standing as well as the country's self-image. This association of sports with bringing honor and respect to Iran and its Islamic revolution helped pave the way for sports' advancement (Chehabi 2002). The official language was shifting; international sporting competitions were no longer dismissed as the domain of "the British and the Americans," as they had been during the first decade of the Islamic Republic. Instead, sports were welcomed anew as a symbolic space in which national pride and allegiance to the Islamic state as its embodiment could be forged and the normalization and return of postrevolution Iran to the international filed could be orchestrated, not just through its association with the long war with Iraq or with regional tensions and rivalries, nor by means of revolutionary propaganda, but through culture and sports.

In a male-dominated public arena, where political institutions were imbued with and formed around masculine norms and values, women had no place in sports fandom and were eventually excluded from sports arenas, first as sportspersons then as sports spectators. The former exclusion was eventually reversed as women's sports grew under state tutelage yet were meticulously circumscribed by it.[4] Nevertheless, when the question of whether or not women's competitive sports should be rehabilitated was eventually settled, another question emerged, that of women's spectatorship. As I argue in this chapter, from a hardly discussed issue (women were routinely, yet informally, not allowed in the stadiums), the question of who could frequent stadiums to watch the games eventually became a vexing issue that was to embroil administrations, different state apparatuses, and even various factions of the clergy in controversy.

Thus, in July 1994, during the Asian Youth Cup preliminary competitions, President Rafsanjani made an announcement that women could attend the games. This change was initiated in a top-down way and constituted one of several similar initiatives launched by President Rafsanjani as he tried to paint a new picture of Iran as open to the world (the creation of the office of the presidential adviser on women's affairs, discussed in chapter 3, is another case in point). In recounting the politics of soccer in Iran, Chehabi (2006) reminds us how the conservative newspapers *Resalat* and *Jomoori Islami* objected to this proposal on the grounds that the vulgar language of the male soccer fans made sports stadiums an unfitting venue for women, and that watching the male soccer players in shorts was also inappropriate for women. Nonetheless, in an attempt backed up by President Rafsanjani's office, on July 18, 1994, the Physical Education Organization designated a special section of the stadium for five hundred women to attend the games. A year later, however, the weekly sports paper *Palevan* published a fatwa (religious ruling) issued by Ayatollah Khamenei, the supreme leader, himself a source of emulation: "An unrelated woman may not look at the naked body of an unrelated man, even if the intent is not deriving lust" (Chehabi 2006, 246). Consequently, the Iranian Soccer Federation—which unlike its counterparts elsewhere is a state agency supervised by the government—repealed its decision.

With the election of Khatami on May 23, 1997, and the coming to power of the reformists—former revolutionaries who had been pushed to the political sidelines in the late 1980s—a new era of political liberalization began. The reformist faction that came to power was backed by twenty million popular votes—77 percent of the electorate—and therefore could claim a popular mandate for its promise to foster a more inclusive polity. The reformist president was the advocate of "dialogue among civilizations" abroad and the promoter of freedom of expression inside the country. Khatami's eight-year presidency was marked by a growing vibrancy of civil society on the one hand, and on the other by increasing adversity and cleavage among different factions within the state and between the Khatami administration and the conservative clerics, particularly those who felt that their authority was undermined by the spread of the reformists' liberal discourse.

It was during the first year of his presidency that Iran played the historic match against Australia mentioned in the opening narrative of this chapter. As the nation prepared for the welcoming ceremony, Khatami and his cabinet were at pains to devise a formula that would allow them to lift the ban on women's entrance into the Freedom Sports Stadium without antagonizing their conservative opponents in Parliament and among the clerics. The Khatami administration could hardly disregard the demands for reform that underpinned its landslide win at the polls, nor could it frustrate the hopes of its dynamic, urban, young base, who still pursued change through engagement and negotiation with the government. The stakes were high, as the fledgling reformist administration would ignore the support female voters extended to it at its peril, especially since Khatami's main campaign slogan was "Iran for *all* Iranians."

The lifting of the ban allowed Khatami and his government to signal the beginning of a new era in which the gates of Freedom were opened to women. This newly experienced freedom, however, was short lived. After the welcoming ceremony, the Khatami administration reinstated the ban, without offering any justification. It was several years later that Mohammad Ali Abtahi, Khatami's vice president, shed some light on the president's apparent about-face. In a newspaper column, Abtahi recalled the opposition that the administration had faced from conservative clerics and the supreme leader's office:

I will never forget the day when, in order to welcome the national team after its victory that led to its participation in the World Cup and generated national ecstasy,
girls and boys headed toward [Freedom] Stadium. That evening we, both in the Presidential Office and in the Physical Education Organization, were under constant
pressure to remove the girls from the stadium. Instead of rejoicing over that victory
we were looking for ways to deal with these pressures. (*Etemad*, April 26, 2006)

Neither Khatami nor his cabinet openly discussed these "pressures" at the time,
since they were intent on pursuing a nonconfrontational approach to the conservatives. Instead of public confrontation, they strove to reach a compromise through
painstaking negotiations and lobbying behind closed doors. Khatami's reform
agenda hinged on maintaining the integrity (or semblance of unity) of the state
and striking a balance among the president, the supreme leader, and the conservative clerics. The ban on women's sports spectatorship was in this conjuncture
framed as a "problem" that needed to be resolved.

The controversy surrounding women's entrance into the Freedom Sports Stadium after Iran's match against Australia was the outcome of a series of transformations I have already hinted at, which brought sports spectatorship, and a possibility of a space for women in it, into the limelight. In the late 1990s soccer had
started becoming a spectator sport with wide appeal to men and women alike. The
football diplomacy following the devastating earthquake in June 1990 contributed
to the sport recovering from the blow it had been dealt in the immediate postrevolutionary era. Having been shunned at the time, soccer's popularity later peaked as
it became a conduit for international sympathy and, ultimately, visibility, and as
the authorities noted its potential to distract and unify. This popularity was
invested in and expanded in the years that followed. Indicative of this progressive
transformation of soccer into a national institution that lent itself to attempts from
power contenders (different factions within the state, as well as the conservative
and reformist political camps) to gain legitimacy and made it a terrain of contestation was the success of the popular weekly TV program *Navad*.[5] The program had
one of the highest viewer rates across the country, and many of its viewers and
participants in its polls have been women. What is more, its host and director,
Adel Ferdosipour, partly recognizing the increasing female following of the sport
(and the show), has not shied away on many occasions from voicing his support
for women's entrance inside the stadiums and as a result has received criticism.

Interestingly, if one focused on societal attitudes, it would become obvious that
the issue of the opening of sports stadiums to women was ridden with ambiguity.
On the one hand, the demand for women to be able to enter stadiums was not yet
widespread. In the course of my interviews, it was difficult to ignore a considerable
gap between opinion and practice; even though a great majority of my interviewees
condemned the ban on women's sports spectatorship, in response to my question

about whether they were prepared to go to Freedom Stadium to watch a match if the ban were removed, only a few responded in the affirmative. For example, Elmira, a twenty-four-year-old student of architecture, characteristically told me:

> I love soccer but never in my wildest dreams have I thought of going to Freedom [Stadium]. Freedom is for a bunch of low-class hooligans [she used the Farsi term *laat o loot*]. I know it's fun to be there. I love to be part of a Mexican Wave. But no! With these fans, I'd rather watch the game at home with my friends.

Interestingly, Elmira's discourse reveals elements underlying both conservative objections and women's reservations regarding women's admission or entrance to the stadiums, notably a classed discourse that associates working-class masculinity with vulgar language, loutish behavior, and violence. Elmira's intimation echoed a widely held predisposition about women's presence in a space thought to be tainted by working-class masculine excesses, as did Banafsheh Arabi, the goalkeeper of Peykan women's futsal team and a soccer fan herself, in an interview:

> Especially during a sensitive match, the male fans use so many curse and insulting words that even if I were a boy I would not want to go to the stadiums. . . . It is one of my wishes to be able to attend a soccer match; however, if this wish were to be realized, I would want to do so in a safe and comfortable environment. (*Iran*, June 7, 2005)

While the ban was publicly problematized, the most decisive call for its repeal was mainly limited to a small segment of the female population in Tehran, mostly those within the city's feminist circles. The discussion about lifting the ban was mainly between these feminist circles and the reformist MPs and the administration, some of whom had identified themselves as advocates of women's rights, whereas some others were consciously responding to what they recognized as the growing demands of their vocal and young base. On the other hand, the ban had acquired symbolic significance way beyond the scope of women's rights activism. As a symbol of change, it resonated among first-time voters, as well as those who had given up hope for change, both constituencies the reformist politicians relied on and strove to continue attracting.

As soccer became popular across the gender divide, it became evident that the debates of the 1990s were merely a warm-up for the political contestations that were to come in the next decade.

THE KICKOFF: SOCCER AS THE DOMESTIC POLITICAL BATTLEFIELD

By the end of President Khatami's first term, the ban on women's sports spectatorship had become a matter of public discussion, as indicated in the multiple outlets that dealt with the issue in the form of cartoons, essays, and opinion pieces

FIGURE 6. Access denied! Courtesy of Mana Neyestani.

(see example from a different era in figure 6). The next round of the political game that was played out on the soccer field took place in the mid-2000s, toward the end of Khatami's second term.

Khatami's efforts to deal with the issue of women's sports spectatorship necessitated dealing with two conflicting constituencies. On the one hand, his strategy needed to keep on board the traditional conservatives, within the state apparatuses as well as among the influential clergy, who saw in any attempts to dilute the de facto ban on women's spectatorship a dangerous instance of creeping liberalism, foreign encroachment on the Islamic foundations of the republic, or/and a threat to their own power. Crossing red lines when dealing with the conservatives was bound to open up a Pandora's box that might destabilize the balances upon which rested the very edifice of the Islamic republic. On the other hand stood a restless, growing base of young voters, the sons and daughters of the revolution, who had grown to be vocal, demanding, and critical; many of them expected an end to the politics of compromise and pragmatism that had marked Khatami's first term and wished for an all-out confrontation with the conservative forces whose politics had circumscribed their lives. Despite Khatami's inclination to pursue incremental and negotiated change, his reliance upon this younger generation, not only for votes but also for legitimacy, could be disregarded only at his peril.

Satisfying both these constituencies at the very same time was a nearly impossible task that required introducing changes while maintaining delicate and precarious balances. This balancing act manifested itself on several occasions in Khatami's and his allies' criticism of what he identified as the backward mind-set of those who were in favor of the ban.

In 2004, at a public gathering, Khatami blamed "society's internalized mentality" for the "discrimination" that women faced when it came to women's sporting activities (*Javan*, July 9, 2004). While he publicly criticized the "particular" societal attitudes that hold women back and keep them on the margins of public spaces and the public sphere at large, he meticulously avoided specifying who holds such a mentality. Upon closer scrutiny of such statements, it becomes clear that the choice of the reformist camp surrounding him was to delegitimize the ideas that supported exclusionary practices such as those women faced when it came to sports participation and spectatorship, but not to directly challenge the authority and position of the conservative circles that deployed them. In all such statements, criticisms remained implicit, indirect, and vague about who held such views and who constituted an obstacle to fuller participation of women in sporting activities. This was not an isolated instance. In 2001 Fatemeh Rakei, then the head of the Women and Family Committee in the reformist-led Sixth Parliament, had attributed the source of the impasse in resolving women's access to Freedom Stadium to what she called the "Talibani approach of some groups":

> Limiting women's access [to sports stadiums] is as irrational as limiting their access to streets, parks, and cinemas. These prohibitions have their roots in some traditional and restrictive approaches to women. Some [groups], with their Talibani mentality, if given the opportunity, will keep the Iranian women inside the homes like the Afghan women. (*Aftab Yazd*, February 28, 2001)

Rakei deployed several tropes in her statement to support the cause of women's inclusion in sports activities. She brought up other areas of social life in which

women had already made a return after the first, more prohibitive, postrevolutionary years, pointing out the absurdity of maintaining sports and stadium access
bans as a remnant of a bygone era of senseless prohibition even according to the
standards of the Islamic Republic itself. But she also attempted to neutralize the
logic behind arguments supporting the ban by likening it to the mentality of an
external "other" that the Islamic Republic had tried to dissociate itself from, and
which public opinion considered as culturally alien, backward, and unsophisti-
cated: the Taliban, the ultraconservative Sunni Islamic fundamentalist political
movement that had until recently held power over much of neighboring Afghanistan's territory. In the realm of the war of ideas, bundling supporting the stadium
ban together with the prohibitive practices and "backward" mentality of the Taliban constituted a powerful indictment of the arguments of the conservative camp
while staying clear of personal attacks. What is more, the evocation of an "enemy"
on the national border by Rakei and others who adopted her line of argument
emphasized the alien character of the insistence on excluding women from the
stadium and wove into the debate a sense of national pride and distinctiveness.
Such discourse demarcates the boundaries between different interpretations of
Islam within a particular Islamic society, underlining the heterogeneity of Islam
and mobilizing echoes of deep-rooted conflicts among various interpretations of
Islam (Mir-Hosseini 1999) that resonate within Iranian society, including its conservative elites.

The potential effects of this type of criticism and of the Talibani mentality anal-
ogy might have helped keep on board the disgruntled, impatient generation of the
daughters and sons of the revolution, and may have made some inroads among
those conservatives receptive to it. But criticism, however muted and vague it may
have been, would not bring about change by itself. The Khatami administration, as
well as some reformists inside and outside Parliament, believed that for the stale-
mate to be overcome, it was imperative to search for some common ground, for
some language intelligible to them and their conservative opponents alike. This
quest was ridden with problems and was by no means uncomplicated.

Government officials and civil society activists did indeed not just criticize
those who blocked the removal of the ban; they also attempted to garner support
for its removal by formulating the right of women to enter Freedom Stadium in
terms of evoking the notion of the collective good. In a 2001 interview, Elaheh
Koolaei, a reformist female MP, speaking in favor of women's entrance to the
sports stadiums, mentioned that such a development "would help both to fulfill
women's need for leisure and to soften the [masculine] space of the stadiums"
(*Javan*, June 30, 2001). Echoing Koolaei's line of argument, the Physical Education
Organization security director, Behzad Katiraei, stated that one of the reasons the
rowdy space of the sports stadiums could not be controlled was that "families—
including women—are not present." In his opinion, transforming the sports sta-

dium into a family space would help reduce the number of security problems and incidents that happened during and after each match. Both Koolaei's and Katiraei's statements, like those made by their opponents, mobilized gender difference to make a point: while the opponents of women's access to stadiums saw the "delicateness" of women as a hindrance to their presence inside the stadium, the proponents of women's access represented it as an instrument to "pacify" the stadium space.

As my interviews with reformist politicians indicate, by adopting the idiom of gender difference that conservative clerics and the more conservative factions of society were customarily deploying, the reformists believed that they could establish common ground with the conservatives and reach a compromise. However, although framing women's rights as legitimate insofar as they advance the collective good might have admittedly provided women with the opportunity to access public spaces (as it did in the case of women's parks), it ultimately enabled those who had the prerogative of defining the collective good to rescind these rights when they deemed them excessive. Indeed, the lack of consensus on what constitutes the collective good, and thus the fragility of any concessions to women, was already in evidence at the time. For example, in a 2010 interview with me, Maryam Behrouzi, a former MP and the head of a conservative advocacy group called Zeynab Society, questioned the positing of women's access to stadiums as a human right, mocked the argument that this was conducive to the collective good, and branded the demands a "whim," and an "obsession with a luxury." Her remarks were not untypical of my other conservative interviewees' comments and demonstrated that should they gain an upper hand in policy making, any concessions to women in terms of access to stadiums could crumble.

Meanwhile, in a variant of this strategy of using a language that instead of antagonizing conservative circles, mobilized themes central to their ideology and discourse, Khadijeh Sepanji, the head of the Women's Soccer Association, attempted to rally support for women to enter sports stadiums as "mothers of the players." She deployed a gendered familial discourse in which women's rights are recognized, but these rights stem from their connections to men (here, male players) as mothers, wives, and daughters.[6] This familial discourse, which was widely used among various members of the reformist camp, also desexualized women as part of the "family." As I argued in chapter 3, this use of the desexualizing trope of "woman as a man's mother, sister or daughter" constitutes not only a means of regulating sexuality, but also a way of rendering women's rights conditional upon their relationship to a man or to the family unit.

While trying to arrive at some understanding with the conservative circles, reformists could not ignore the growing number of female sports fans lining up outside the doors of sports stadiums, large and small, demanding entry. Through loosening social controls, Khatami's reformist government quietly suspended the ban on women's spectatorship of almost all sports, but not soccer and wrestling, the two most popular national sports.[7] Worried about provoking the conservative clerics and coming under attack by various opposing conservatives, they deliberately avoided media publicity. In 2010, during my fieldwork, I attended several matches at national basketball and volleyball tournaments, alongside tens, and sometimes, if the match was important, hundreds of other women. Inside the stadium, the TV cameramen informed me that they had received instructions not to transmit any images of women so as not to incite a reaction from the clerics, so they had their cameras facing away from women. "Out of sight, out of mind!" joked one cameraman. It is significant to note that these instructions had come from the state-owned Iranian TV, whose head was appointed by, and therefore accountable to, not the reformist government, but the supreme leader. The state, caught between two of its radically different constituencies—the conservative clerics and the young Tehrani women with rising expectations and "a sharp consciousness of injustice, of social inequity between the sexes" (Kurzman 2008)—struck a delicate balance. The reformists settled on an unspoken suspension of the ban in some areas. On the other hand, the supreme leader and the circles close to him used their control over the state media to keep the "transgression" invisible and "off the record," thus denying their opponents any symbolic gains.

Back in the soccer pitch, however, the situation remained tense as the continued ban on women's entry to soccer stadiums was perceived as a sign of indecisiveness on the part of the Khatami administration by those supporters who were pushing for some form of showdown with the conservatives, who in turn saw it as a sign of weakness. This tension manifested itself at the end of Khatami's second term, when yet another international game, just like the one with Australia during his first term, sparked controversy just as a crucial presidential election was looming.

Iran was facing Bahrain in the 2006 World Cup qualifiers, and the match was to be held in Tehran on June 8, 2005, one week before the 2005 presidential elections. Foreign reporters had flooded into the country to cover both the World Cup qualifiers and the election campaign. The reformist camp was caught between a rock and a hard place, relentlessly monitored and subjected to criticism from conservative circles in Parliament and in the state but also under pressure from its increasingly frustrated and impatient constituency, among them vocal women's rights activists and members of Khatami's own cabinet, to make a symbolic historic move by officially eliminating the ban on women's sports spectatorship and championing women's rights.

Khatami's administration had failed to deliver on many of its promises, not least because its proposals faced continuous opposition from the conservatives, who controlled other branches of the government and state apparatuses, and also from the Guardian Council, which kept vetoing the bills that were passed by the reformist-dominated Sixth Parliament. As a prominent reformist figure and a former member of the Khatami administration told me, reformists were desperately in need of a symbolic gesture that would allow them to build the momentum to bring out their base to vote again in order to maintain their now precarious lead over conservative candidates, but also to withstand pressures from unelected state apparatuses that were bent on frustrating the reform process. Thus the elections, together with the game, provided a political opportunity structure for various social and political actors to further their cause and for the presidential candidates to gain popularity. Various reformist politicians and presidential candidates used their limited authority in the liminal space opened by the forthcoming elections to highlight their support for women's access to sports stadiums. They deployed the publicity opportunity the soccer match provided to rally support and push their agenda to the fore.

The issue of women's entry into the stadiums was used by Hashemi Rafsanjani, for example, who was running for president again after having served from 1989 to 1997. Rafsanjani used his campaign speeches to steer a middle path, similar to that Khatami tried to maintain, to simultaneously emphasize the importance of shari'a restrictions and suggest that women, "while observing [religious and ethical] principles, could be present inside the stadiums" (*Iran*, May 1, 2006). In an attempt to distinguish the reformist proposition from Rafsanjani's, Mostafa Tajzadeh, a politician and member of the steering committee of the Islamic Iran Participation Front, the country's leading reformist party, founded in 1998, challenged the alleged Islamic premise of the ban on women's access in an interview: "Today our women are prohibited from entering the stadium, a prohibition that does not have any basis in shari'a. It will only be a few years before this issue is resolved and not used as an electoral slogan" (*Toseh*, May 5, 2005).

In the meantime, the conservatives continued to vehemently oppose women's sports spectatorship. Their justifications clustered around two distinct themes: that the stadiums lacked security and that the removal of the ban was not a priority issue. Criticizing Rafsanjani's backing of women's entrance into the stadiums, *Siasat-e Rooz*, a conservative newspaper, published an editorial reminding Rafsanjani of the "inappropriateness" of the stadium space:

> It is necessary that we remind [Rafsanjani] that inside soccer stadiums the most famous and popular of our soccer players, such as Ali Daei, are the target of the worst insults by the soccer fans. Many get injured in the crowd and in their rush for seating. How could you even demand that women be present in such stadiums? (*Siasat-e Rooz*, May 4, 2005)

Ironically, despite the caring veneer of such an argument, in this context, protecting women from inappropriately behaving men did not entail reining in the offending behaviors and their perpetrators, but instead imposing restrictions on their potential victims. This inconsistency notwithstanding, this expression of concern about safety was not entirely baseless. A few months earlier, on March 26, 2005, following a World Cup qualifying match between Iran and Japan, five people had been trampled to death in Tehran; many others were injured, and eighty-six buses were damaged in crowd violence (BBC News 2005). To a certain extent, then, the conservatives' position that the stadium was an "inappropriate" space for women fit with women's perceptions of and experiences in sports stadiums.

Nevertheless, and despite the reservations of many women and the relatively tepid support for the ban to be lifted, out of the scattered objections of a few feminist journalists grew a small but organized feminist campaign known as the White Scarf Girls. In contrast to the occasional, less elaborate form of private resistance by a few women cross-dressing as men and attempting to sneak into the stadium, the White Scarf Girls marked the first official and collective opposition to the ban on Iranian women's sports spectatorship. The match with Bahrain in 2005 marked the official formation of the White Scarf Girls Campaign, which demanded "half of Freedom for women."[8] A dozen feminist journalists, along with several women's rights activists—some of whom were interested in attending soccer matches and some of whom found in this ban a symbolic opportunity to challenge the state's regulation of women's public presence in general—activated their support network within the state and the civil society. Many of the reformist presses were already run by members of the administration and reformists in Parliament. Thus, by siding with the reformist state actors, the White Scarf Girls were able to orchestrate the publication of a series of opinion pieces that not only questioned the ban and demanded equal access to Freedom Stadium, but also ushered into the domain of visibility what used to be an issue that had not attracted the sustained and passionate support of the broader public. The publicity afforded to the ban on women encouraged more women to join the campaign in front of the gates of Freedom in order to attend the match between Iran and Bahrain and raised awareness of the symbolic importance of the ban. Khatami's two female cabinet members—Zahra Shojaee, the presidential adviser on women's affairs, and Masoomeh Ebtekar, the head of the Environment Protection Organization—offered their support and lobbied with other authorities to pave the way for women's entrance to Freedom Stadium.

The White Scarf Girls protest challenged the conventional wisdom that visualized civil society and the state in Iran pitted against each other in a conflict premised on irreconcilable and mutually exclusive interests and objectives. Their action brought into sharp relief something that I alluded to earlier: Theirs was not an accidental or ephemeral alliance that blurred the boundary between feminists or women's rights activists and the state; it rather revealed the fact that the demarcating line between the two is hard to discern. The reformist women who were themselves supporters of women's rights and/or were responding to demands from below were on most occasions part of the state, holding positions in its various apparatuses.

FIGURE 7. White Scarf Girls facing the police. Courtesy of Mansour Nasiri.

As has already become clear in my discussion of this, as well as other case studies, not only has the boundary between state and civil society been permeable and unclear, but the unity and integrity of the state whose semblance Khatami, driven by the pragmatic imperative of bringing about negotiated, incremental reform, tried to preserve, also needs to be brought into question. Referring to the cabinet's efforts to reach an agreement with the conservative clerics and their representatives on ways to handle the ban, Abtahi later revealed that the clerics refused to offer their support and instead threatened to declare the government religiously illegitimate. Indeed, the ban controversy far extended the confines of women's rights (however these were understood by different parties) and acquired the characteristics of a proxy fight in the context of the larger political rivalry between the reformers, on the one hand, and the judiciary, the police, and the religious arbiters on the other. The reformist administration found itself in an extraordinarily tenuous position. Instead of officially removing the ban, Khatami settled for the symbolic gesture of taking Shojaee and Ebtekar to the game. Similarly, Mohsen Mehralizadeh, then the head of the Physical Education Organization and a reformist presidential candidate, exploited the advantages of his position and took a group of twenty female employees to the VIP section, making them hold his campaign banners and placards. Under such conditions of threat, then, the reformists' indecisive gestures actually were understood as significant.

Meanwhile, outside the stadium another game was under way. The White Scarf Girls, together with a group of fifty women who had responded to their call, gathered, blocking the path of the cars bringing the Bahraini players to the stadium, holding up placards (see figure 7) that read, "Women's Right: Half of the Freedom."

The police tried to intervene and make them scatter, but they rushed toward the gate, trying to force themselves in.

Their strategy was effective in that they managed to attract the attention of foreign reporters, who were quick to report both on the ban and on the women's clash with the police. With these foreign reports, the ban, previously formulated as a domestic problem, shifted to an issue on an international scale. After the first half of the game was over, President Khatami and his staff received reports about the chaos outside the stadium gates, at which point the president demanded that the White Scarf Girls be let in.

Khatami's era, however, ended a month later with no official permission for women to enter the stadiums. Women had won the battle but not the war. They managed to get in and watch the match, but they did not manage to effect a change in policy. These unsuccessful attempts left traces of disillusionment among women's rights and other political activists. The reformists were losing their hold on the state apparatuses, but the conservative camp coming into power with the election as president of Ahmadinejad, one of the main leaders of the nonclerical conservative Alliance of Builders of Islamic Iran, would soon find itself beset by growing internal divisions.[9]

BICYCLE-KICK GOAL: USING SOCCER AGAINST THE CLERGY

Raising eyebrows all around, on April 26, 2006, a year into his presidency, Ahmadinejad kicked the ball in the opposite direction from the direction he was facing and scored a bicycle-kick goal against the conservative segment of the clerics. He reversed the ban that was in place and in a directive sent to the Physical Education Organization, demanded that a special section be reserved for women, so as to create a "healthier atmosphere" in stadiums. It was a step unprecedented in the thirty-year history of the Islamic Republic. Ahmadinejad's directive seemed not only out of character, but also out of step with political reality in the Islamic Republic. His political opponents among reformists and feminists and his supporters among the conservative clerics alike were surprised and suspicious of his intentions.

In his letter to the head of the Physical Education Organization, Ahmadinejad wrote:

> As you are aware, the final soccer matches are extremely popular. Especially during sensitive national matches and major league matches, millions watch the games and tens of thousands, including families, who are interested in and enthusiastic about the game come together to watch the games inside the stadium. Contrary to the common perception and some groups' propaganda, experience has shown that a large presence of women in public spaces guarantees the prevalence of safety, ethics,

and chastity within these spaces. Women have been present on the frontline of all the major events in recent decades. Today they are the epitome of a presence that not only is lively and constructive but also preserves the values and sacredness of women and their particular responsibilities. Thus, it is necessary that for both national and important matches, the organization, taking into account our esteemed women's dignity, assigns one of the most desirable sections inside the stadium to women and families. I am certain that our cherished women, who are the guardians of women's chastity and dignity and who have, in all stages, supported the Islamic revolution, today, too, will be the vanguards of creating a healthy and safe social environment inside the stadiums. (*Keyhan*, April 28, 2006)

This directive created much controversy. It misses the point to scrutinize it, as some quickly did, for evidence of budding but slyly downplayed antiwoman tendencies within Ahmadinejad's government and among its conservative backers (Shahrokni 2010). Rather than signaling the new government's approach to women's issues, it indicated Ahmadinejad's attempt to declare his independence from the conservative clergy and the traditional conservatives. This "declaration of independence" was made possible by Ahmadinejad's exploitation of the failure of the reformists to fulfill their promises in delivering goods and rights to the youth, and, to some extent, to women, in order to build a constituency that was not confined to his core conservative base. At the same time, the directive revealed a new face of his administration to the world. International pressure on Iran had been escalating both because of Ahmadinejad's controversial statements about Israel and because of intensifying disputes about Iran's nuclear program. Lifting the ban on women's access to soccer stadiums would have ameliorated the domestic fallout from Iran's increasingly tense foreign relations under his leadership.

Not surprisingly, the announcement of the directive on Iranian state television created something of an uproar among conservative clerics in the holy city and seat of the clerical establishment of Qom, who saw the step as encroaching upon their power (Slackman 2006). The conservative clerics made their distress known in private meetings and through their public platforms in mosques and elected office as intimated to me by a conservative parliamentarian. Mobilizing their religious authority, they dismissed the directive as "un-Islamic." Mohammad Taqi Rahbar, the Friday prayer imam of Isfahan and also Isfahan's representative in Parliament, declared that according to shari'a, "just as it is forbidden for men to look at women's naked body, it is forbidden for Muslim women to look at men's naked legs" (*Sharq*, April 27, 2006). Similarly, Ayatollah Fazel Lankarani, one of the sources of emulation, emphasized that "a woman's looking at a man's body, even if not out of lust or for pleasure, is not permitted."[10] But he went further to express his concerns about the "mingling of men and women inside the sports stadiums," which according to him would be "inevitable" in public sports spaces (*Jomhoori Islami*, April 27, 2006).

Conservative newspapers listed the names of the sources of emulation who had objected to the directive, demanding that the president respect their fatwas and withdraw his statement. Ayatollah Ostadi, the Friday prayer imam of Qom, criticized the state television for announcing the news about the president's decision to remove the ban but not covering the objections raised by the sources of emulation and other clerics in Qom (*Abrar*, May 6, 2006).

Boushehr MP Shokrollah Attarzadeh suggested that "Mr. Ahmadinejad should be humble enough to accept his wrongdoing, obey the *hawza* (seminary center for the training of Shi'a clerics) and the clergy, and revoke his statement" (*Sharq*, May 2, 2006). Similarly, Ali Abbaspour, the head of the Education and Research Commission in Parliament, warned Ahmadinejad that "in occasions of discrepancy between the *hawza* and the clergy on the one hand, and the government on the other hand, it is the clergy's approach that should be taken into account" (*Aftab Yazd*, May 3, 2006).

Ahmadinejad's challenge was seen as an attempt to destabilize the intricately balanced political system and the position of the clergy in it; as such, it set in motion a chain reaction. Remarkably, it temporarily brought together the different factions within the conservative clergy and their political allies, as well as even segments of the reformist clerical camp, against the threat the president's action posed to the notion and practice of clerical guardianship (the authority of the clerics over the Islamic state). In the face of the threat, more reform-minded clerics (even those who had in the past expressed themselves against the ban, like former president Rafsanjani) found themselves siding for tactical reasons with the traditional conservative clerical Combatant Clergy Association (*rowhâniyat-e mobârez*), which favored unchallenged power for the clergy.

President Ahmadinejad, however, seemed determined to stand by his words and despite all the pressures, did not revoke his statements. The high-ranking clerics were riled, to say the least, that they had not been consulted about the decision and that even after they had expressed their disapproval, Ahmadinejad did not pay attention. Fearing their authority would be eclipsed, they condemned the administration for "promoting Islam minus the clergy" (*Sharq*, May 8, 2006). Ayatollah Bayat Zanjani, one of the high-ranking clerics in Qom, asked, distraught, in an interview: "Have the lawmakers in this country become self-sufficient in extracting the religious opinion? Since when does the Islamic Republic of Iran make such sensitive decisions without consulting with the clergy?" (*Etemad*, May 7, 2006). They had recognized there was a power struggle under way, and having largely put their differences aside, they were trying to forge new alliances and maintain their share of power.

But there was something conspicuously missing from this controversy. Totally absent from these disputes was the status of women and the fate of their right to sports spectatorship. The clerics and the students of *hawza* were more concerned about Ahmadinejad's confrontational approach and feared that if they showed no reaction, then "this kind of behavior would persist and become institutionalized." Students of *hawza* organized several gatherings in opposition to the government, which had come to power through their backing, and threatened to withdraw their support (*Jomhoori Islami*, April 27, 2006). The influential Society of Seminary Teachers of Qom dedicated one of its regional meetings to discussing the problematic character of women's entrance into sports stadiums.[11] Yet in none of the reports or statements that were published in the aftermath of their convention did the clerics engage with the question of women's entrance into the stadium. Rather, their final statement harshly criticized the government and expressed their regrets and concerns about the president's recent moves. The three representatives of Qom in Parliament also wrote a letter to the president requesting the annulment of the statement:

> We say this with good intentions that these kinds of decisions will leave the selfless friends of the revolution with a sour taste and a broken heart. As representatives of Qom, the city of *jihad* [a Muslim's duty to struggle for a just cause] and *ijtihad* [independent reasoning and decision-making process in Islamic law], we expect you to boldly revoke your statement and respond to the concerns. You should look to the ingenious and authentic friends of Islam and the revolution and not to your advisers who make these decisions on your behalf. This could seriously undermine your praiseworthy efforts in implementing Islamic rule and in serving the poor. (*Sharq*, May 2, 2006)

But Ahmadinejad seemed to be quite willing to antagonize the clerics. Having joined together to oust the reformists from power, the nonclerical conservatives were now trying to consolidate their authority over state power, thereby turning a former relationship of alliance into one of rivalry. Originally supported by the clerical establishment, Ahmadinejad turned around and effectively "bit the hand that fed him," calculating that the clerics would have little other option than to climb down, as they knew their position as lone claimants to the state would be untenable. The controversy came to an end only when Ayatollah Khamenei, the supreme leader, intervened to ask Ahmadinejad to retract his statements.

Although Ahmadinejad complied, his open confrontation with the clerics had a number of implications: First, pitting the clerics and "their impenetrable fatwas" against women allowed Ahmadinejad to transfer the blame for the discrimination to the clerics (*Sedaye Edalat*, May 14, 2006), ultimately contributing to the reproduction of the comfortably accepted assumption about how Islam and the clerics hinder the improvement of women's status. Second, it led to the marginalization of the clerics and the curtailment of their formerly unquestionable authority over the central government. By postponing the annulment of his decision, Ahmadinejad demonstrated to the clerics and the sources of emulation that after victory in the elections, their opinions would not be important, and that unless the supreme leader intervened, their fatwas would have no effect on the government's decisions. Third, it attempted to resolve the tension between religious guardianship and the authority of the parliament that had caused considerable ambiguity with regard to the affairs of the state since the Revolution, by suggesting a hierarchy of decision-making processes whereby laws passed by Parliament were superior to fatwas and proposals by officials or MPs, thus challenging the unofficial gravitas clerics had in policy making.

This open confrontation underscored the tension between the clerical establishment and the state. In a public statement, Mehdi Koochakzadeh, a conservative MP close to Ahmadinejad, drew a line between fatwas and laws and emphasized:

> Only the Parliament can through the passage of laws prohibit women from entering the stadiums. We cannot do this with the fatwas of the sources of emulation. Their fatwas are to be respected and observed by *their* followers [and not all citizens; emphasis added]. Thus, if sources of emulation, the MPs, and the officials believe that because of our customs it is not appropriate for women to enter the stadium and that they should be banned from doing so, they would have to ask the Parliament to pass a law, and then whoever breaches the law could be punished. (*Aftab Yazd*, April 27, 2006)

Ali Akbar Javanfekr, the president's press adviser, highlighted another aspect of this tension: "The concerns raised and expressed by the clerics [*ulama*] and the sources of emulation are seriously considered by the government, but there are legal hierarchies and procedures that should also be taken into account" (*Jomhoori Islami*, May 7, 2006). Here Javanfekr is pointing out the diverging priorities of the sources of emulation and the government.

The conservative newspaper *Abrar* reported that in a private gathering Ahmadinejad had "told some of the people in his circle that 'these gentlemen [the clerics] should take a walk in the street to realize what's going on'" (*Abrar*, May 24, 2006). Such statements underscored the irrelevance of religious rulings to people's everyday lives and demands. Ahmadinejad and his cabinet members further diminished the clerics' authority by highlighting the remoteness of their opinions and statements from the day-to-day concerns of a government that was trying to "navigate international pressure, counter Western negative propaganda and conspiracy to initiate a war against Iran." For example, Mohammad Naser Biriya, the president's adviser on clerical affairs, stated at a conference held at one of the provincial branches of the Islamic Propaganda Organization:

> We [the administration] arrived at this decision [to remove the ban on women's sports spectatorship] to counter the enemy's plot of war. It was a positive decision. We had been informed that some groups had recorded images of women cross-dressed as men, who had attempted to sneak into the stadium. The foreign TV sta-

tions had planned to show these images during the World Cup matches. On the other hand, we had heard that the United States is planning to use lack of freedom as an excuse to wage a war against our country. In order to counter these plans we came up with the decision to remove the ban on women's sports spectatorship. (*Mardomsalari*, July 8, 2006)

Ahmadinejad's directive that women should have a section within sports stadiums was not his only attempt to decouple the government from the clergy and position himself as a popular champion against his former allies. Several times during his terms in office (2005–13) he surprised his supporters and opponents alike with a political bicycle kick, scoring a goal against the clerics by reversing a position to champion the "democratic rights" of Parliament and women's rights. For example, on August 16, 2009, Ahmadinejad announced that he would nominate at least three women to be ministers in the new cabinet. Not only was it a step unprecedented in the thirty-year history of the Islamic Republic, but it was also a considerable challenge to the widespread belief among the conservative clergy that placing women in high office is contrary to God's will (Shahrokni 2009).

At the end of the day, the issue of women's access to the soccer stadium proved to have become a fixture in Iranian political debates, a veritable apple of discord. The case of Ahmadinejad's openings and clash with the conservative religious circles demonstrates that even a conservative president had to gain popularity by making symbolic and concrete gestures toward opening up spaces for women or attempting to address women's demands.

SCALING UP AND PLAYING DEFENSE

As already seen in my discussion of women's parks, national politics and rifts are not self-contained; they spill over and shape local spaces and dyanmics but can also go upward and shape international dynamics. They affect international interactions and become factors in the shaping of foreign policy and diplomacy just as international governance affects the domestic arena.

Ahmadinejad's claim that his overturning the ban to women's access to stadiums was a way of protecting the country from war was not wholly cynical. On October 25, 2005—two months into his presidency and six months prior to his directive about women's sports spectatorship—while speaking to an audience of about four thousand students at "The World without Zionism" event, Ahmadinejad had described Israel as a "disgraceful blot" that should be "wiped off the map" (MacAskill and McGreal 2005). There are controversies about what he actually said in Farsi and its connotations.[12] Nonetheless, his speech had ramifications. Iran had once again won the entry ticket to the World Cup, which was to be held from June to July 2006 in Germany, and Ahmadinejad had expressed interest in attending the soccer extravaganza. In response, some German authorities lobbied against him and demanded that he not be given a permit to enter Germany. That the Iranian vice president, Mohammad Aliabadi, had already been granted a visa was referred to as "scandalous" by some German TV presenters (*Deutsche Welle* 2006). Ahmadinejad's reaction to the international uproar was similar to his reaction to the clerics and domestic uproar. He stood by his previous statements questioning the Holocaust, watched the World Cup matches from his TV in Tehran, and said that he "was not at all surprised" because he was aware that "there is a very active worldwide network of Zionists, also in Europe" (*Guardian*, May 28, 2006).

As events unfolded, it became obvious that a new round of animosity between Iran and the West had begun. Whereas Khatami and his predecessor, Rafsanjani, had attempted to reintegrate Iran into the international community and greet the world with a friendly face, Ahmadinejad's comments about Israel and the Holocaust, which coincided with the US Senate's adopting a regime-change policy toward Iran, turned the clock back to the earlier years of the Islamic Republic. Ahmadinejad was labeled "the Hitler of the 21st century" by Germans, who orchestrated a demonstration against him ahead of the World Cup match between Iran and Mexico. Carrying and waving Israeli flags, the protesters chanted pro-Israel slogans and held signs that read "Give Ahmadinejad a red card" (*Spiegel Online International* 2006).

At the same time that Western activists were attempting to exert pressure on Iran over the ban on women, *Offside*, a film by Jafar Panahi, an internationally acclaimed Iranian filmmaker, premiered at the 2006 Berlin Film Festival, prior to the World Cup championship game, and was awarded the Silver Bear Jury Grand Prix. *Offside*, inspired by an incident in which Panahi's daughter was refused entry to the soccer stadium, depicts the story of a group of young Iranian women who disguise themselves as men and sneak into Freedom Stadium to watch the World Cup qualifying match between Iran and Bahrain. The term *offside* refers to the position of a player of the team that has possession of the ball if he is closer to the goal line than both the ball and the second-to-last defender, if he is in the opposition half of the field. If a player finds himself in an offside position, he is in banned territory. As the offside position is relative to the configuration of other players. the area that is off-limits to a player is constantly moving. Panahi had used the soccer match as a metaphor to show the discrimination against women on a larger scale. In one scene, he shows the female fans, who are denied entry and are kept behind the gates, relying on a male guard's report of the game. "A fine feminist metaphor there," wrote Philip French (2006) for the *Guardian*. The film highlights how Iranian women, by pushing for their demands and for the removal of the ban, are way ahead of their opponents but also that the playing field is constantly in a state of flux. Although the film was banned from being shown in Iran, its success in the West contributed to Iran being shamed on the international stage once again over the issue of women's access to sports stadiums.

These developments may have afforded wider publicity to the White Scarf Girls' cause, but they did not get them access to Freedom. Nevertheless, taking advantage of the turbulent international relations and placing their hopes in the international arena for FIFA and AFC, the women attempted to internationalize an until that moment low-intensity domestic issue. By laying off the pass to FIFA, the AFC, and the International Olympic Committee, the White Scarf Girls attempted to set them up as their teammates and form transnational support networks. As their first step, they wrote a letter to the three organizations appealing to them to use their influence to put an end to gender discrimination. The letter was deemed by conservative circles as an unacceptable attempt to undermine Iran's sovereignty—a sensitive issue the conservatives used to rally support among their constituencies—and was framed by the conservative press as an invitation for "foreign intervention into [Iran's] domestic affairs" that would undermine Iran's sovereignty (*Jomhoori Islami*, August 21, 2006). In the letter, the White Scarf Girls requested that the international sport organizations step in to terminate "gender discrimination" and to "protect Iranian women's rights":

> During the past two years we have tried to convince the Iranian sports authorities that they should respect *our* [women's] *rights as citizens* and not to ban us from attending soccer matches inside the stadiums. In return, however, not only have the authorities not provided us with the opportunity to watch the matches, but they have also confiscated our cameras and personal belongings and have even arrested some of our members. Their excuse for such an obvious form of gender discrimination is that women's safety and security cannot be guaranteed inside the stadiums. While this statement seems to apply to all women, it is important to note that non-Iranian women are allowed to freely enter and wander around Freedom Stadium. We believe that gender discrimination is, under no circumstances, justifiable and that if, as sports authorities claim, the problem is women's lack of security inside the stadium, then we expect that the Iranian soccer authorities make necessary provisions in this regard. Considering all this, we demand that you investigate the issue and use your authority to end gender discrimination against female football fans [in Iran]. (Emphasis added.)

As a result of this letter, international sporting organizations joined the game. In the name of protecting Iranian women's rights, these organizations put pressure on Iran to remove the ban and threatened to refuse Iran the privilege of hosting international competitions. A reformist newspaper reported, "After thirty years the Islamic Republic of Iran ha[d] reached a point where it [had become] inevitable not to respond to the key questions that were raised in social, cultural and political arenas." The report went on to suggest that "as a modern religious state, it [was] necessary that Iran meet the expectations set forth by both its various constituencies and by the Muslim world," highlighting once again Iran's ambition to take a leading role in the "Muslim world" (*Etemad-e Melli*, August 21, 2007).

Following the issuance of this letter, the AFC demanded that Iran comply with AFC regulations, remove the ban, and demonstrate its commitment to the "no discrimination" rule that is shared and respected by all the members of the AFC and FIFA. Mohammad Bin Hammam, then the head of the AFC, expressed that in his opinion the ban on women attending soccer matches was "a sign of [gender] discrimination." He went on to state: "All I can say is that if Iran was to ever host one of the AFC tournaments, they will have to give permission to women to attend the matches" (*Etemad-e Melli*, August 24, 2008).

Seyyed Reza Akrami of the conservative Combatant Clergy Association stated in an interview that the government should not submit to foreign pressure "even if it results in the dismissal of Iran from international competitions." Speaking to a reporter, Akrami added: "When, in West, they remove the marriage ban for priests, cardinals, bishops and nuns, we will also remove the ban on women to enter sports stadiums" (*Etemad Daily*, July 9, 2006). However, Ali Kaffashian, then the head of the Iranian Soccer Federation, stated that Iran was "fully ready to follow all the requirements and instructions from the AFC." But instead, Iran came to an agreement with the AFC and FIFA. While Iranian women were still kept outside the gates of Freedom, foreign women continued to be allowed to attend international soccer matches that took place in Iran. Iran thus managed to reach a compromise with FIFA whereby Iranian women's issues were treated as domestic issues, just as household matters and family problems were, while Iran continued to provide foreign women with a space inside the stadium. Iranian women who were interested in attending sports matches continued to disguise themselves as men and sneak into the stadium. The struggle outside the stadiums also continued and eventually spilled over into other sports (such as volleyball) and other spaces where soccer matches were broadcast live (such as movie theaters and cafes). From the authorities' perspective, the women remained "offside," and if caught by the guards would be given a red card and expelled.

During Ahmadinejad's second term (2009–12), the contestation between the state and these international sports organizations escalated to the point where attempts to enter the stadium were framed as a "threat to national security." In fact, the state had come to respond to this outside pressure as an infringement on its jurisdiction, thereby transforming the once-divisive domestic issue into a matter of national sovereignty and security that the different segments of the state and the political élite could rally around, further asserting and consolidating their authority. Notable here is that the Ahmadinejad administration, which had been willing to use the stadium issue as a means to challenge clerical authority, now was perfectly willing to use it to ally (again) with the clergy and consolidate national authority.

In 2011, and as the tensions continued to rise, FIFA and the AFC, the very organizations that had stepped in to protect Iranian women's autonomy against the state and demand respect for women's right to attend soccer matches as fans, banned the Iranian national women's team from playing in an Olympic qualifying game because the players were wearing hijab (which is compulsory in Iran). As Dubois (2012) indicates, "the team was literally minutes away from entering the field when they were told they could not play." FIFA justified the ban on the basis of regulations that prohibit the presence of "politics or religion" on uniforms and not on the basis of regulations that disallow any piece of clothing that jeopardizes the players' safety.

The Iranian state, through the statements of Ahmadinejad, retaliated. He referred to FIFA officials as "dictators" and "colonialists" who intended to "impose their lifestyle on others." Just as the officials at FIFA and the AFC had promised the White Scarf Girls to protect their rights and to guard their autonomy against the encroachments of the Iranian state, Ahmadinejad promised women "to deal with those who carried out this ugly job" and to "follow and protect the rights of [his] girls" (Dorsey 2012).

As the Iranian government, eagerly undertaking to avenge the injustice suffered by the Iranian women athletes, and the very international organizations that had mobilized to demand that Iranian women be allowed to enter soccer stadiums, were flexing their muscles by arguing over what constitutes women's rights and making claims about their ability to protect "their girls" from the abuses and violation of their rights by the "other," Iranian women found themselves yet again left out of the stadium, this time not only as spectators but also as soccer players, reduced to the position of the subaltern prevented from not only speaking, but also playing. The doors of Freedom were shut in their faces both at home and abroad. Iran fought for women's access to international competitions and eventually managed to resolve the "hijab problem" with FIFA, but inside its borders women were, and still are, effectively prohibited from attending men's soccer matches.

The political game played on the soccer field was thoroughly gendered. In contrast to other public spaces, where women have slowly returned after the consolidation of the Islamic Republic (such as in the cases I discussed previously in this book), the seats of the soccer stadium have remained consistently elusive to them. However, the nature of the justification for their exclusion has not proven to be equally consistent, as it has ranged from the evocation of Islamic morality, to concerns over women's well-being, to concerns about public safety. Similarly, the arguments for women's inclusion have for a variety of reasons been diverse and not logically consistent. They have involved references to the rights of women as mothers and daughters, to women as appendages to men, and to the family unit, as well as evocations of the national good and of state security or of women's human rights. Various state actors and the conservative clerics, along with the international sporting organizations, have fought to secure their share of political power and authority, or to undermine that of others, by claiming and asserting control over Iranian women's bodies and the rules that regulate their movements in public spaces such as sporting arenas. The complex political game devised by men, largely played by men alone, and whose rules are arbitrated by men, have been played on the bodies of women used by state actors, incumbents, and contenders alike to assert, reinforce, and challenge their authority. It could be argued that women's access to the stadium had become a field of competition on which whoever managed to have the last word would yield power over their political opponents. Having said that, women have not been mere outsiders, shut out of the inner workings of the state; on occasion they have engaged in alliances with state actors or themselves have been part of these state actors. Ultimately, however, their engagement and activism have been circumscribed by the gendered character of the political universe they have to operate in.

Re-placing Women, Remaking the State

Gender, Islam, and the Politics of Place Making

In his meeting with members of Tehran City Council on January 13, 2014, Ali Khamenei, Iran's supreme leader, praised Tehran Municipality for its expansion of green spaces, construction of new highways and bridges (facilitating transportation), and production of exercise and sports spaces. The leader stated that "despite hostile pressures from the World's superpowers, and all the other kinds of pressures [we have been enduring], we can resolve the problems our country is facing and move forward." Pointing out the existence of conflicting political views within the city council and alluding to rifts in the local authority-state relationship, he insisted that if all individuals and institutions worked to serve the people, such differences would be inconsequential. He stated that in order to do this, the city council should not just supervise the municipality but also support it, and affairs and projects should be pursued based on mutual understanding and fraternity, and with serving the people as a guiding principle. Referring to the central government and the Tehran Municipality, he emphasized the importance of mutual cooperation between the two. Supreme leader Khamenei suggested that the municipality, then led by conservative politician and formerly Iran's chief of police, Mohammad Baqer Qalibaf, should cooperate with the government, led by the reformist president Rouhani.

The leader's statements marked a process that had been ongoing for a while: the move from a revolutionary, heavily ideological approach to politics toward a much more service-oriented understanding of the functioning of state institutions, and the need for coordination and collaboration among state agencies and different levels of governance, from the central administration to the local, municipality, level.

In that same meeting the supreme leader, acknowledging the difficulties of imagining and constructing a modern Islamic urban center, stated that Tehran was nowhere close to representing an Islamic city. This statement was revealing, not only of the complexities that urban development presented under international sanctions and isolation, but also of the challenges of integrating into the notion of urban development the ideological imperative of building an Islamic city and its practical repercussions. The recognition of the complications of a project whose seeds were planted in the 1979 revolution that toppled the monarchy in Iran prompted the leader to urge the city council and urban planners to pay closer attention to the public appearance and architecture of Tehran. Tehran's features, he claimed, "do not represent those of an Islamic city." Moving away from the architectural façade of the city toward the elements that facilitate living and moving in it, he concluded his remarks by highlighting the importance of designing and constructing the urban environment in a way that would be conducive to and enable an Islamic lifestyle.[1]

Khamenei's speech highlights the following features of life in Iran. First is the transformation of the state, over the past forty years, into a functionally, financially, and politically differentiated cluster of institutions and apparatuses, from central government to specialized agencies and institutions of urban governance. The latter in particular, due to their proximity to the loci of everyday life of the citizens, have been transformed into a progressively significant political arena. Increasingly, the day-to-day affairs of the city have become a matter of national politics, which in turn are also played out at the local level and in everyday city spaces. Over the years urban governance has been a source of tension, but it has become increasingly so since the 1990s and, as indicated in the leader's comments, reached a peak when urban development projects were delayed or never materialized as a result of political rifts. As we saw in the case of the BCT in chapter 2, the initiative of putting women drivers behind the wheels of its buses was opposed and canceled because critics of the president undermined it, and as we saw in chapter 3, the opening of women-only parks was delayed due to conflicts between Tehran Municipality and the government, which were staffed by members of opposing factions. Similarly, as we saw in chapter 4, the stadium doors remained closed despite years of pressure from women's movements activists and negotiations between various state bodies and FIFA, as each party advanced different interests and objectives.

The leader's comment also indicates a concomitant change over the same period in implicating Islam by the state. This change entailed a move from Islam as a guiding principle and source of legitimacy of the Iranian state, "political Islam," toward what Mohammad Ayatollahi Tabaar (2018) refers to as "the politics of Islam": a complex articulation of Islam with different interests within the state and society that opened up processes of its negotiation and redefinition, coupled with an increase in service provision and quality of life mentalities.

These exchanges between the leader, the mayor, and the members of Tehran City Council reflect several themes that this book has sought to unpack. In what follows I discuss these themes from the perspective of their intersection with the "woman question," the quest for a place for women in the Iranian society, and the pragmatics of urban governance and statehood in the Islamic Republic of Iran. Specifically, I trace the shifting intersection of discourses of gender, statehood, and Islam over the past four decades, demonstrating how they constitute, reproduce, and challenge one another on the terrain of the city.

IN SEARCH OF A BLUEPRINT

In his attempt to express both the objectives and the challenges of creating an Islamic urban space, the leader's choice of Tehran is not accidental and definitely has a history. When the Islamic Republic was established, the capital city gained symbolic significance. At the outset Tehran became a stage on which the Islamic credentials of the state and the society it allegedly represented were supposed to be played out. It was on this stage that women were included as unwitting protagonists in a play whose script was being written during its staging. Women were (and are) regarded as the embodiment of Islamic morality, and indeed, a visible one at that. Situated at the very heart of city making, they were deemed to have great emblematic value in providing, or rather constituting tangible markers of, "the Islamic" in the city, of rendering the urban space a distinctive character of its own, separating it from "non-Islamic" alternatives. Thus, from day one of the establishment of the Islamic state, discussions were in earnest over the appropriate place of women in society and in search of how women should occupy particular social spaces in the city. Needless to say, such debates over the possibilities and limitations that delineate gendered urban space have had a significance far exceeding the confines of urban planning; they spoke to broader contestations over the position of women in the Iranian society and over their place in the process of state building. Or, in other words, state building has been inextricably linked to gendered processes of city and place making.

Islamization has been central to the self-definition and legitimacy—domestic and international alike—of the Islamic Republic. Thus, the production of new spatial arrangements that would mark the qualitative distinctiveness of the revolutionary and postrevolutionary order from that of the ancien régime became a priority; the setting of gender boundaries, and in particular their translation into spatial orders, gained symbolic significance. The state strove to govern not just space, but also (gendered) bodies and the way these were included in it; ultimately, the very project of statehood became bound to them. In fact, it is no exaggeration to point out that the Islamic character of Tehran, leaving the façades of the buildings and the martyrs' memorials aside, has largely been built on mandatory veiling and gender segregation.

Through these policies, the state presented, inserted, and situated itself as the arbiter of gender boundaries and defined the contours of women's bodies and their movement in the city. Mandatory veiling and gender segregation, with their tenuous association to Islamic morality as constructed in a context of male domination, became linked to the texture of everyday life in the city and through this, ultimately, to the branding of the Islamic Republic. The late Pahlavi era used the image of scantily clad women as a means of boosting the state's "modern" or "Western" credentials, and the Islamic state relied again on women, veiled and spatially circumscribed this time, to showcase the new Islamic order; women became once more a walking billboard advertising the identity of the state.

As indicated in the case studies, the state tied itself to space through things and in the process endowed these things with meaning (Appadurai 1986): the metal bar that divides the bus space and separates women from men on their bus rides (chapter 2); the walls that keep women inside the parks, distant from the "prying eyes of men" (chapter 3); the gates that keep women outside the sports stadiums, away from men's rowdy behavior (chapter 4). These objects, along with, in some instances, fences, curtains, signs, and posters, were all installed as a way of signifying the new gender order established by the Islamic state. They were allusions to and potent markers of the power of the state as the arbiter of gender boundaries. Within these new spaces of state power, urban life, bodily motions, movements, and rhythms had to be Islamized as well. But even when not enclosed by park walls, or when not in the women's section on the bus, women live (and therefore constitute) the gender order of the Islamic state through other objects such as the veil. Veiling carries in itself unwritten expectations, prescriptions, and rules of behavior as well as potentialities expressed in the intricacies and modalities of the practice. Wearing different types of body and head covers restricts and enables different types of movement, different rhythms, and different ways of being in (a) place as a woman; it is this very difference of "being placed in the city" as a woman that the state sought to bring about. The state thus assumed the role of a conductor positioning men and women in different parts of the public space, directing their movements in space, synchronizing and regulating the performances of the human bodies it lays claim on. As we saw in chapter 3, the state lent its authority to rendering certain bodily movements unacceptable and ultimately prohibited; for example, stretching in public parks was no longer tolerated in the years that followed the revolution, making parks inhospitable places for women. But these rules and regulations were not conforming to some sort of preconceived (Islamic) notion of what is acceptable and what is not; rather, they were based on improvisation. In 2009, in a short phone conversation with me, Valiollah Chahpoor, the director of the Bus Company of Tehran in the early years of the postrevolutionary phase, said: "It's not like there was a manual about Islamization of the bus space. We did what we thought was right, what we were told was right. Did we make mistakes along the way? Yes, we did. It was all an experiment. We were creating the manual as we went."

The "Islamic" and the process of Islamization itself are hardly predetermined, coherent projects. Lacking an authoritative blueprint or model for emulation, the Islamic city has been a vision to be discovered, to take shape through a complex process of searching for its features, its aesthetics, and its functionalities. It had to be located in religious and historical sources, in lived experiences and practices that constitute repositories of traditions, religious and nonreligious, in life in a modern, globalized world. The Islamic city has been, and still is, a project of translation. First, the line between the Islamic/religious and the secular itself had to be drawn, and that was largely a matter of a political decision, a response to contingency as much as a product of design (Agrama 2010). Then, the "non-Islamic" needed to be translated in ways that were compatible with or integral to the Islamic space to be constructed. Building the Islamic city relied on the domestication of the foreign into the familiar, in the appropriation of the scriptural and historical past into practical spatial structures and practices.

This raises the question of who translates all this into "Islamic" elements. The answer is far from simple. The clerical establishment as the bastion of religion, despite its internal differentiation and polyphony, has had a significant role in giving guidance as to what is Islamic. However, as noted in various case studies, there is not one coherent single interpretation of gender and Islam (Mir-Hosseini 1999), and as chapter 4 suggests, interpretation often becomes entangled with power and politics.

It is fairly clear that from the outset, two discursive strategies within the Islamist movement and the emerging state developed. One was symbolically coded in Fatemeh, Prophet Mohammad's daughter, whose domestic role and traditional sense of propriety are combined with a more effective public role. In her famous Fadak Sermon, Fatemeh, forced by circumstances, decided to step out of her domestic environment and speak to the newly elected caliph, who was in the mosque among a crowd, against injustice, albeit from behind a curtain that was erected between her and the crowd. A second one was coded in Zaynab, Fatemeh's daughter, with an emphasis on women's public role as active participants in and builders of the ideal community. Zaynab accompanied her husband and sons to the battlefield, and when they were martyred, she kept their memories alive by giving public sermons encouraging people to revolt against tyranny. Much of policy orientation and reorientation over the following decades was related to the pull and push of these two distinct discursive strategies.

In the case studies I have discussed, this space of power and politics constitutes the arena where other actors who find it incumbent upon themselves to define or to guard the Islamic come to the foreground. Tehran Municipality has had to maneuver this muddy terrain, and as we saw in chapter 3, also the mayor's office, but different divisions within it or under its supervision have had to work within what they perceive as Islamic. The leader's verdict has in many cases been the last word about where the boundary between Islamic and non-Islamic is drawn. As shown in chapter 4, in the confrontations between President Ahmadinejad and the conservative clerics around the appointment of women ministers and the granting of access to Freedom Stadium to women, it was the leader's words that ended the controversy and determined the boundaries of the "proper."

In view of the lack of a definitive blueprint and of the multiplicity of actors involved in its definition, the process of Islamization has been haphazard, as indicated in the preceding discussion. Chapters 2 and 4 are particularly interesting in this respect. They clearly make the case for seeing the "Islamic" as the product of negotiation and struggles, as different actors engage competitively in its definition, drawing and redrawing gender boundaries, such as the bus barrier that still separates the spaces allocated to women and men in Tehran's buses but has been moved back and forth many times, or the issue of access to stadiums, which has been the subject of considerable acrimony and confrontation.

We often fall into the trap of looking at this constellation of disparate interpretations, this cacophony of practices as unified by a logic of the state, a logic that presupposes its reification and reliance on a reasoning that promotes an essentialized notion of Islam. However, the leader's comments about the importance of designing and constructing the urban environment in a way that is conducive to, and enabling of, an Islamic lifestyle constitute an indication of how Islam is implicated differently by the state in different moments.

With reference to gender segregation, the narratives in this book show that it has been transformed from a means of imposing an Islamic lifestyle to a means of enabling a lifestyle that can be deemed Islamic. Through the narratives we see how gender segregation was once used as a moralizing tool, only to be reframed more recently as a quality-of-life-enhancing measure. It is in this light that, I suggest, one should see and make sense of what I refer to as an inclusive regime of gender segregation: the various initiatives to provide women with more comfortable and safe rides on the city buses, create exclusive, women-friendly exercise spaces in the city's parks, or secure women's sections inside the sports stadiums.

By the same token, the various initiatives undertaken by the state and local government have acquired the quality and rationality of services (which retain an Islamic dimension or an association with Islam). So in a way, reading the travails of gender segregation through the narratives unfolding in this book can provide clues to how to read Islam and the Islamic in Iran and beyond: as mediated through the imperatives of governance and statehood. The Islamic character of the state (and its local, urban manifestations), aside from its dependence on processes of experimentation and invention, has had to reconcile diverse imperatives, such as technocratic exigencies, pragmatic considerations regarding the viability of the state, and international influences and conditionalities, and to accommodate and adopt novel forms of governance, most notably the neoliberal model and the role of the market in it.

As the city changes, so does the relationship of religion and space. Islam is redefined through its exposure to, fusion with, and contrast to these different pressures, trends, and developments; in the process it redefines the place of women, giving different meanings to the practice of gender segregation and its localized applications in different spaces and distinct social contexts. Interestingly, as the revolutionary state and the actors associated with it linked their "Islamic credentials" to a set of practices, including gender segregation, they produced a set of ideological and practical contours that shaped the state itself. In other words, the state was in dire need of grounding itself in the ideology it produced and was ultimately both enabled and constrained by it. This apparent paradox, whereby the state is both an ideology producer and a construct of that very ideology, means that the Islamic state and the Islamic city could be perceived as the products (and not just the producers) of gender segregation.

The Islamic city that the state has put at the epicenter of its urban development policies remains central, yet the role of gender and religion and the interaction of the two vary and change, finding their expression in different regimes of gender segregation, characterized by a different balancing of exclusion and inclusion.

Here it is important to remember a number of important points. First, whatever regime of gender segregation becomes dominant, women remain at the heart of city making and state building. Regulating their place, administering their bodies, or serving their needs makes them a key element in the Islamic character of the urban space and of the state. As the place of women is changing in this process, as women are redefined by the Islamic institutions, these and the Islam they are embodying become the object of negotiation and change: Islam redefines the place of women, and women redefine Islam, as I discuss in more detail in what follows.

The cases examined in this book question visualizing the state and its policies as the product of a coherent and unified organization. The internal differentiations within the state bureaucracy and the disagreements, or even conflicts, between different state apparatuses and agencies often contradict this image. The state is in fact made up of a multitude of components, and it is the product of the continuous dialogue, interaction, and confrontation with what makes it up. Furthermore, it is the product of similar interactions with interlocutors within and outside Iran, different social and political actors in the domestic field, and other governments, but equally important, of institutions of international governance in the global arena. It is this continual dialogue and exchange that gives the state its flexibility, and at the same time fragility. Rather than a static entity, it should be seen as an assemblage of components, practices, and interactions, in a permanent state of flux.

It is thus important that we develop a methodology of "disaggregating the state" (Morgan and Orloff 2017), delve beneath the semblance of wholeness and unity of the state, and adjust our analytical toolkit to look past it, to explore its fragments: the various actors within and around the state and the actual everyday practices they engage in.

This is what I do in the next section.

ACCOMMODATING GENDER BOUNDARY CRISES

Throughout this book I have traced these very transactions that make the state, in this case the Islamic state, and what it has been at given moments of its evolution. I have done this through the dual lens of the relationship between the state (in its multifacetedness) and its female citizens, and the way the former orders and administers urban space. In my analysis of this state-women-space nexus, I have sketched key aspects of the shifting character of the state as it gradually evolved from a revolutionary ideological construct to a postrevolutionary, problem-solving machine. I have demonstrated how a state that emerged out of a revolution that claimed to be inspired by Islam sought its legitimacy in convincing its citizens and the international community of its ideological purity and commitment. As the state consolidated itself, it was faced with practical issues relating to improving living conditions and responding to the needs of its population. Thus it had to engage in a process of transformation from an institutional constellation predominantly preoccupied with ideological concerns to one confronted with concrete political and practical concerns and the need to address these through both administering its citizens and providing services for them, or engaging in processes of practical problem solving. This not necessarily linear and uninterrupted transformation of the state was, I argue, marked by a shift from prohibition to provision.

This section centers on the state's flexibility by examining how the state, in reaction to shifts in gender order, has evolved over time. It provides an account of the institutional workings of the state that made the trajectory from one regime of gender segregation to the other possible. The development of an inclusive gender segregation regime, as discussed in chapter 1, was set against the background of a set of significant factors: on the one hand the exigencies of shifts in the political economy (discussed in some detail in chapter 2) and the external influences stemming from the circulation of both globalized norms and commodities (discussed in chapter 3), and on the other hand international pressures and internal political struggles that became more pronounced as the state diversified in functional terms (as highlighted in chapter 4). These developments led to the reconfiguration of the state policy process context and had significant impacts on policy regimes in Iran, which eventually had to address a wider range of demands and deal with a broader spectrum of problems or "social pathologies." It was against this background that the Iranian state expanded its deployment of provisionary policies.

Regarding its relationship to its female citizens, the state continued pursuing gender segregation, but the content and meaning of the latter changed considerably. State apparatuses maintained, expanded, and developed policies that relied less on "prohibiting" women from being present in mixed spaces and more on "providing" them with women-only spaces. I have pointed out that this progressive moving away from the prohibitive dimension of the state was partially due to the contestation and testing of the gender boundaries by women in their daily interactions and movements in the city. Protest against the oppressive character of the state's segregation practices, as well as, more commonly, the expression of a need for better provision, led the state to produce better and more desirable gender-segregated spaces. Instead of pursuing politically and ideologically costly, prohibitive segregation policies, the state opted for a more inclusive process, relying on channeling women's desires and aspirations within the gender-segregated order.

As already discussed, even in the case of the soccer stadium, where prohibition persisted, women's exclusion was eventually framed more in terms of "prohibiting in order to serve," as the state's inability to provide security for women inside the stadium. In addition, more of the state actors joined the call for provision of a gender-segregated space within the stadiums, and in recent years there has been some improvement; in an intricate balancing act, during the 2018 World Cup women were let inside the Freedom Stadium, not to watch players in action, but to watch the match live on big screens.

This approach entailed dealing with demands for inclusion and provision, not through recourse to desegregation but through the development of new segregated spaces characterized by a philosophy of provision, such as women's universities, bus services as well as bus sections, and women's parks and exercise areas. This process was not driven by a clear methodology; it was not smooth, it encountered setbacks, and as already suggested, it relied on trial and error.

In the course of the discussion of the case studies examined previously, I have demonstrated that three major factors contributed to and necessitated this shift. First, after the stage of revolutionary exceptionalism passed and postrevolutionary fatigue prevailed, the Islamic Republic had to respond to both domestic and global exigencies that entailed the "normalization" or "routinization" of the state's operation in the domestic arena and the projection of an image of a "modern" state at the international level. Whereas in the early days after the revolution the newly formed state was concerned with establishing its control over Iran's territory and developing an Islamic order, once this concern dissipated, especially after the end of the eight-year war with Iraq, the state found itself caught up in a web of unexpected consequences resulting from its earlier policies. For example, in my case studies it became clear that mandatory veiling law led to a series of complications that were summarized by the "experts" as health problems, such as depression, joint diseases, and obesity. These "sick bodies" needed to be taken care of. Added to that, the state's urban development project had satisfied certain needs, such as housing provision for an expanding city population, but had led to shrinking living space, environmental degradation, proliferation of cars, and heavy traffic. Urban mobility was constricted. Citizens needed and demanded an enhanced public transportation system. These "constricted" and "frail," yet demanding and revolting, bodies, the products of earlier decisions and policies, could not be ignored, and their needs were to be addressed (and admittedly defined) by the state in its postrevolutionary phase. On the other hand, the inability of the state to deploy such strategies and to frame problems as needs, as in the case of closed stadium gates, undermined its effectiveness in resolving a gender boundary crisis in the country's soccer stadiums.

Second, the sisters of the revolution who had fought for the new Islamic order experienced segregation as disappointment, and in some cases as exclusion by their putative brothers, while the younger generation of the daughters of the revolution—or more accurately a growing number of them, especially in Tehran—facing the lack of provision in meeting their professional, educational, and recreational aspirations, saw it as an ultimately alienating imposition that restricted their life chances and ambitions. Moreover, women's rising levels of education, economic independence, and public presence led to their developing a sense of entitlement to city spaces and voting with their feet. For all women, practical issues related to unhindered mobility and access to places of work, education, consumption, and leisure, as well as health and well-being concerns, also gave rise to demands. Various scholars have pointed out that the populist streak was strong in the revolution from the start; therefore the Islamic Republic has had to constantly find ways of satisfying the populations' aspirations and demands (Abrahamian 1982, 1993). As such, women's demands for broader access to public spaces could no longer be dismissed or overlooked. As time passed, the state found it futile to impose a gender-segregated spatial order through prohibition in the face of external and bottom-up pressures and shifted to coupling the practice with the idiom of provision.

Third, despite its emphasis on combating imperialism in its political, economic, and cultural variants, the Iranian state did not exist in a vacuum. It had become difficult for the state to keep global influence at bay and insulate women from global discourses and trends, while the need for Iran to integrate into the global and regional systems made it sensitive to external pressure and scrutiny. For example, as discussed in chapter 3, the global rise of the discourse on healthy bodies and women's right to health crept in, producing women's desire for fit bodies. Global discourses of women's rights and gender equality have also been generative of actions at the local level, as documented in chapter 4 in the discussion of White

Scarf Girls. Furthermore, the changing role of international organizations in shaping the Iranian state's policies cannot be ignored. Chapter 2 discussed the role of the IMF and the World Bank in the privatization of state-owned companies, chapter 3 highlighted the role of WHO in the spread of urban health initiatives in Tehran, and chapter 4 pointed out tensions between FIFA and the AFC with the Iranian Sports Organization, as well as President Ahmadinejad.

These transactions and transformations unsettled the initial gender order imposed by the state and created what I call gender boundary crises. A gender boundary crisis occurs when too many things grow and form outside the state's control zone, when bodies and behaviors fall outside the state-sanctioned gender boundaries, in effect undermining the state's regulatory authority. In the cases I have discussed, the state faced multiple contestations of the gender boundaries it sanctioned and that on occasion set off a chain reaction of crises. In several instances the spaces the state defined and demarcated with the aim of containing gendered bodies were not sufficient and did not correspond to the needs of a changing society or to the aspirations of the women they sought to accommodate. The one-third of the bus space became too little, too hot, and too uncomfortable. The state's sanctioned disposition of female bodies and the limits on women's ability to exercise could no longer suppress their growing desire to engage in healthy lifestyles and pursue leisure activities, and the closed-doors policy of the stadiums could no longer remain unquestioned. These tensions, these skirmishes over thresholds, barriers, fences, doors, and walls, created crises underlined by an increasing dissatisfaction among the female population and led to challenges.

As I have argued, the state had to accommodate these "unruly" bodies, this new generation of women that was increasingly mobile, progressively vocal, and ever more demanding. Throughout the case studies we observed the state in action as it negotiated different pressures and navigated changing contexts. The state changed in response to the changing conditions within and outside it. Indeed, the process of adjustment to these new circumstances, the expectations generated by women in particular, presented the state with an unprecedented challenge. In order to navigate such a fragmented field, the state has had to constantly reorient itself to the different interests that it claims to represent and the different needs that it purports to satisfy. Confronted with a gender boundary crisis and serious challenges both externally and internally to its role as boundary maker, the state has opted for adaptation and change by adopting accommodative strategies that I label *outsourcing, scaling down,* and *scaling up.* These types of gender regulation are premised upon different contingencies and the recognition of the entry into the political arena or the ascendance in it of new social forces.

The practice of *outsourcing* consists of transferring the management of the gender boundary to the private sector, engaging it in the act of governing (as described in the process of public transport privatization in chapter 2). This strategy allows the state to feature as an ultimate regulator, setting expectations and limitations, but exposes the private, nonstate sector that is charged with combining service provision with the implementation of gender segregation targets for public scrutiny. Failure thus is more easily perceived not as state failure but as the inability of the private service providers to meet customer expectations. Outsourcing allows the state to retreat from tension or conflict with its citizens and transfer gender boundary crises outside of what is defined as "the state space." The state retains its regulatory role in supervising the workings of the private companies, while simultaneously shifting the blame about any backlashes (for example, about lack of respect for Islamic ethics on the buses and the mingling of men and women) onto the private sector.

Scaling down entails transferring and resolving a gender boundary crisis from the national level to the local level (usually the level of local governance and service provision, as discussed in the case of municipalization in chapter 3). As the state expands its tentacles all the way to the neighborhood level, it also challenges the erstwhile clear-cut boundary between state and society. The presence of frontline state employees—everyday representatives of the state—such as doctors and exercise instructors, experts at the local level, facilitates a sense of proximity and familiarity and "domesticates" aspects of state power in the eyes of the citizen (Ghannam 2002; Ismail 2006). At the same time, in order to expand its regulatory power, the state invests in producing healthy citizens and a habitable environment. By investing in the gender boundary crisis, the state shifts its regulatory competence to "responsible" and "rational" individuals who cooperate with, or even embrace, municipality-sponsored projects.

Scaling up is the process of transferring a gender boundary crisis from the local to the national level, that is, elevating a local problem (such as women's access to a stadium in Tehran) to a problem of national security. Here, the national and the international can intersect, as the case of the involvement of FIFA in the stadium access crisis and the broader debates on women's right to sports participation suggests. Chapter 4 highlighted how the tension between FIFA and the Iranian state was read as an attempt to undermine the sovereignty of the Islamic Republic and as such deepened the connection between demands for gender equality and national security.

The book thus offers a picture of a flexible yet fragile state that has managed to respond and adapt to internal and external pressures, whose access to resources has expanded over time, and which has developed a bureaucratic infrastructure in the postwar reconstruction era, which has acted to bring various state actors together and has stabilized the balance between state and nonstate actors. In addition, the enlistment of technocrats into the state—such as the transportation expert at the bus company or the doctors at the municipality's health department—has made it possible for civil administrators to diagnose societal problems and frame policy alternatives to address them. In diagnosing problems, the so-called experts and technocrats reformulate gender boundary crises as social problems, "pathological conditions" that warrant intervention by various state organizations (Steinmetz 1999, 31). For example, access to exercise space can be a political issue but could be framed and handled as a technical and medical decision. Reformulating the gender boundary crisis as a technical or medical issue helps de-escalate political tensions and shape a problem space to which the state has a solution. The paradox in this, as discussed previously, is that interventions to address such technical and "depoliticized" issues open up spaces for the articulation of further demands, contestation, and ultimately, politicization of domains that had hitherto remained outside the state's purview.

The state has to provide more and respond to demands and expectations; in order to provide, it has to stretch itself too far into everyday life. It is at these extreme edges that its power is being challenged. As the state extends its reach and jurisdiction into the previously unregulated and obscure corners of everyday life, it encounters and has to engage with more groups and their claims. The result is much more negotiation, friction, and, occasionally, conflict. Likewise, when the state fails to provide, frustration spreads to a wider part of the population. In this sense, the state "governs" too much and as such undermines itself.

As shown in the case studies, the state's ability to govern efficiently and to regulate and provide depends on the resources at its disposal and the mechanism of redistribution it uses. If these start falling apart, especially in a failing economy, as Keshavarzian (2015) points out, the state could find itself deprived of the means to generate consent and of the compliant citizenry it craves. In such instances, it becomes more difficult for the state to satisfy needs and demands, as various waves of protests in Iran indicate. When the repertoire of "hegemony through consent" is exhausted, the state might turn to the application of prohibitive measures and resort to the routine use of more repressive tactics in order to secure domination.

Nonetheless, the case studies in this book do not just capture a movement from prohibition to provision (or the oscillation between the two); they also shed light on alternative ways of looking at the state and chronicle a narrative of state maturation. The case studies suggest that in order to adequately understand the role of the state— in Iran and elsewhere—one needs to refocus from the state understood *stricto sensu* to the state writ large; my discussion of strategies, policies, and contestation on the part of women has demonstrated that the Iranian state cannot be made sense of if analysis fails to incorporate actors at its "edges," where it intersects with the mundane and the everyday. Ultimately, the successful reproduction of the state and its hegemony has involved an interchangeably expanding, contracting, and changing shape, including and coopting women and then excluding them, putting them in place and taking them out of place, and in the process also restructuring the positions and power of different state (and nonstate) actors and components.

WOMEN IN AND OUT OF PLACE

Throughout the book I have shown how the state and other political actors unevenly draw on the "Iranian woman" as an ideological construct to support and advance their political agendas.[2] Yet as I have pointed out, the multifacetedness, and even fragmentation, of the state has had considerable implications for how female citizens are addressed; different state actors and apparatuses approach and define women differently, thus leading to multiple, and occasionally contrasting, ways in which "Iranian women" are implicated in city-making processes and state practices. Furthermore, as I have also pointed out, Iranian women, depending on their class, age, and other social markers of difference, experience the city differently and engage with the state in distinctive ways, producing a wide array of claims, needs, and demands.

By adopting the accommodative strategies that I have explained in the previous section, the state responds to these various, sometimes conflicting demands and in doing so produces two distinct sets of effects: First, as the state adopts new accommodative strategies and in a context of changing circumstances, new groups of women enter the frame of governance and start to bargain with the state, make demands, or reinforce their power position. In response, the state is compelled to expand its service provision function and capacity and further stretches itself to contain, control, and regulate both upward and downward. Each response to such demands on the part of the state brings a series of reconfigurations; it produces new identifications and new modes of belonging to the city and enables new sets of claim making that shift the terms of engagement with the state. As I have argued, women initially laid claims as sisters of the revolution, as moral subjects, demanding the dignity they were promised in the Islamic order. Eventually, and with the shift from addressing women as moral subjects to citizens with tangible needs, rights, and demands, women could mobilize around other categories: as mobile citizens and clients of privatized services, as citizens and clients in need of health-related and welfare services, and as spectators of national celebrations such as the sporting matches. As such, they laid claims on different parts of the city and demanded full access to various corners of it. Second, despite this fragmentation, the state continuously lives off of and invests in constituting and addressing women as a unified and cohesive category. The statements delivered by state officials are permeated with elements promoting a unitary vision of the Iranian "woman" who has served the state and needs to be served by it.

The state thus sets in motion a chain of contradictory reactions to claims; on the one hand, it recognizes the multiplicity and diversity hidden in the category "woman" and engages in action that increasingly fragments the discourses addressing women's needs. On the other hand, the state also responds in ways that achieve the opposite effect: it constantly attempts to bring all these fragments and stitch them together in a coherent category, that of the "Iranian woman." What we see here is that the state strives to constantly regulate and contain women's bodies and movements within the boundaries of the "proper," but simultaneously invests in and claims credit for women's expanded access to public spaces. The state appropriates and reframes the product of demands and contestations and presents their achievements as the achievements of itself, the Islamic state. The state, in other words, produces and at the same time is reproduced through these contradictions; it mobilizes its productive and enabling capabilities to respond to demands, in the process addressing women in multiple ways and creating differentiations; yet it tends to bring together the fragments its productive power engenders to construct women as an undifferentiated category.

However, discursive formations and their material effects are contingent and marked by a series of ruptures and recuperations; they shift with changing state mandates, with the effect that new discursive spaces are continually emerging, colliding, and disappearing. Women's lives, as noted in the case studies, are shaped and affected by competing discourses that demarcate the boundaries of the "proper," define women's rights and needs, and delineate the confines of the "possible."

Women occupy an untenable space governed by religious, market, and state imperatives and framed by competing discourses. These imperatives and discourses are disabling and enabling, and women live in this in-between-ness, in spaces where their bodies are simultaneously constricted (because, for instance, their movements are limited within certain spaces) and expanded (because, for example, women-only spaces are subjected to lesser degrees of surveillance). They have little choice but to adjust their movements to these imperatives but can also mobilize the latter to their benefit and attempt to influence the drawing of the contours of their movements. The case studies offer several examples of how women have lived in the "margins" while at the same time mobilizing their very marginality and reterritorializing it, transforming it from a handicap to a resource. There are ample examples in this book: the members of the One Million Signature Campaign using the seemingly apolitical, and rather unsupervised, space of the park for their activism (chapter 3); the sisters of the revolution drawing on the very revolutionary and Islamic discourses that had led to their exclusion from a public library in Qom in order to challenge the prevailing conservative policies and demand the restoration of their dignity, which had been taken away by the very discourses that had promised to restore it in the first place (chapter 1); or the female sports fans who settled for their own invisibility, accepting that they would not be shown on TV or be able to talk to the media, in exchange for access to men's sporting matches (chapter 4). By mobilizing these competing discourses, women have appropriated space, articulated conflicts, and responded to ideologies in locally meaningful ways, albeit remaining in positions of relative marginalization when confronting the state and its predominantly male gaze and mind-set.

If cities contain gender-segregated sites of confinement, these spaces, like every other space, also carry within them seeds of empowerment; they can become sites of potentiality. The story of Neda's mother I recounted in chapter 2 reveals, for example, how the gender-segregated bus space made it possible for her to move from one neighborhood to the other, laying claim to more of the city space. Like the bus space, women appropriate an array of other spaces, from the women-only park, to the movie theater, to the women's section of the library or the university lecture hall, to lay claim to, and deepen, their citizenship.

Women's engagement with the state, be it in the form of contestation or of a less adversarial expression of needs, aspirations, and desires, has the effect of configuring urban spaces in particular ways, reshaping Tehran in both material and symbolic ways, redrawing its geography. But this is only part of what this array of demands and requests does; it also demystifies the way the state presents itself by shedding light on the complex politics unfolding as a response, hidden in discourses about the position of women in the Iranian society. It uncovers the ways in which different users embody, reject, or appropriate women's causes and aspirations.

Through these processes, the city becomes a veritable laboratory, a surface upon which visions of the state, of society, and ultimately of the city itself are crafted. Different groups of women thus imprint their identity on city spaces and assert that public spaces do not belong only to those in positions of power. In fact, women's tactics and their reterritorialization of space and reappropriation of discourses available to them have also created space for new claims and demands to emerge and gain relevance and currency, for new groups and solidarities to be instrumentalized in political struggles. By placing women at the center of city-building and state-making projects, women's issues have been further politicized, creating opportunities for political struggle at the very loci wherein gender boundaries are drawn. Factions within the state have been reaching and do reach out to these new groupings in order to increase their political capital, either to bring about change or to entrench themselves against different segments of the state. Women and "their place" have become issues that have prompted political reconfigurations both within the state, and between the state, its components, and social actors, ultimately reproducing hegemonic alignments.

As my discussion of the ways in which women's issues have been articulated in Iranian politics, and more specifically the politics of space, indicates, women have found themselves in different "positions" in the city and vis-à-vis the state over time. One can describe these different positions through the use of a series of telling metaphors: women *jumped on the wagon* of the state, as did the sisters of the revolution—the women who helped to topple the shah and build the Islamic republic in its early years—and as did loyal supporters of the state among the subsequent generations. At times women were *pulled onto the wagon*, as was the case for those women who became the state's interlocutors, unwitting or even willing policy beneficiaries or participants in state projects. These included those who benefited from the new, segregated bus lines in Tehran and those who used and enjoyed the women-only parks. There have been instances when women *fell off the wagon*, such as the less-affluent female bus passengers being left to wait for slower and more congested transport while the better off ones passed them by in the newer buses and more exclusive BRT lines. Finally, some women even opted to *stay off* (or *get off*) *the wagon* and not to participate in the power games played by the state and its various components.

These distinctions indicate that some women are included and benefit from state policies more than others; not benefiting from policies can equally be a choice or something inflicted upon certain women. The terms inclusion and exclusion do not readily convey the complexity and multiplicity of experiences, gratifications, and predicaments of being in and out of place, what I call *differential exclusion and inclusion*. What is more, it is worth noting that the very same women might find themselves in different positions on this continuum of inclusion and exclusion, of being, or feeling, "in and out of place," in different contexts and moments, and they may experience both prohibition (for instance, they may be banned from entering a stadium) and provision (they might benefit from leisure and recreation services in women only parks) at the very same moment or at different times. Women find themselves or are "in place" when they are in the space the state has designated for them, and they are "out of place" when they reject that designation of space or otherwise negotiate the way they inhabit it. "In place" might seem to be a relationship of deference and acceptance and "out of place" one of resistance. But the interplay of power and resistance is riddled with ambivalence, as women are able to be both in and out of place at once, and in multiple contexts.

A note of caution is in order here. This multiplicity of positions women occupy vis-à-vis the state makes it imperative to decenter the notion of woman as much as it is important to retain it and deploy it in our analyses. Yet it is also important to bear in mind that talking about the state and women as external to each other also needs to be subjected to scrutiny. Indeed, the best way of visualizing and making sense of the relationship between the two is positing them not in terms of a binary and mutually exclusive relationship, but rather in terms of a continuum on which the state and women cannot be fully separated; they co-constitute each other, and at times the boundaries between the two fade away. As we have seen, female officials have been crucial in advancing perspectives and making gains for women. From the female state functionaries in the Piroozi Sports Complex who chose to work for the right to access to sports for women by creating a space with and within the constraints posed by the Islamic Republic, to the reformist officials who provided support to the White Scarf Girls during the soccer stadium crisis, to the osmotic relationship between state and civil society actors, it is clear that women are both inside the state apparatuses and outside of them. Thus it is sometimes quite difficult to discern the already blurred line between policy makers and policy consumers, despite the analytical usefulness of such a distinction.

As this book winds toward its conclusion, it is important to note that there is not one coherent gender politics of the state. The Iranian state, or any state for that matter, does not devise policies that are pro-women or against them, because it simply does not have the unity and coherence to render such an utterance meaningful (Haney 2000; Htun 2010). While in the "eyes" of the state women are supposed to have a specific place in a system of gender difference and to be kept within its confines, the exigencies of domestic and international political, economic, and bureaucrastic circumstances on occasion require the state not to rigidly police gender boundaries. As pointed out, even when the rigid rules continued to apply on paper, their implementation at times became more relaxed, to the point that the policies of the state and its approach to handling women's issues were informed by what I would call flexible sexism. As the state itself is not coherent, but rather a complex balancing act among its different components, various incumbents, diverse interests, and disparate ideologies, it is imperative that our analyses do not merely disaggregate "it" but also consider the multiplicities of its effects, impacts, and interventions. Only then can we talk about the various ways in which different segments within the state address women, recognize or dismiss them, include or exclude them, and ultimately set them in and out of place.

1. THE POLITICS OF GENDER SEGREGATION IN IRAN

1. It is important to note that whereas the appearance and conduct of women was scrutinized and regulated on the grounds of morality—women as ethical subjects—that of men was mostly scrutinized for political reasons. Culturally informed notions of propriety carried within them institutionalized and accentuated patriarchal norms and regulatory aspects.

2. There is much controversy about what makes an Islamic city. See, for example, Hourani and Stern (1970) and Eickelman (1974). For a different take on the Islamic city, see AlSayyad and Massoumi (2010).

3. President G. W. Bush, in his State of the Union address on January 29, 2002, labeled Iran, Iraq, and North Korea the "Axis of Evil," which he claimed was arming itself to threaten the peace of the world.

4. See, for example, Khosravi (2007), Mahdavi (2009), and Moaveni (2007). For a critical account, see Moruzzi (2008).

5. According to a research report published by the Center for Strategic Studies (2014), the research arm of the President's Office, in 2006, 24.3 percent of Tehrani women said that chador would be the covering of their choice (a much lower percentage than in provincial towns); by 2014 that number had decreased to 14.7 percent. Furthermore, while in 2006, 34.7 percent of Tehranis considered that hijab (veiling) was an individual choice and not a matter warranting state intervention, in 2014 close to half of Tehranis (49.2 percent) referred to veiling as something that should be left to individual choice.

6. Bank Melli (2010).

7. There are similar initiatives in provincial cities and towns. For a report on a women-only carwash in Tabriz. see *Tabnak* (2012), and in Qom, see Young Journalists Club (2018).

8. Vice Presidency for Women and Family Affairs (2014).

9. See, for example, Vakil (2011). For journalistic accounts with the same approach, see articles by Mouri (2014) and Faramarzi (2007).

10. There are now more than five women-only parks in Tehran, and dozens of them across the country.

11. For a historical discussion of gender segregation in other Middle Eastern contexts, see Asma Afsaruddin's (1999) edited volume.

12. Leslie Peirce (1993) makes the same point about women's lives under the Ottomans.

13. For a study of the origins of Iran's modern girls' schools, see Rostam-Kolayi (2008).

14. I use the term *public space* to denote a physical space imbued with social relationships and interactions, embodying constraints and resources for action and given meaning by those who utilize it. Not every public space is necessarily a *public sphere*. The public sphere is a domain of social life in which citizens engage in communication and interaction, defining matters of general interest and dealing with them and in the process forming a "public" (Habermas 1989). As such, the public sphere does not depend on the physicality of public spaces, and the communicative action that constitutes it turns social individuals into a "public."

15. Iran's Constitutional Revolution was a protracted process that unfolded between 1905 and 1911. It was largely the product of concern among the kingdom's (mainly male) nobility, religious authorities, and educated elite over increasing foreign influence and the inefficient and corrupt administration of Mozaffar ad-Din Shah of the Qajar dynasty. It led to royal concessions and the establishment of a parliament (Abrahamian 1982, 91).

16. Karimi (2013) demonstrates how the "modern" rules and tenets, along with the influx of new household goods and spread of consumer culture, led to changes in the Iranian home and domestic architecture. For a discussion of urban change and development under the Pahlavis, see Ehlers and Floor (2007).

17. It is worth noting that, according to Bahramitash (2013), the pink-collar clerical jobs the regime approved of were reserved for literate, urban women of higher status, while most women (and girls) in the paid workforce held low-status jobs as carpet weavers or domestic servants.

18. Scholars have documented similar developments in postsocialist cities. See, for example, Rose-Redwood, Alderman, and Azaryahu (2018) and Light (2004).

19. *Eghtesad-e Irani* (2014).

20. For works that address the Pahlavis' deveiling project, see Sedghi (2007); Zahedi (2007); and Najmabadi (2000).

21. For a discussion of gender segregation in Iranian universities, see Rezai Rashti (2015) and Shahrokni and Dokouhaki (2012).

22. For a summary of Ayatollah Khomeini's approach to gender segregation at Iranian universities, see the following post (#43027) on his web portal from May 1, 2013: "I want to know Imam's view on gender segregation."

23. See Paidar (1997, 297). Also, for an analysis of how state ideology and compensatory programs politicized war widows, see Zahedi (2006).

24. To clarify, women have access to sports stadiums and, indeed, there are some stadiums for women. The ban discussed in this book is a ban on women's spectatorship of men's sports.

25. See, for example, Fenster (2007) on gender segregation in an orthodox district in Jerusalem, and Dunckel-Graglia (2013) on women-only taxis in Mexico.

26. Gender-segregated spaces in Iran have remained unexamined, but scholars who write about women in Iran occasionally refer to gender segregation policies and practices of the Islamic Republic of Iran, mostly to highlight the regime's discriminatory approach toward women. See Afary (2009); Kian (1995); and Mir-Hosseini (1999).

27. For a similar discussion about how gender segregation might facilitate women's integration into public spaces and spheres, see Mazumdar and Mazumdar (2001).

28. The literature on gender includes a rich treatment of boundaries defined as "the complex structures—physical, social, ideological and psychological—which establish the differences and commonalities between women and men, among women, and among men, shaping and constraining the behavior and attitudes of each gender group" (Gerson and Peiss 1985, 318). Gender boundaries are objectified forms of gender differences manifested in unequal access to and unequal distribution of resources (material and nonmaterial) and social opportunities. As this book suggests, access to city spaces constitutes such an instance of access to resources and opportunities. I argue that gender segregation is the consolidation of gender difference in physical forms. It is a form of gender boundary making. As such, gender segregation needs to be considered in the broader context of gender boundary making practices in the city that feminist geographers have for a long time paid attention to.

29. The Ayatollah Mar'ashi Najafi library holds more than seventy-five thousand volumes, including over thirteen thousand rare manuscripts, and as such is the first of its kind in Iran and the third in the Islamic World. See "Library of Ayatollah Marashi Najafi" (2013, 1:96–100).

30. The use of the terms *brothers* and *sisters* indicates an Islamic revolutionary discourse.

31. There was no point in pretending otherwise. The way I was read by my interlocuters partially depended on how I presented myself to them. Their reading of me also depended on the kinds of tropes that were dominant and available to them.

2. BOUNDARIES IN MOTION: SISTERS, CITIZENS, AND CONSUMERS GET ON THE BUS

1. Public education in Iran is free. However, in response to an increasing demand for higher education places, private universities have mushroomed all over the country. Private universities are not free, and their tuition fees are constantly on the rise.

2. For a detailed account of the "fluidity" of the Iranian public sphere, see Shahrokni (2010), and for an analysis of the specificities of Iranian public spheres/spaces, see Bayat (1997).

3. Elsewhere, I have referred to this process as "patriarchal accommodations"; see Andrews and Shahrokni (2014).

4. The Islamic Republic established several charity foundations to provide support for poor families and to help them regain financial stability. Among these are the Foundation of the Dispossessed and Disabled and the Imam Khomeini Relief Foundation.

5. Articles 29 to 31 of the Iranian Constitution stipulate that the government is obliged to provide welfare benefits, including healthcare, free education, and affordable housing, for each and every citizen of the country."

6. Quoted in *Entekhab* (2013).

7. Stated at the web portal of Iran Khodro, http://www.ikco.ir/fa/Intro.aspx.

8. For an analysis of the impact of traffic zones, see Salarvandian, Dijst, and Helbich (2017, 965–82).

9. For a thorough assessment of the social, political, and economic effects of the Iran–Iraq War, see Takeyh (2010).

10. The historical narrative in this section and the next one is partially reconstructed from the information I collected through my interviews with bus drivers and one of the experts at Traffic and Transportation Organization of Tehran.

11. The Islamic Republic has often used the provinces as testing grounds for its more controversial initiatives. The pilot plan is usually implemented in lightly populated provinces to gauge the severity of the reaction among (sometimes radically) different constituencies. If successful, the plan is then extended to larger provinces and the capital city.

12. Here *hezbollah* should not be confused with the Lebanese political party Hezbollah. The term literally means "the party of God," and the BCT is referring to Iran as a nation that serves as the party of God.

13. For an analysis of similar effects in higher education, see Mehran (2003, 269–86).

14. The imam was Ayatollah Khomeini.

15. For a discussion of fertility rate trends in Iran, see World Bank (2010).

16. For an overview of divorce trends in Iran since the revolution, see Aghajanian (1986), and more specifically in the 1990s, Aghajanian and Moghadas (1998) and Aghajanian and Thompson (2013).

17. Employed population by gender figures for 1966–2011 were retrieved from Management and Planning Organization of Iran (2015); data on women's participation in the workforce are from World Bank (2019).

18. Women's week starts off by celebrating the birth of Fatimah, the Prophet's daughter.

19. See *Hamshahri* (December 9, 2010), http://www.hamshahrionline.ir/news/122001. For an assessment of the impact of pollution in Tehran, see Karimzadegan et al. (2008).

20. See also see Atlas of Tehran Metropolis (2006).

21. For Khatami's economic plan, see also Behdad (2001).

22. I use "Maziar" as a pseudonym to protect the anonymity of the official in question, as he requested not to be identified.

23. Hamidi (2013).

24. See Turquoise Partners (2011) and *Global Mass Transit Report* (2011).

3. HAPPY AND HEALTHY IN MOTHERS' PARADISE: WOMEN-ONLY PARKS AND THE EXPANSION OF THE STATE

1. Veiling in Iran is compulsory by law. All women (of any religion or nationality) must cover most if not all of their hair and wear some type of outer garment over their clothes when appearing in public.

2. Friday is considered the weekend in Iran. At the time of this research, boys who were eight years old or younger were allowed in the park; this indicates the arbitrariness of gender boundaries, because according to the law, which is based on Islamic jurisprudence, boys reach puberty at around 15 lunar years (around 14.5 solar years) or whenever they start

showing signs of puberty, at which point it becomes a religious obligation for unrelated women to wear hijab in front of them.

3. Primary and secondary schools are gender-segregated, though most universities are coed. Uniforms are required in most boys' schools and in all girls' schools. The girls' uniform consists of a long dress and headscarf (bright colors in elementary, darker colors in junior high and high school). According to Islam, women are supposed to cover their heads and bodies in the presence of unrelated men, but despite the absence of males, schoolgirls must remain covered while at school. The rationale given is that it is difficult to keep the prying eyes of men away, and that the practice of veiling should become a habit through continuity.

4. Translation: "Hey lady, I gave you my heart / broke everyone else's heart."

5. Note that dancing in public is formally banned in Iran.

6. For a discussion of this campaign, see Sameh (2010, 2014).

7. That these spaces were labeled as feminine, and therefore apolitical is neither new nor unique to Iran. Black churches during the civil rights movements in the United States also were labeled as religious and thus apolitical; as such they provided spaces that were loosely monitored/supervised and where new forms of collectives and resistance could develop.

8. This encounter took place just before the 2009 presidential elections in Iran.

9. Hoodfar and Sadr (2010) discuss how the Islamic Republic shifted from adopting pronatalist polices to implementing one of the most successful family planning programs in the non-Western world. On Iran's education policies, see Mehran (1990).

10. Tehran Municipality, Center for Budget and Statistics (May 1999).

11. For a discussion of Iran's municipal beautification programs, see Zarkar (2016).

12. See Keshavarzian (2005); Siavoshi (1992); Takeyh (2006).

13. Ayatollah Ruhollah Khomeini died on June 3, 1989 and was succeeded by Ayatollah Ali Khamenei.

14. For a study of the impacts of cultural globalization on youth culture and consumption patterns of Iranians, see Jafari (2007).

15. "Marriage crisis" refers to the increasing age of marriage for both men and women, caused at least in part by the increasing expense of beginning a new household. See also the High Council of Iranian Youths Collection of Bills (2009).

16. Saturdays are not part of the weekend in Iran.

17. See Behdad (2001); Boroujerdi (2004); Khajehpour (2002).

18. Morteza Alviri (for a period of thirty-two months between 1999 and 2001), Mohammad Hassan Malekmadani (for a period of ten months between 2001 and 2002), and Mohammad Hossein Moghimi (for a period of four months between 2002 and 2003).

19. Interestingly, the politically left-leaning *Salam* (February 12, 1999), the centrist *Ettelaat* (February 23, 1999), and -leaning *Resalat* (April 16, 2003) take similar positions on the "problem."

20. The Islamic Propagation Organization, Women's Social and Cultural Council, Tehran Municipality, the Presidential Center for Women's Affairs and Participation, the High Council of Iranian Youths, and Islamic Republic of Iran Broadcasting.

21. This report was published as part of a news story in *Ettelaat* (May 17, 2004).

22. Note that women still have access to all the other parks. In addition, the municipality is gradually increasing the number of women-only parks across the city.

23. This is a reference to the title of Emily Brontë's 1847 novel.

24. See *Hamshahri Online*(2012).

25. See, for example, Moaveni (2008, 2009).

26. See Foucault (1991, 100).

4. SOCCER GOALS AND POLITICAL POINTS: THE GENDERED POLITICS OF STADIUM ACCESS

1. Figures provided by FIFA suggest that 85,000 people were in the Melbourne Cricket Ground on that day (FIFA 2012).

2. See Murray (1997).

3. See FIFA (2015/2016).

4. For a comprehensive account of women's sports in Iran (and beyond), see Hoodfar (2016).

5. *Navad* (meaning Ninety, referring to the ninety minutes of the soccer match) was launched at the end of the 1990s and broadcast from Iran's Channel 3, a channel with considerable major sports events coverage. The show was exclusively dedicated to soccer and to covering local, national, and international news relevant to the sport and soon became extremely popular.

6. This strategy has been used elsewhere with varying levels of success. See, for example, Berkovitch (1999).

7. Unlike soccer, however, wrestling enjoys little popularity among women. The combination of the lack of women's demand for access with the revealing outfits worn by wrestlers kept the ban in place.

8. For a detailed account of the White Scarf Girls and their activities, see Afzali (2016).

9. Although discussing the significance of the election of Mahmoud Ahmadinejad in bringing to the fore the divisiveness and diversity within the conservative segments of Iran's political class is not within the remit of this book, nor can it be accomplished in the space of a footnote, it is important to mention that his nonclerical background, his association with the nonclerical conservative Alliance of Builders of Islamic Iran, and his pursuit of agendas that pitted him against the conservative clergy caused uneasiness within the conservative clerical establishment.

10. Source of emulation, or *Marja-i Taqlid*, is a central element of Shia Islam whereby those Imams formally recognized as just and knowledgeable specialists in the field of the Islamic law provide authoritative guidance and a source of inspiration and emulation among the faithful.

11. The Society of Seminary Teachers of Qom was founded in 1961 by the leading Muslim clerics of Qom city to promote a revolutionary interpretation of Islam, such as the idea of Islamic government. After the 1979 revolution the society assumed the responsibility of keeping the regime's registrar of who counts as a grand ayatollah (source of emulation), ayatollah, and hojjatoleslam. It currently heads the Supreme Council of Qom Hawzas and proposes judges to the judiciary system.

12. For an extensive overview of these controversies, see Cole (2007); Steele (2006); and Kessler (2011).

5. RE-PLACING WOMEN, REMAKING THE STATE:
GENDER, ISLAM, AND THE POLITICS OF PLACE MAKING

1. The Mayor and the Members of Tehran City Council Meet with the Leader of the Revolution." January 13, 2014. http://farsi.khamenei.ir/news-content?id=24963.

2. Taking cues from postcolonial and post-structural feminist literature, I have looked at the ways in which the category "woman" has been discursively constituted in historically specific ways. Yuval-Davis and Anthias (1989), for example, refer to five ways in which women are discursively constituted and utilized by nation-state leaders as (a) ensuring the biological reproduction of state and nation, (b) being central in cultural reproduction and transmission (c) assuming a frontier function, (d) being signifiers of national difference, and (e) participating in national liberation struggles.

Abrahamian, Ervand. 1982. *Iran between Two Revolutions.* Princeton, NJ: Princeton University Press.

———. 1993. *Khomeinism: Essays on the Islamic Republic.* Berkeley: University of California Press.

———. 2009. "Why the Islamic Republic Has Survived." *Middle East Research and Information Project* 39 (Spring 2009). www.merip.org/mer/mer250/why-islamic-republic-has-survived.

Abu-Lughod, Janet. 1987. "The Islamic City—Historic Myth, Islamic Essence, and Contemporary Relevance." *International Journal of Middle East Studies* 19: 155–76.

Abu-Lughod, Lila. 1990. "The Romance of Resistance: Tracing Transformations of Power through Bedouin Women." *American Ethnologist* 17 (1): 41–55.

———, ed. 1998. *Remaking Women: Feminism and Modernity in the Middle East.* Princeton, NJ: Princeton University Press.

———. 2002. "Do Muslim Women Really Need Saving? Anthropological Reflections on Cultural Relativism and Its Others." *American Anthropologist* 104 (3): 783–90.

Adelkhah, Fariba. 2000. *Being Modern in Iran.* New York: Columbia University Press.

Afary, Janet. 2009. *Sexual Politics in Modern Iran.* Cambridge, UK: Cambridge University Press.

Afsaruddin, Asma, ed. 1999. *Hermeneutics and Honor: Negotiating Female "Public" Space in Islamic/ate Societies.* Cambridge, MA: Harvard University Press.

Afzali, Nasrin. 2016. "Gaze Reversed: Iranian Women's Campaign to Be Football Spectators." In *Women's Sports as Politics in Muslim Contexts,* edited by Homa Hoodfar, 161–84. London: Women Living Under Muslim Laws.

Aghajanian, Akbar. 1986. "Some Notes on Divorce in Iran." *Journal of Marriage and Family* 48 (4): 749–55.

Aghajanian, Akbar, and Ali Asghar Moghadas. 1998. "Correlates and Consequences of Divorce in an Iranian City." *Journal of Divorce & Remarriage* 28 (3–4): 53–71.

Aghajanian, Akbar, and Vajda Thompson. 2013. "Recent Divorce Trend in Iran." *Journal of Divorce & Remarriage* 54: 112–25.

Agrama, Hussein Ali. 2010. "Secularism, Sovereignty, Indeterminacy: Is Egypt a Secular or a Religious State?" *Comparative Studies in Society and History* 52 (3): 495–523.

Ahmed, Leila. 1992. *Women and Gender in Islam: Historical Roots of a Modern Debate.* New Haven, CT: Yale University Press.

Alaedini, Pooya, and Mohamad Reza Razavi. 2005. "Women's Participation and Employment in Iran: A Critical Examination." *Critique: Critical Middle Eastern Studies* 14 (1): 57–73.

Alamdari, Kazem. 2005. "The Power Structure of the Islamic Republic of Iran: Transition from Populism to Clientelism, and Militarization of the Government." *Third World Quarterly* 26 (8): 1285–1301.

Allen, Heather. 2013. "An Integrated Approach to Public Transport in Tehran, Islamic Republic of Iran: Case Study prepared for Global Report on Human Settlements." Case study prepared for the United Nations' *Global Report on Human Settlements 2013.* www.unhabitat.org/grhs/2013.

AlSayyad, Nezar, and M. Massoumi. 2010. *The Fundamentalist City?* London: Routledge.

Amin, Camron, M. 2002. *The Making of the Modern Iranian Woman: Gender, State Policy, and Popular Culture, 1865–1946.* Gainesville: University Press of Florida

Amir-Ebrahimi, Masserat. 2006. "Conquering Enclosed Public Spaces." *Cities* 23 (6): 455–61.

Anderson, Benedict. 1983. *Imagined Communities: Reflections on the Origin and Spread of Nationalism.* New York: Verso Press.

Andrews, Abigail, and Nazanin Shahrokni. 2014. "Patriarchal Accommodations: Women's Mobility and Policies of Gender Difference from Urban Iran to Migrant Mexico." *Journal of Contemporary Ethnography* 43 (2): 148–75.

Appadurai, Arjun, ed. 1986. *The Social Life of Things: Commodities in Cultural Perspective.* Cambridge. UK: Cambridge University Press.

Arjomand, Said A. 1988. *The Turban for the Crown: The Islamic Revolution in Iran.* Oxford: Oxford University Press.

———. 2009. *After Khomeini: Iran under His Successors.* Oxford: Oxford University Press.

Afshar, Haleh. 1985 "The Iranian Theocracy." In *Iran*, edited by Haleh Afshar, 220–43. London: Palgrave Macmillan.

Ataian, Setareh. 2011. "Analyse des dépenses en transport urbain des ménages à Téhéran." *Les Cahiers scientifiques du transport*, AFITL, 95–122.

Avishai, Orit, Lynne Gerber, and Jennifer Randles. 2012. "The Feminist Ethnographer's Dilemma: Reconciling Progressive Research Agendas with Fieldwork Realities." *Journal of Contemporary Ethnography* 42 (4): 394–426.

Ayatollahi Tabaar, Mohammad. 2018. *Religious Statecraft: The Politics of Islam in Iran.* New York: Columbia University Press.

Bahramitash, Roksana. 2003a. "Islamic Fundamentalism and Women's Economic Role: The Case of Iran." *International Journal of Politics, Culture, and Society* 16: 551–68.

———. 2003b. "Revolution, Islamization, and Women's Employment in Iran." *Brown Journal of World Affairs* 9 (2): 229–41.

———. 2013. *Gender and Entrepreneurship in Iran: Microenterprise and the Informal Sector.* New York: Palgrave Macmillan.

Banakar, Reza, and Benoosh Payvar. 2015. *Gender and Domination: Interviews with Female Taxi Drivers*. London: I. B.Tauris.

Banuazizi, Ali. 1994. "Iran's Revolutionary Impasse: Political Factionalism and Social Resistance." *Middle East Report* 191: 2–8.

Bayat, Asef. 1997. *Street Politics: Poor People's Movements in Iran*. New York: Columbia University Press.

———. 2007. "A Women's Non-Movement: What It Means to Be a Woman Activist in an Islamic State." *Comparative Studies of South Asia, Africa and the Middle East* 27 (1): 160–72.

———. 2010. "Tehran: Paradox City." *New Left Review* 66 (November–December 2010). https://newleftreview.org/II/66/asef-bayat-tehran-paradox-city.

———. 2011. "Tehran: Paradox City 1." *Frontline* (PBS), January 30, 2011. www.pbs.org/wgbh/pages/frontline/tehranbureau/2011/01/tehran-paradox-city-1.html.

Beaumont Justin, and Christopher Baker, eds. 2011. *Postsecular Cities: Space, Theory, and Practice*. New York: Bloomsbury Publishing.

Behdad, Sohrab. 2001. "Khatami and His 'Reformist' Economic (Non-)Agenda." *Middle East Report Online*, May 21. https://merip.org/2001/05/khatami-and-his-reformist-economic-non-agenda/

Behrouzan, Orkideh. 2016. *Prozak Diaries: Psychiatry and Generational Memory in Iran*. Stanford, CA: Stanford University Press.

Berkovitch, Nitza. 1999. *From Motherhood to Citizenship: Women's Rights and International Organizations*. Baltimore, MD: Johns Hopkins University Press.

Boroujerdi, Mehrzad. 2004. "The Reformist Movement in Iran." In *Oil in the Gulf: Obstacles to Democracy and Development*, edited by Daniel Heradstveit and Helge Hveem, 63–71. London: Ashgate.

Boudagh, M., and P. Ghaemmaghami. 2011. "The Typology of Traditional Houses in Tabriz," in *Structural Studies, Repairs and Maintenance of Heritage Architecture XII*, edited by C. A. Brebbia and L. Binda, 87–99. UK: WIT Press.

Brookshaw, Dominic Parviz. 2013. "Women in Praise of Women: Female Poets and Female Patrons in Qajar Iran." *Iranian Studies* 46 (1): 17–48.

———. 2014. "Qajar Confection: The Production and Dissemination of Women's Poetry in Early Nineteenth-century Iran." *Middle Eastern Literatures* 17 (2): 113–46. www.tandfonline.com/doi/abs/10.1080/1475262X.2014.928040.

Brown, Wendy. 1992. "Finding the Man in the State." *Feminist Studies* 18 (1: 7–34).

———. 1995. *States of Injury: Power and Freedom in Late Modernity*. Princeton, NJ: Princeton University Press.

Bush, G. W. 2002. State of the Union Address (transcript). https://georgewbush-whitehouse.archives.gov/news/releases/2002/01/20020129-11.html.

Carnoy, Martin. 1986. *The State and Political Theory*. Cambridge, UK: Cambridge University Press.

Chatterjee, Partha. 1993. *The Nation and Its Fragments: Colonial and Postcolonial Histories*. Princeton, NJ: Princeton University Press.

Chehabi, H. E. 1991. "Religion and Politics in Iran: How Theocratic Is the Islamic Republic?" *Daedalus* 120 (3): 69–91.

———. 2002. "A Political History of Football in Iran." *Iranian Studies* 35 (4): 371–402.

———. 2006. "The Politics of Football in Iran." *Soccer and Society*. 7 (2–3): 233–61.

Cheheltan, Hassan. 1991. *Talar-e'Aineh*. Tehran: Negah.

Cole, Juan. 2007. "Ahmadinejad: 'I Am Not Anti-Semitic.'" *Informed Comment: Thoughts on the Middle East, History and Religion*, June 26. www.juancole.com/2007/06/ahmadinejad -i-am-not-anti-semitic.html.

Collins, Patricia Hill. 1986. "Learning from the Outsider Within: The Sociological Significance of Black Feminist Thought." *Social Problems* 33 (6, October–December): S14–S32.

Connell, R. W. 1990. "The State, Gender, and Sexual Politics." *Theory and Society* 19 (5): 507–44.

Crampton, Jeremy W., and Stuart Elden. 2007. *Space, Knowledge and Power: Foucault and Geography*. Burlington, UK: Ashgate.

Dash, Veena, and Deborah Poole, eds. 2004. *Anthropology in the Margins of the State*. Santa Fe, NM: School of American Research Press.

Domosh, Mona, and Joni K. Seager. 2001. *Putting Women in Place: Feminist Geographers Make Sense of the World*. New York: Guilford Press.

Dorsey, James. 2012. "Muslim Players Win Hijab Battle in Their Struggle for Women's Rights." *Huffpost Sports*, March 7. www.huffingtonpost.com/james-dorsey/iran-womens-soccer -hijab_b_1318549.html.

Dreyfus, Hubert L., and Paul Rabinow. 1982. *Michel Foucault, Beyond Structuralism and Hermeneutics*. Chicago: University of Chicago Press.

Dubois, Laurent. 2012. "The Hijab on the Pitch." *The Feminist Wire*, August 3. https://the feministwire.com/2012/08/the-hijab-on-the-pitch

Dubowitz, Mark, and Emanuele Ottolenghi. 2013. "Iran's Car Industry: A Big Sanctions Buster." *Forbes*, May 13. www.forbes.com/sites/energysource/2013/05/13/irans-car-industry-a-big -sanctions-buster/

Dunckel-Graglia, Amy. 2013. "'Pink Transportation' in Mexico City: Reclaiming Urban Space through Collective Action against Gender-Based Violence." *Gender & Development* 21 (2): 265–76

Ehlers, Eckart, and Willem Floor. 2007. "Urban Change in Iran, 1920–1941." *Iranian Studies* 26 (3–4): 251–75.

Ehsani, Kaveh. 1999. "Municipal Matters: The Urbanization of Consciousness and Political Change in Tehran." *Middle East Report* (212): 22–27. doi:10.2307/3012909.

———. 2009. "Survival through Dispossession: Privatization of Public Goods in the Islamic Republic." *Middle East Report* 250. https://merip.org/2009/03/survival-through-disposs ession/

Eickelman, Dale. 1974. "Is There an Islamic City? The Making of a Quarter in a Moroccan Town." *International Journal of Middle East Studies* 5: 274–94.

Erdbrink, Thomas. 2011. "Tehran's Coffee Shops Offer Private Retreat." *Washington Post*, November 11.

———. 2013. "Annual Buildup of Air Pollution Chokes Tehran." *New York Times*, January 6. www.nytimes.com/2013/01/07/world/middleeast/tehran-is-choked-by-annual-buildup -of-air-pollution.html.

Farahmand-Razavi, Arman. 1994. "The Role of International Consultants in Developing Countries: Lessons from Tehran (Iran)." *Transport Policy* 1 (2): 259–68.

Faramarzi, Scheherezade. 2007. "Iran's Rising Conservatives Roll Back Women's Right." *Los Angeles Times*, April 29.

Fenster, Tovi. 2007. "Gender, Religion, and Urban Management: Women's Bodies and Everyday Lives in Jersusalem." In *Women, Religion, and Space: Global Perspectives on Gender and Faith*, edited by Karen M. Morin and Jeanne Kay Guelke, 41–61. Syracuse, NY: Syracuse University Press.

Fine, Gary Alan. 1993. "Ten Lies of Ethnography: Moral Dilemmas in Field Research." *Journal of Contemporary Ethnography* 22 (3, October): 267–94.

Fisk, Robert. 1996. "Tehran's Tree-Loving Mayor Has a Taste for Democracy." *Independent*, March 18. www.independent.co.uk/news/world/tehrans-treeloving-mayor-has-a-taste -for-democracy-1342714.html.

Foucault, Michel. 1980. *Power/Knowledge: Selected Interviews and Other Writings 1972–1977.* Edited by Colin Gordon. New York: Pantheon Books.

———. 1991. "Governmentality." In *The Foucault Effect: Studies in Governmentality with Two Lectures by and an Interview with Michel Foucault*, edited by Graham Burchell, Colin Gordon, and Pete Miller, 87–105. Chicago: University of Chicago Press.

———. 1995. *Discipline and Punish: The Birth of the Prison.* New York: Vintage.

———. 2007. *Security, Territory, Population: Lectures at the Collège de France 1977–1978.* Basingstoke, UK: Palgrave Macmillan.

Fraser, Nancy. 1990. "Rethinking the Public Sphere: A Contribution to the Critique of Actually Existing Democracy." *Social Text* (25/26): 56–80.

French, Philip. 2006. "Iran 1 Female Fans 0." *Guardian*, June 11. www.theguardian.com/film /2006/jun/11/features.review2.

Frey, James H., and D. Stanley Eitzen. 1991. "Sport and Society." *Annual Review of Sociology* 17: 503–22.

Gardner, Carol Brooks. 1995. *Passing By: Gender and Public Harassment.* Berkeley: University of California Press.

Gerson, Judith, and Kathy Peiss. 1985. "Boundaries, Negotiation, Consciousness: Reconceptualizing Gender Relations." *Social Problems* 32 (4): 317–31.

Ghamari-Tabrizi, Behrooz. 2013. "Women's Rights, Shari'a Law, and the Secularization of Islam in Iran." *International Journal of Politics, Culture, and Society* 26 (3): 237–53.

Ghannam, Farha. 2002. *Remaking the Modern: Space, Relocation, and the Politics of Identity in Global Cairo.* Berkeley: University of California Press.

Global Mass Transit Report. 2011. July 1. www.globalmasstransit.net/archive.php?id=7086.

Goffman, Erving. 1959. *The Presentation of Self in Everyday Life.* New York: Anchor Books.

Gramsci, Antonio. 1971. *Selections from the Prison Notebooks.* New York: International Publishers.

Gross, Zehavit, Lynn Davies, and Al-Khansaa Diab, eds. 2013. *Gender, Religion and Education in a Chaotic Postmodern World.* Dordrecht: Springer Netherlands.

Habermas, Jurgen. 1989. *The Structural Transformation of the Public Sphere: An Inquiry into a Category of Bourgeois Society.* Translated by Thomas Berger. Cambridge, MA: MIT Press.

Hall, Stuart, Chas Critcher, Tony Jefferson, John Clarke, and Brian Roberts. 2013. *Policing the Crisis: Mugging, the State and Law and Order.* New York: Palgrave.

Haney, Lynne A. 2000. "Feminist State Theory: Applications to Jurisprudence, Criminology, and the Welfare State." *Annual Review of Sociology* 26 (1): 641–66.

Harris, Kevan. 2012. "The Brokered Exuberance of the Middle Class: An Ethnographic Analysis of Iran's 2009 Green Movement." *Mobilization: An International Quarterly* 17 (4, December): 435–55.

———. 2017. *A Social Revolution: Politics and the Welfare State in Iran.* Oakland: University of California Press.

Harvey, David. 2000. *Social Justice and the City.* Athens: University of Georgia Press.

Hayden, Dolores. 1981. *The Grand Domestic Revolution: A History of Feminist Designs for American Homes, Neighborhoods, and Cities.* Cambridge, MA: MIT Press.

Hoodfar, Homa, ed. 2016. *Women's Sports as Politics in Muslim Contexts.* London: Women Living Under Muslim Laws.

Hoodfar, Homa, and Samad Assadpour. 2000. "The Politics of Population Policy in the Islamic Republic of Iran." *Studies in Family Planning* 31 (1): 19–34.

Hoodfar, Homa, and Shadi Sadr. 2010. "Islamic Politics and Women's Quest for Gender Equality in Iran." *Third World Quarterly* 31 (6): 885–903.

Hosseini, Seyed Reza, Ali Nik Eteghad, Ezequiel Uson Guardiola, and Antonio Armesto Aira. 2015. "Iranian Courtyard Housing: The Role of Social and Cultural Patterns to Reach the Spatial Formation in the Light of an Accentuated Privacy." *ACE: Architecture, City and Environment* 10 (29): 11–30.

Hourani, A. H., and S. M. Stern, eds. 1970. *The Islamic City: A Colloquium.* Philadelphia: University of Pennsylvania Press.

Htun, Mala. 2003. *Sex and the State: Abortion, Divorce, and the Family under Latin American Dictatorships and Democracies.* Cambridge, UK: Cambridge University Press.

Ismail, Salwa. 2006. *Political Life in Cairo's New Quarters: Encountering the Everyday State.* Minneapolis and London: University of Minnesota Press.

Jafari, Aliakbar. 2007. "Two Tales of a City: An Exploratory Study of Cultural Consumption among Iranian Youth." *Iranian Studies* 40 (3): 367–83.

Jaynes, Gregory. 1979. "Iranian Women: Looking Beyond the Chador." *New York Times,* April 22, SM10.

Jonathan, C. R. 1979. "Women Protest in Iran, Shout 'Down with Khomeini.'" *Washington Post,* March 9.

Kandiyoti, Al-Ali, and Spellman Poots, eds. 2019. *Gender, Governance and Islam.* Edinburgh: Edinburgh University Press.

Karimi, Pamala. 2013. *Domesticity and Consumer Culture in Iran: Interior Revolutions of the Modern Era.* New York: Routledge.

Karimzadegan, H., M. Rahmatian, D. D. Farhud, and M. Yunesian. 2008. "Economic Valuation of Air Pollution Health Impacts in the Tehran Area, Iran." *Iranian Journal of Public Health* 37 (1): 20–30. http://ijph.tums.ac.ir/index.php/ijph/article/view/2068.

Keshavarzian, Arang. 2005. "Contestation without Democracy: Elite Fragmentation in Iran." In *Authoritarianism in the Middle East: Regimes and Resistance,* edited by Marsha Pripstein Posusney and Michelle Penner Angrist, 63–88. Boulder, CO: Lynne Rienner Publishers.

———. 2007. *Bazaar and the State in Iran: The Politics of the Tehran Marketplace.* Cambridge Middle East Studies 26. Cambridge, UK: Cambridge University Press.

———. 2015. "The Iran Deal as Social Contract." *Middle East Report,* 277.

Kessler, Glenn. 2011. "Did Ahmadinejad Really Say Israel Should Be 'Wiped off the Map'?" *Washington Post,* October 5. www.washingtonpost.com/blogs/fact-checker/post/did

-ahmadinejad-really-say-israel-should-be-wiped-off-the-map/2011/10/04/gIQAB JIKML_blog.html.

Khajehpour, Bijan. 2002. "Protest and Regime Resilience in Iran." *Middle East Report Online*, December 12. www.merip.org/mero/mero121102.

Khatib, Gandom. 2014. "Tehran's Underground Speakeasies." *Daily Beast*, July 15.

Khatib-Chahidi, J. 1981. "Sexual Prohibitions, Shared Space, and Fictive Marriages in Shi'ite Iran." In *Women and Space: Ground Rules and Social Maps*, edited by Shirley Ardener, 112–35. Oxford: Berg.

Khosravi, Shahram. 2007. *Young and Defiant in Tehran*. Philadelphia: University of Pennsylvania Press.

Kian, Azadeh. 1995. "Gendered Occupation and Women's Status in Post-Revolutionary Iran." *Middle Eastern Studies* 31 (3): 407–21.

Koehler, Benedikt. 2011. "Female Entrepreneurship in Early Islam." *Economic Affairs* 31: 93–95.

Kraus, Christopher. 2010. "The Sources of Anti-Americanism in Iran: A Historical and Psychological Analysis." *Valley Humanities Review* (Spring). http://portal.lvc.edu/vhr/2010/krause.html.

Kurzman, Charles. 2004. *The Unthinkable Revolution in Iran*. Cambridge, MA: Harvard University Press.

———. 2008. "A Feminist Generation in Iran?" *Iranian Studies* 41 (3): 297–321.

Ladier-Fouladi, Marie. 2002. "Iranian Families between Demographic Change and the Birth of the Welfare State." *Population* 57 (2): 361–70.

Lamont, Michele, and Virag Molnar. 2002. "The Study of Boundaries in the Social Sciences." *Annual Review of Sociology* 28: 167–95.

Le Renard, Amelie. 2008. "'Only for Women': Women, the State and Reform in Saudi Arabia." *The Middle East Journal* 62 (4): 610–29.

———. 2014. *A Society of Young Women: Opportunities of Place, Power, and Reform in Saudi Arabia*. Stanford, CA: Stanford University Press.

Lefebvre, Henri. 2009. *State, Space, World: Selected Essays*. Edited by Neil Brenner and Stuart Elden. Minneapolis: University of Minnesota Press.

"Library of Ayatollah Marashi Najafi, The." 2013. Iran's Manuscript Libraries, The Parliament's Library, 1:96–100. http://archive.ical.ir/files/english/pl-01-28.pdf.

Light, Duncan. 2004. "Street Names in Bucharest, 1900–1997: Exploring the Modern Historical Geographies of Post-Socialist Change." *Journal of Historical Geography* 30 (1): 154–72.

Mahdavi, Mojtaba. 2011. "Post-Islamist Trends in Postrevolutionary Iran." *Comparative Studies of South Asia, Africa and the Middle East* 31 (1): 94–109. Project MUSE.

Mahdavi, Pardis. 2009. *Passionate Uprisings: Iran's Sexual Revolution*. Stanford, CA: Stanford University Press.

Management and Planning Organization of Iran. 2015. http://irandataportal.syr.edu/wp-content/uploads/Employed-Population-by-Gender-1966-2011.xlsx.

Massey, Doreen. 1994. *Space, Place, and Gender*. Minneapolis: University of Minnesota Press.

Mazumdar, Shampa, and Sanjoy Mazumdar. 2001. "Rethinking Public and Private Space: Religion and Women in Muslim Society." *Journal of Architectural and Planning Research* 18: 302–24.

McAdam, Douglas. 1999. "Conceptual Origins, Current Problems, Future Directions." In *Comparative Perspectives on Social Movements, Political Opportunities, Mobilizing Structures, and Cultural Framing*, edited by Douglas McAdam, John D. McCarthy, and Mayer Y. Zald, 23–40. Cambridge, UK: Cambridge University Press.

MacAskill, Ewen, and Chris McGreal. 2005. "Israel Should Be Wiped Off Map, Says Iran's President." *Guardian*, October 27.

McDowell, Linda. 1999. *Gender, Identity and Place: Understanding Feminist Geographies*. Minneapolis: University of Minnesota Press.

McElrone, S. M. 2005. "Nineteenth-Century Qajar Women in the Public Sphere: An Alternative Historical and Historiographical Reading of the Roots of Iranian Women's Activism." *Comparative Studies of South Asia, Africa, and the Middle East* 25 (2): 297–317.

Mehrabi, Masood. 1989. *History of Cinema in Iran (From the Beginning to 1979)*. Tehran: Nazar.

Mehran, Golnar. 1990. "Ideology and Education in the Islamic Republic of Iran." *Compare: A Journal of Comparative and International Education* 20 (1): 53–65. doi:10.1080/03057929 00200105.

———. 2003. "The Paradox of Tradition and Modernity in Female Education in the Islamic Republic of Iran." *Comparative Education Review* 47 (3): 269–86.

Meijer, Roel. 2010. "The Gender Segregation (Ikhtilat) Debate in Saudi Arabia: Reform and the Clash between Ulamah and Liberals." *Journal for Islamic Studies* 30: 2–32.

Meyer, Armin Henry. 2003. *Quiet Diplomacy: From Cairo to Tokyo in the Twilight of Imperialism*. Lincoln, NE: iUniverse.

Miller, Kristin J. 1996. "Human Rights of Women in Iran: The Universalist Approach and the Relativist Response." *Emory International Law Review* 10: 779–832.

Mills, C. Wright. 1959. *The Sociological Imagination*. Oxford: Oxford University Press.

Mir-Hosseini, Ziba. 1999. *Islam and Gender: The Religious Debate in Contemporary Iran*. Princeton, NJ: Princeton University Press.

Mitchell, Timothy. 1991. "The Limits of the State: Beyond Statist Approaches and Their Critics." *The American Political Science Review* 85 (1, March): 77–96.

Moaddel, Mansoor. 1986. "The Shi'i Ulama and the State in Iran." *Theory and Society* 15 (4): 519–56.

———. 2010. "Religious Regimes and Prospects for Liberal Politics: Futures of Iran, Iraq and Saudi Arabia." *Futures* 42: 532–44.

Moallem, Minoo. 2001. "Transnationalism, Feminism and Fundamentalism." In *Women, Gender, Religion: A Reader*, edited by Elizabeth Anne Castelli and Rosamond C. Rodman, 119–49. New York: Palgrave Macmillan.

———. 2005. *Between Warrior Brother and Veiled Sister: Islamic Fundamentalism and the Politics of Patriarchy in Iran*. Berkeley: University of California Press.

Moaveni, Azadeh. 2007. *Lipstick Jihad: A Memoir of Growing up Iranian in America and American in Iran*. New York: PublicAffairs.

———. 2008. "Should a Pious Muslim Practice Yoga?" *Time*, November 20. www.time.com/time/world/article/0,8599,1862306,00.html.

———. 2009. "How to Work Out while Muslim—and Female," *Time*, August 16. www.time.com/time/magazine/article/0,9171,1924488,00.html.

Moghadam, Valentine. 1988. "Women, Work, and Ideology in the Islamic Republic." *International Journal of Middle East Studies* 20 (2): 221–43.

———. 1992. Patriarchy and the Politics of Gender in Modernising Societies: Iran, Pakistan and Afghanistan. *International Sociology* 7(1): 35–53.

———. 1999. "Revolution, Religion, and Gender Politics: Iran and Afghanistan Compared." *Journal of Women's History* 10 (4): 172–95.

———. 2003. *Modernizing Women: Gender and Social Change in the Middle East*. Boulder, CO: Lynne Rienner.

———. 2004. "Patriarchy in Transition: Women and the Changing Family in the Middle East." *Journal of Comparative Family Studies* 35(2): 137–62.

Moghissi, H. 2009. "Women and the 1979 Revolution: Refusing Religion-Defined Womanhood." *Comparative Studies of South Asia, Africa and the Middle East* 29 (1): 63–71.

Montazeri, M., and T. Hashemi. 2009. "Bus Rapid Transit in Tehran." In "Big Changes for the Bus," special issue, *UITP Public Transport International Newsletter* (September / October).

Morgan, Kimberly J., and Ann Shola Orloff. 2017. *The Many Hands of the State: Theorizing Political Authority and Social Control*. Cambridge, UK: Cambridge University Press.

Moruzzi, Norma Claire. 2008. "Trying to Look Different: *Hijab* as the Self-Presentation of Social Distinction." *Comparative Studies of South Asia, Africa and the Middle East* 28 (2): 225–34.

Moruzzi, Norma Claire, and Fatemeh Sadeghi. 2006. "Out of the Frying Pan, Into the Fire: Young Iranian Women Today" *Middle East Report* (241, Winter): 22–28.

Mouri, Leila. 2014. "Gender Segregation Violates the Rights of Women in Iran." International Campaign for Human Rights in Iran. www.iranhumanrights.org/2014/09/gender-segregation/.

Murray, Les. 1997. *Australia vs Iran (2:2) WCQ in 1997*. YouTube, published by Socceroos Video Archive on July 2, 2012. www.youtube.com/watch?feature=player_embedded&v=PR6NWJDq6bo.

Naficy, Hamid. 2012. *A Social History of Iranian Cinema*. Volume 1, *The Artisanal Era, 1897–1941*. Durham, NC: Duke University Press.

Najmabadi, Afsaneh. 1991. "Hazards of Modernity and Morality: Women, State and Ideology in Contemporary Iran." In *Women, Islam and the State: Women in the Political Economy*, edited by Deniz Kandiyoti, 48–76. London: Palgrave Macmillan.

———. 1993. "Veiled Discourse-Unveiled Bodies." *Feminist Studies* 19 (3): 487–518.

———. 2000. "(Un)veiling Feminism." *Social Text* 18 (3): 29–45.

———. 2005. *Women with Mustaches and Men without Beards: Gender and Sexual Anxieties of Iranian Modernity*. Berkeley: University of California Press.

———. 2013. *Professing Selves: Transsexuality and Same-Sex Desire in Contemporary Iran*. Durham, NC: Duke University Press.

Navai, Ramita. 2014. *City of Lies: Love, Sex, Death and the Search for Truth in Tehran*. London: Weidenfeld & Nicolson.

Osanloo, Arzoo. 2009. *The Politics of Women's Rights in Iran*. Princeton, NJ: Princeton University Press.

Paidar, Parvin. 1997. *Women and the Political Process in the Twentieth Century*. Cambridge, UK: Cambridge University Press.

Peirce, Leslie. 1993. *The Imperial Harem: Women and Sovereignty in the Ottoman Empire*. Oxford: Oxford University Press.

Public Culture Council. 2011. "List of Bills Passed by Public Culture Council between 1987 and 2011." http://pcci.farhang.gov.ir/fa/desision/fehrest.

Rezai Rashti, Goli. 2015. "The Politics of Gender Segregation and Women's Access to Higher Education in the Islamic Republic of Iran: The Interplay of Repression and Resistance." *Gender and Education* 27 (5): 469–86.

Rezai Rashti, Goli, Mehran Golnar, and Shirin Abdmolaei, eds. 2019. *Women, Islam, and Education in Iran.* New York: Routledge

Rock-Singer, Aaron. 2016. "The Salafi Mystique: The Rise of Gender Segregation in 1970s Egypt." *Islamic Law and Society* 23 (3, June): 279–305.

Rose, Nikolas. 2001. "The Politics of Life Itself." *Theory, Culture & Society* 18 (6): 1–30.

Rose-Redwood, Reuben, Derek Alderman, and Maoz Azaryahu, eds. 2018. *The Political Life of Urban Streetscapes: Naming, Politics, and Place.* New York: Routledge.

Roshan, Gholamreza R., Saeed Zanganeh Shahraki, David Sauri, and Reza Borna. 2010. "Urban Sprawl and Climatic Changes in Tehran." *Iranian Journal of Environmental Health Science and Engineering* 7 (1): 43–52.

Rostam-Kolayi, Jasamin. 2008. "Origins of Iran's Modern Girls' Schools: From Private/National to Public/State." *Journal of Middle East Women's Studies* 4 (3): 58–88.

Sadeghi-Boroujerdi, Eskandar. 2013. "The Post-Revolutionary Women's Uprising of March 1979: An Interview with Nasser Mohajer and Mahnaz Matin." https://iranwire.com/en/features/24.

Saghafi, Morad. 2005. "Three Sources of Anti-Americanism in Iran." In *With Us or Against Us: Studies in Global Anti-Americanism,* edited by Tony Judt and Denis Lacorne, 189–297. New York: Palgrave Macmillan.

Salarvandian, Fatemeh, Martin Dijst, and Marco Helbich. 2017. "Impact of Traffic Zones on Mobility Behavior in Tehran, Iran." *Journal of Transport and Land Use* 10 (1): 965–82.

Sameh, Catherine. 2010. "Discourses of Equality, Rights and Islam in the One Million Signatures Campaign in Iran." *International Feminist Journal of Politics* 12 (3–4): 444–63. doi:10.1080/14616742.2010.513113.

———. 2014. "From Tehran to Los Angeles to Tehran: Transnational Solidarity Politics in the One Million Signatures Campaign to End Discriminatory Law." *Women's Studies Quarterly* 42 (3/4): 166–88. www.jstor.org/stable/24364999.

Sansarian, Eliz. 1982. *The Women's Rights Movement in Iran Mutiny, Appeasement, and Repression From 1900 to Khomeini.* Santa Barbara, CA: Praeger.

Sayeed, Asma. 2013. *Women and the Transmission of Religious Knowledge in Islam.* Cambridge, UK: Cambridge University Press.

Scheper-Hughes, Nancy. 2000. "Ire in Ireland." *Ethnography* 1 (1): 117–40.

Sciolino, Elaine. 1992. "Teheran Journal: From the Back Seat in Iran, Murmurs of Unrest." *New York Times,* April 23.

———. 2003. "Daughter of the Revolution Fights the Veil." *New York Times.* April 2.

Sedghi, Hamideh. 2007. *Women and Politics in Iran: Veiling, Unveiling, and Reveiling.* Cambridge, UK: Cambridge University Press.

Sehlikoglu, Sertac. 2016. "Exercising in Comfort: Islamicate Culture of *Mahremiyet* in Everyday Istanbul." *Journal of Middle East Women's Studies* 12 (2): 143–65. https://read.dukeupress.edu/jmews/article/12/2/143-165/42878.

Shaditalab, Jaleh. 2005. "Iranian Women: Rising Expectations." *Critique: Critical Middle Eastern Studies* 14 (1): 35–55.

Shahidian, Hameed. 2002a. *Women in Iran: Gender politics in the Islamic Republic.* Westport, CT: Greenwood Press.

———. 2002b. *Women in Iran: Emerging Voices in the Women's Movement.* Westport, CT: Greenwood Press.

Shahrokni, Nazanin. 2009. "All the President's Women." *MERIP (The Middle East Report)* 253: 1–6.

———. 2010. "The Politics of Polling: Polling and the Constitution of Counter-Publics during 'Reform' in Iran." *Current Sociology* 60 (2): 202–21.

———. 2014. "The Mothers' Paradise: Women-only Parks and the Dynamics of State Power in the Islamic Republic of Iran." *Journal of Middle East Women's Studies* 10 (3): 87–108.

———. 2019. "Protecting Men and the State: Gender Segregation in Iranian Universities." In *Women, Islam, and Education in Iran,* edited by Goli Rezai Rashti, Mehran Golnar, and Shirin Abdmolaei, 142–56. New York: Routledge.

Shahrokni, Nazanin, and Parastoo Dokouhaki. 2012. "A Separation at Iranian Universities." *Middle East Report Online,* October 18. www.merip.org/mero/mero101812.

Shams, Alex. 2014. "Urban Space and the Production of Gender in Modern Iran." Ajam Media Collective. February 23. https://ajammc.com/2015/02/23/urban-space-production-gender-iran/.

Shariati, Ali. 1971. *Fatima Is Fatima.* Translated by Laleh Bakhtiar. Tehran: The Shariati Foundation. www.playandlearn.org/eBooks/FatimaIsFatima.pdf.

Shavarini, Mitra. 2005. "The Feminisation of Iranian Higher Education." *International Review of Education* 51 (4): 329–47.

Shirazi, Faegheh. 2019. "The Education of Iranian Women." In *Women, Islam, and Education in Iran,* edited by Goli Rezaei Rashti, Mehran Golnar, and Shirin Abdmolaei, 142–56. New York: Routledge

Siavoshi, Sussan. 1992. "Factionalism and Iranian Politics: The Post-Khomeini Experience." *Iranian Studies* 25 (3–4): 27–49.

Sinaiee, Maryam. 2008. "All-Female Park Opens in Tehran." *National* (UAE), September 2. www.thenational.ae/news/world/middle-east/all-female-park-opens-in-tehran.

Slackman, Michael. 2006. "Iran Chief Eclipses Power of Clerics." *World Security Network,* May 27. www.worldsecuritynetwork.com/Other/Slackman-Michael/Iran-Chief-Eclipses-Power-of-Clerics.

Steele, J. 2006. "Lost in Translation." *Guardian,* June 14. www.guardian.co.uk/commentisfree/2006/jun/14/post155.

Steinmetz, George. 1999. *State/Culture: State-Formation after the Cultural Turn.* Ithaca, NY: Cornell University Press.

Strobl, Staci. 2008. "The Women's Police Directorate in Bahrain: An Ethnographic Exploration of Gender Segregation and the Likelihood of Future Integration." *International Criminal Justice Review* 18 (1): 39–58.

Tabari, Azar. 1980. "The Enigma of Veiled Iranian Women." *Feminist Review* 5 (1): 19–31.

Takeyh, Ray. 2003. "The Iran-Iraq War: A Reassessment." *Middle East Journal* 64 (3): 365–83.

———. 2006. *Hidden Iran: Paradox and Power in the Islamic Republic.* New York: Times Books/Henry Holt.

Thompson, Elizabeth. 2003. "Public and Private in Middle Eastern Women's History. *Journal of Women's History* 15,(1, Spring): 52–69.

Thrift, Nigel, J. 2000. "It's the Little Things." In *Geopolitical Traditions: A Century of Geopolitical Thought*, edited by David Atkinson and Klaus Dodds, 380–87. London: Routledge.

Tohidi, Nayereh. 1991. "Gender and Islamic Fundamentalism: Feminist Politics in Iran." In *Third World Women and the Politics of Feminism*, edited by Chandra Talpade Mohante, Anna Russo, and Lourdes M. Torres, 251–71. Bloomington: Indiana University Press.

———. 2007. "'Islamic Feminism': Negotiating Patriarchy and Modernity in Iran." In *The Blackwell Companion to Contemporary Islamic Thought*, edited by Ibrahim M. Abu-Rabi, ch. 36. Oxford: Blackwell.

Turquoise Partners. 2011. *Iran Investment Monthly* 5 (53). www.turquoisepartners.com /media/1139/iim-feb11.pdf.

Vakil, Sanam. 2011. *Women and Politics in the Islamic Republic of Iran: Action and Reaction.* New York: The Continuum International Publishing Group.

Varmaghani, Hosna, Soltanzadeh Hossein, and Mozayan Dehbashi Shani. 2016. "The Relationship between Gender and Space in the Public and Private Realms in the Qajar Era." *Bagh-e Nazar* 12 (37, February–March): 31–40.

White, Adam. 2013. *The Everyday Life of the State: A State-in-Society Approach.* Seattle: University of Washington Press.

Wilman, Mike, and Bob Bax. 2015. "The Automotive Industry in Iran: A Critical Analysis." In *Reintegrating Iran with the West: Challenges and Opportunities*, edited by Mohammad Elahee, Farid Sadrieh, and Mike Wilman, 57–74, Bingley, West Yorkshire, UK: Emerald Publishing.

Woodward, C. Vann. 2002. *The Strange Career of Jim Crow.* Oxford: Oxford University Press.

Woolf, Virginia. 1929. *A Room of One's Own.* New York: Harcourt, Brace and Company.

World Bank (2010). "Fertility Rates, Islamic Republic of Iran (Births per Woman)." https:// data.worldbank.org/indicator/SP.DYN.TFRT.IN?locations=IR.

———. (2019). "Labor Force, Female (% of Total Labor Force)." https://data.worldbank.org /indicator/SL.TLF.TOTL.FE.ZS?locations=IR&view=chart.

Yeganeh, Nahid. 1993. "Women, Nationalism, and Islam in Contemporary Political Discourse in Iran." *Feminist Review* 44: 3–18.

Young, Iris Marion. 2003. "The Logic of Masculinist Protection: Reflections on Current Security State." *Signs: Journal of Women in Culture and Society* 29 (1, Autumn): 1–25.

Yuval-Davis, Nira, and Floya Anthias. 1989. *Women-Nation-State.* London: Palgrave Macmillan.

Zahedi, Ashraf. 2006. "State Ideology and the Status of Iranian War Widows." *International Feminist Journal of Politics* 8 (2): 267–86.

———. 2007. "Contested Meaning of the Veil and Political Ideologies of Iranian Regimes." *Journal of Middle East Women's Studies* 3 (3): 75–98.

Zarkar, R. 2016. "A Mural Erased: Urban Art, Local Politics and the Contestation of Public Space in Mashhad." *Urbanisation* 1 (2): 166–79.

NEWSPAPERS, MAGAZINES, AND NEWS AGENCIES

Abrar, May 6, 2006
Abrar, May 24, 2006

Abrar, November 13, 2008
Aftab Yazd, February 28, 2001
Aftab Yazd, April 27, 2006
Aftab Yazd, May 3, 2006
Agence-France Presse, June 17, 2008
Eghtesad-e Irani, May 13, 2014
Etemad, April 26, 2006
Etemad, May 7, 2006
Etemad, December 17, 2006
Etemad Daily, July 9, 2006
Etemad-e Melli, August 21, 2007
Etemad-e Melli, July 29, 2008
Etemad-e Melli, August 24, 2008
Ettelaat, February 23, 1999
Ettelaat, May 17, 2004
Ettelaat, May 15, 2008
Guardian, May 28, 2006
Iran, July 2, 2001
Iran, October 27, 2004
Iran, June 7, 2005
Iran, May 1, 2006
Iran, July 1, 2007
Iran, May 23, 2018
IRNA, June 18, 2011
Javan, June 30, 2001
Javan, July 9, 2004
Jomhoori Islami, December 28, 1992
Jomhoori Islami, April 27, 2006
Jomhoori Islami, May 7, 2006
Jomhoori Islami, August 21, 2006
Keyhan, November 30, 2003
Keyhan, April 28, 2006
Mardomsalari, July 8, 2006
Resalat, April 16, 2003
Resalat, May 17, 2006
Reuters, May 21, 2007
Salam, February 12, 1999
Sedaye Edalat, May 14, 2006
Sharq, December 6, 2003
Sharq, April 10, 2006
Sharq, April 27, 2006
Sharq, May 2, 2006
Sharq, May 8, 2006
Siasat-e Rooz, May 4, 2005
Toseh, May 5, 2005
Zan-e Rooz, June 20, 1981

Zan-e Rooz, August 8, 1981
Zan-e Rooz, August 29, 1981
Zan-e Rooz, October 15, 1982
Zan-e Rooz, November 17, 1984
Zan-e Rooz, March 7, 1986
Zan-e Rooz, March 13, 1987
Zan-e Rooz, January 20, 1988
Zan-e Rooz, January 20, 1989
Zan-e Rooz, October 21, 1989
Zan-e Rooz, November 10, 1989
Zan-e Rooz, November 17, 1989
Zan-e Rooz, November 24, 1989
Zan-e Rooz, December 13, 1991
Zan-e Rooz, June 11, 1993
Zan-e Rooz, August 3, 1996
Zan-e Rooz, September 13, 2003
Zan-e Rooz, December 5, 2003
Zan-e Rooz, December 24, 2006

ONLINE SOURCES

Websites

Atlas of Tehran Metropolis. 2006. "Car Ownership per Household in Tehran." http://atlas
    .tehran.ir/Default.aspx?tabid=294.
Bank Melli. 2010. "In an Innovative Move, Bank Melli Launched Its First Women Only
    Branch," June 7. http://bmi.ir/Fa/shownews.aspx?nwsId=5094.
Center for Strategic Studies. 2014. "Report of the Expert Meeting on Hijab." www.css.ir
    /Media/PDF/1396/11/14/636532375414083535.pdf.
FIFA. 2012. "Australia vs Iran: Celebration and Heartbreak." Accessed June 6, 2012. www
    .fifa.com/classicfootball/matches/qualifiers/match=8705/index.html.
FIFA. 2015/2016. "Laws of the Game." https://img.fifa.com/image/upload/datdzopms85gbnq
    y4j3k.pdf.
Iran Khodro. n.d. "An Introduction to Iran Khodro." www.ikco.ir/fa/Intro.aspx.
Hamidi, Milad. 2013. "The Footprints of Feminism and Female Chauvinism on BRT Buses
    in Tehran." *Men's Rights Blog*, April 16. http://mensright.mihanblog.com/post/225.
Vice Presidency for Women and Family Affairs, The. 2014. "The Urban Space of Tehran Is
    Still Not Optimal for Women," May 18. http://women.gov.ir/fa/news/6644.

Specific Articles

BBC News. 2005. "Five Die after Iran Football Game," March 26. http://news.bbc.co.uk/2
    /hi/middle_east/4383939.stm.
Deutsche Welle. 2006. "Germans Protest against Ahmadinejad, Racism as Cup Opens," June
    11. www.dw.de/germans-protest-against-ahmadinejad-racism-as-cup-opens/a-2051820.
Eghtesad-e Irani. 2014. "What Is the Budget for Mosques in Iran?," May 13. http://www
    .ireconomy.ir/fa/page/12663.

Entekhab. 2013. "Interview with Ibrahim Asgharzadeh: 'Hoveyda also Spoke Like Ahmadinejad,'" April 27. www.entekhab.ir/fa/news/108187.

Hamshahri Online. (2012), "Tehran Is No Longer a Masculine City," July 7. www.hamshahri online.ir/news/175309.

Hurriyet Daily News. 2000. "Iran Gives Schoolgirls Choice of Uniform Color," July 19. Accessed December 20, 2012. www.hurriyetdailynews.com/iran-gives-schoolgirls-choice -of-uniform-color.aspx?pageID=438&n=iran-gives-schoolgirls-choice-of-uniform -color-2000-07-19.

Kanoon-e Zanan-e Irani. 2007. "The First Female Bus Driver in Tehran," January 4. http:// ir-women.com/2740.

"The Mayor and the Members of Tehran City Council Meet with the Leader of the Revolution." January 13, 2014. http://farsi.khamenei.ir/news-content?id=24963.

Spiegel Online International. 2006. "'The Hitler of the 21st Century': German Jews Give Ahmadinejad the Red Card," June 11. www.spiegel.de/international/the-hitler-of-the -21st-century-german-jews-give-ahmadinejad-the-red-card-a-420760.html.

Tabnak. 2010. "Title," June 1. www.tabnak.ir/fa/news/101949.

Tabnak. 2012. "Photos: Women's Carwash in Tabriz," July 23. www.tabnak.ir/fa/news/260020.

Young Journalists Club. 2018. "The Opening of the First Women's Carwash in Qom," August 28. www.yjc.ir/fa/news/6648606.

INDEX

Abbas Abad hills, 57, 72 *fig*, 78

Abtahi, Mohammad Ali, 87, 97

accommodation, 34; patriarchal accommodations, 129n3

AFC (Asian Football Confederation), 84, 105–107, 119

agency: women's, 7

Ahmadinejad, Mahmood: and Alliance of Builders of Islamic Iran, 132; as challenger to the conservative clerics, 75, 84, 98–107, 114; as mayor, 71, 74; as president, 3, 27, 74, 75, 84, 98–107, 119

Akrami, Seyyed Reza, 106

Aliabadi, Mohammad, 104

Alimohammadi, Fereshteh, 73, 76

Alliance of Builders of Islamic Iran, 98, 132n9

al-Zahra University, 45

Andarooni, 6, 8

angels of the home, women as, 60

antiamericanism, 36

antiwesternism, 67, 69, 85, 105

antizionism, 104

axis of evil, 2, 127n3

Ayatollah Khamenei, 27, 67, 86, 87, 94, 101; and Tehran City Council, 109. *See also* Supreme Leader

Ayatollah Khomeini, 1, 35, 131n13; and the chador, 10; and the dispossessed, 35; and gender segregation, 11, 12, 128n22; and the

post-Khomeini era, 65; and sisters of the revolution, 35; and sports, 85

Ayatollahs. *See* clerics

Azizi, Khodadad, 82–83

Badmagerian, Ardasheh (Ardeshir Khan), 6

Baharestan Square, 42

ban: dance, 131n5, soccer stadium, 24, 83, 84, 87–89, 91, 92, 95, 99, 103, 125; women's sports, 85, wrestling, 94, 132n7. *See also* women's access to soccer stadiums

barefooted, 35, 48, 55

Bin Hammam, Mohammad, 106

birooni (semipublic space in the home), 6, 8

bodies: sexualized, 74

bureaucracy, 115; infrastructure of, 34, 120; logic of, 5

Bus Rapid Transit (BRT): Bogota, 51; Tehran, 30, 34, 51–55, 125

buses, 23, 24; infrastructure of, 30, 31, 36–37; segregation in, 3, 4, 11, 12, 22, 24, 26, 30–57; women-only, 3

Carter, Jimmy, 36

chador, ix, 1, 2, 3, 33, 41, 55, 56, 127; as flag of the revolution, 10. *See also* veil

Chahpoor, Valiollah, 38, 42, 112

chastity: institutionalization of, 2

Cheheltan, Amir Hassan, 7

Chitgar Park, 66
Chizar neighborhood, 31
Cinema Khorshid, 6
citizen: healthy, 80; and state power, 120
citizenship, 56, 59, 124, 129; alternative spheres of, 59; and female subjecthood, 21; secular liberal, 5; urban, 64, 65, 66
city: partitioning of, 5
cityscape, 10, 65
clerics, 3, 24, 28, 71, 75, 84, 87, 88, 93, 94, 97, 98, 99, 100, 101, 102, 103, 104, 107, 113, 114, 132n9, 10, 11
Combatant Clergy Association, 100, 106
communicative action, 128n14
compulsory veiling, 70, 74, 76, 78, 111
conservative: clergy, 94, 97, 99, 100, 103, 106, 107, 114; clergy and other conservatives, 94, 98, 99, 101; factions, 90, 91, 93, 99, 101, 106, 107; media, 95, 100, 102, 105; parliamentarians, 94, 95; policies, 123
Constitutional Revolution, 7, 128
contestation, 5, 12, 80–84, 88–89, 106, 111, 117, 119–124
crossdressing, 102
cultural defense, 69
cultural invasion (western), 66–70, 78

Daei, Ali, 82, 95
Dastjerdi, Marzieh Vahid (Health Minister), 3, 80
daughters of the revolution, 19–20, 91, 118
desegregation, 117; policies of, 7–10
desexualization: of public spaces, 74; of women, 43
deveiling: as official state policy, 8–10, 128; as a violent process, 8
discursive regimes, 5
double-decker buses, 39–40
dress codes: Islamic, 9; secular, 9

Ebtekar, Masoomeh, 96–97
Ekbatan neighborhood, 61
electoral fraud, 27
'Elm o San'at Technical University, 31
Ettelaat Institution, 22
ethnography, xiv, 23, 28–29
Europe, 6–8, 28, 104
exclusion, 4, 10, 14, 15, 18, 19, 20, 21, 34, 86, 91, 92, 107, 117, 118, 121, 123, 126; balancing with inclusion, 17, 115, differential, 125; spaces of, 5

Ferdosipour, Adel, 88
female micro entrepreneurs, 15

femininity, 33; and private space, 20; in the city, 44
fieldwork, 22–29
FIFA (Fédération Internationale de Football Association), 81, 84, 105–107, 110, 119–120, 132; banning women's soccer team, 107; hijab problem, 107
Fonda, Jane, 77
Fordism, 17
framing: women's exercise as makrūh (religiously unacceptable), 20; women's rights, 93
Freedom Sports Stadium (Azadi Stadium), 4, 13, 21, 23, 80, 81, 83, 87–89, 91–92, 96–97, 104–107, 114, 117

gender as binary, 33
gender boundaries, 4, 7, 12, 111, 112, 114, 117, 119, 123–124, 125, 126; contestation of, 5, 7, 12, 66; physicality of, 19, 40; policing of, 126; porosity of, 17, 125; transgression of, 31; unsettling of, 7, 66
gender domination, 5, 21, 84, 112; logics of, 20
gender order, 4, 20, 41, 45, 112, 116, 119
gender roles, 45
gender segregation, 128; at Alborz mountain range, 11; in the Caspian Sea, 10, 11fig; at Dizin, 11; in Egypt, 14; in healthcare, 3–4, 22; in Jerusalem, 128; in Mexico, 128; in the 1980s, 20, 21, 47; policies, 13, 16, 18, 20–22; proactive, 20, 21; reactive, 20, 21; regime of, 20, 21fig; as regulation of bodies, 74; and religious morality, 56, 112, 114; in Saudi Arabia, 14; as social practice, 13, 14, 35, 74, 111, 112, 115; spatial dimensions of, 39, 41, 46, 47, 56; and state building, 114–115; as state project, 20–22; temporal dimensions of, 12; in the 2000s, 20, 21
gendered subjects: and power, 85; and prohibition, 116, 118
geopolitics, 17
Germany: anti-Ahmadinejad protests, 104
Ghafourifard, Hassan, 60–61
globalization: effects of, 16, 78, 131n14
governmentality: liberal, 18
Green movement, 27
Guardian Council, 94

Habibi, Shahla, 61, 67–68
haram (religiously forbidden). See also makruh 38, 60
hawza, 100–101, 132n11
headscarf, 58, 131n2

hegemony, 22, 121
heterosociality, 7–8
hijab, 38, 59, 67, 68, 70, 127, 130–131n2; bad hijab, 67, 78
Hijab Complex, 61
homosociality, 7
hostage crisis, 36
Hoveyda, Amir Abbas, 36–37
human rights, 17, 107
Hussein, Saddam, 36

Imam Khomeini Relief Foundation, 129n4
in and out of place, 125, 126
inclusion, x, xiii, 5, 15, 17, 19, 20, 21, 26, 56, 91, 107, 115, 117, 125; spaces of, 5, 20
international: actors, 84; governance, 103, 115, 116; media, 85, 132; organizations, 52, 79, 80, 84, 105–110, 115, 119; pressures, 21, 84, 99, 102, 110
International Monetary Fund (IMF), 44, 49, 119
International Olympic Committee, 105
Iran: as modern state, 71, 105, 112, 117; –Iraq war, 10, 43, 58
Iranian: cinema, 6; media, 22, 94, 99–100, 123; theater, 6–8
Iranian Soccer Federation, 87, 106
Iran National (Iran Khodro), 36
Isfahan, ix, x, 40, 77, 99
Islamic: city, 2, 5, 10, 110, 113, 115, 127; morality, 1, 5, 10, 19, 21, 34, 54–56, 66, 75, 80, 107, 111, 112, 127; revolution, 1, 2, 10, 17–19, 34–37, 44, 62, 64, 75, 85–86, 91–92, 99, 101–102, 110, 112, 115–117, 122–124
Islamic Propaganda Organization, 102
Islamic Republic, 2, 5, 6, 9, 10, 12, 14, 17, 18, 20, 21, 36–8, 43–44, 47, 50, 60, 67, 70, 75, 77–78, 83, 86, 91–92, 98, 100, 103–105, 107, 111, 117, 120, 124–125; branding of, 112; as populist, 43, 118; self image of, 4, 111
Islamic Revolution: as populist, 43, 118
Islamist movement, 113
Islamization: of the bus space, 42; project, 9, 132, 41, 42, 47, 111, 113–114; of space, 112;

Javanfekr, Ali Akbar, 102

Karbaschi, Gholanhossein, 62–65, 69
Katiraei, Behzad, 92–93
Khadem, Rasool, 24–26, 76
Khatami, Mohammad, 48, 49, 69–71, 83–84, 87–98, 104, 130
Kiarostami, Abbas, 85

Koochakzadeh, Mehdi, 102
Koolaei, Elaheh, 92–93

Laleh Park, 62
left behind. See poor.
liberalism, 2, 3, 69, 91
Life, and Nothing More (Movie), 85

makruh (discouraged), 20, 61
male guardianship: transformation into state protection, 5
man, becoming a, 33
manhood, 33
Manjil and Rudbar, earthquake, 85
martyrs, 10, 18, 43, 44, 58, 65, 111, 113
masculinity, 20; working class, 89
medicalization discourse, 78–80
Mehralizadeh, Mohsen, 97
Mellat Park, 62
Men's Rights Association, 52
middle class, 5, 9, 22, 25, 54–55, 63
Milani, Tahmineh, 76
Ministry of Education, 70
Ministry of Health, 79
Ministry of Interior, 38
Ministry of Science, Research, and Technology, 27
modern: city, 34, 110; woman, 7
modernity, 7–9; alternative, 9; early, 7; Islamic, 9; western, 9
modernization, 8, 10
modesty: institutionalization of, 2
Mofid Children Hospital, 55
Mohammad Reza Shah, 8–9, 11, 36, 85, 124
Moshir, Zahra, 76
Mostafavi, Reza, 19, 60
Mothers' Paradise Park, xiv, 4, 13, 25–26, 57–80
movements: body, x, 10, 20, 26, 112, 123; social, xiv, 27, 92, 110
moving in the city, 5, 41–42, 47, 55, 66, 74, 108, 112, 117, 123

Narmak neighborhood, 31, 33
nation, nationalism, 25, 41, 71, 75, 82–83, 86, 88, 92
national security, 27, 106, 120
Navad, TV program, 88, 132n5
Nazarali, Parvaneh, 9, 10
new woman: molded by the Iranian Revolution, 9–13; under the Qajar dynasty, 7; under the Pahlavi dynasty, 7–9

non-islamic, 19, 11, 113, 114
nuclear program, 1, 2, 99

Offside (movie), 104
offside (soccer term), 104, 106
One Million Signature Campaign, 59, 123
Ottoman Empire, 14, 128
outsourcing, 119–120

Pahlavi dynasty, 8–10, 35–36, 112, 128nn16, 20
Panahi, Jafar, 104
panopticon, 17
Park des Princes, 61
Paykan, 36
Physical Education Organization, 87, 88, 92, 97, 98
pink-collar jobs, 9, 128
Piroozi Sports Complex, ix, 125
political: boundaries of, 85
poor, 6, 35, 37, 56, 101
power: pastoral, 22, 80; pragmatics of, 21;
    spatiality of, 17
privatization, 34, 44, 49–51, 119, 122
prohibition: provision, 5, 20–21, 78, 116, 121, 125;
protection, 5, 19, 38, 59, 78; as service provision,
    78; discourse of, 5, 22, 89; masculinist, 22
provision, 5, 18–21, 45, 49, 50, 53, 56, 69, 71, 73,
    78–80, 110, 116, 117, 118, 120–122, 125
protest: and Green Movement, 27; as individual
    acts of disobedience, 12; and spaces of con-
    testation, 12; and White Scarf Girls, 96–98,
    105, 107, 125;
public iconography, 10
public sphere, 4, 9, 33, 59, 77, 91, 128n14, 129n2;
    female, 6–7, 59; male, 6–7
purification, moral, 2

Qajar dynasty, 6–8, 128n15
Qalibaf, Mohammad Baqir, 52, 74–77, 109
Qods Square, 30
Qom, 18, 75, 99–101, 123, 127n7, 132n11

Rafsanjani, Hashemi, 43, 44, 48, 62, 66, 86, 87,
    95, 100, 104
Rakei, Fatemeh, 91–92
regulation, 5, 21, 34, 70, 80, 96; modes of 5, 20,
    21, 78, 80, 119
reform, 9, 69, 83, 87, 95, 100
reformists, 3, 4, 27–28, 34, 65, 69–71, 73, 76, 79,
    82, 87–89, 91–99, 101, 105, 109, 125
Resalat, 30–31
resistance, 2, 28, 29, 52, 80, 96, 125; romance of, 2
revolution of the "barefooted," 35

rhetoric: of care and service provision, 18
Rouhani, Hassan, 84, 109
Rumi, 23

Sadrazam Nouri, Zahra, 41
scaling down, 78, 79, 119, 120
scaling up, 119, 120
Second Students' Sports Olympiad, ix, x
securitization (of women's issues), 106, 107, 120
Sepanji, Khadijeh, 93
sexism, flexible, 126
sexual harassment, 77
sexuality, 74, 93
Shahid Beheshti University, ix
Shojaee, Zahra, 71, 73, 96, 97
sisters of the revolution, 18, 19, 20, 118, 122, 123,
    124
soccer, 132; diplomacy, 85, 103–104; and domestic
    politics, 89–108; and nation building, 85–86,
    88; women's attitudes towards, 89
Society of Seminary Teachers of Qom, 101, 132n11
The Sound of Music (movie), 58
Source of emulation (*Marja-i Taqlid*), , 87,
    99–102, 132n10
space: administering and ordering of, 5, 39, 54;
    appropriation of, 45, 68, 124; creation of,
    68, 124; desexualized, 64; domestic, 6–8,
    63, 65–66; feminine, 6, 45, 47, 56, 68, 71;
    feminist, 45; gendered, 6, 41, 111; gender seg-
    regated, 26, 34, 38, 41–42, 45, 117, 124; Islamic,
    4, 39, 41–42, 46, 111–113, 115; liminal, 82, 95;
    masculine, 6, 19, 34, 43, 47, 89, 92, 95–96;
    politics of, 17, 57–58, 68, 124; private, 6–8, 20;
    public, 6–8, 4, 14, 19–20, 47, 56, 58, 70, 74,
    80; reterritorialization of, 124; symbolic, 86;
    urban, 66, 111, 115–116, 124
sports spectatorship, 83–91, 94–96, 100, 102–103
state: authoritarian, 17; disabling, 5, 18, 80, 123;
    enabling, 5, 18, 80, 123; Islamic, 4, 5, 9, 10, 21,
    34, 43, 85, 86, 100, 111–116, 123; patriarchal,
    17; post-revolutionary, 4, 22, 92, 111, 116, 118;
    as producer of a gender-segregated spatial
    order 5, 118; resilience of, 17; theocratic, 17
state power: modalities of, 4
subjecthood: female, 20, 21, 33, 80; moral, 80
Supreme Leader, 86–87
surveillance, 5, 8, 123

taa'hod (loyalty) , 50
Tabriz, 40
Tajzadeh, Mosatafa, 95
takhassos (expertise), 50

Taleghani Park, 67, 68

Taliban, 91, 92

Tarasht neighborhood, 42

Tehran: City Council, 3, 22, 24, 27, 73, 76, 109, 111; Education and Training Organization of, 70; Parks and Green Space Organization, 71, 76

Tehran Municipality: Department of Health, 79, 80; Women's Sports Offices, 80, 84

un-islamic, 60, 75, 99

United Nations Human Settlements Programme (UN-Habitat), 50, 52, 53

US-led sanctions, 36, 43, 48, 82, 110

Vahdat Hall, 23

Valiasr, 45

Vasiri, Colonel Alinaqi, 6

veil, veiling, 1, 9, 10, 12, 25, 26, 33, 42, 57, 67, 70, 71, 74, 76, 78, 111, 112, 117, 127n5, 130n1, 131n3

Velayat Park, 80

westernization, 19, 66–70, 85, 112

westoxicated, 19

women: as customers, 3, 55; as signifiers of Iran's modernity, 8–9; as subjects of of Islamic morality, 10, 34, 55, 80; as symbols of Islamic morality, 1, 10, 111

women-only: bank branches, 3; buses, 3, 40, 45–47, 50, 51, 56; businesses, 3; cafes, 3; carwash, 3; cinemas, 6; metro compartments, 26; parks, xiv, 3, 4, 13, 20, 23, 57, 59, 60, 62, 70-7880, 110, 124, 125, 128, 131; sports stadium, 21; swimming facilities, 10; taxis, 128; theaters, 6, 8; universities, 45, 117, 128; spaces, 3, 6, 13, 19, 26, 70, 123

women's: access to public space, x, 2, 19, 20, 29, 70, 118, 123; access to stadiums, 24, 29, 76, 83, 85, 91, 93, 95, 103, 105, 107, 114, 120, 123, 128; bodies, fragility and vulnerability of, 22, 67, 84; dignity, 6, 19, 78, 99, 122, 123; education, 8, 18, 43, 44, 61, 73, 118, 130; equal access to stadiums, 96; entrance into the workforce, 9, 43, 44, 73, 128n17, 130n17; invisibility, 8, 15, 33, 123; leisure-time activities, 60, 69; outdoor exercise as a solution to public health problems, 118–120, 122; outdoor exercise as *makrūh* (religiously unacceptable), 20, 61; stadium access as political competition, 108; visibility, 2, 3, 4, 8, 15, 20, 33, 53, 111

women's interests as state interests, 77

Women's Soccer Association, 93

World Bank, 44, 50, 66, 119, 130

World Health Organization (WHO), 50, 79, 119

The World without Zionism event, 103

Wuthering Heights, 71, 72*fig*

Zanan, x, xi, 22

Zan-e Rooz, 22, 38, 40, 45, 56, 61

Zeinab Society, 27

Founded in 1893,
UNIVERSITY OF CALIFORNIA PRESS
publishes bold, progressive books and journals
on topics in the arts, humanities, social sciences,
and natural sciences—with a focus on social
justice issues—that inspire thought and action
among readers worldwide.

The UC PRESS FOUNDATION
raises funds to uphold the press's vital role
as an independent, nonprofit publisher, and
receives philanthropic support from a wide
range of individuals and institutions—and from
committed readers like you. To learn more, visit
ucpress.edu/supportus.